*International Political Economy Series*

General Editor: **Timothy M. Shaw**, Professor of Political Science and International Development Studies, and Director of the Centre for Foreign Policy Studies, Dalhousie University, Halifax, Nova Scotia

Titles include:

Henry Veltmeyer, James Petras and Steve Vieux
NEOLIBERALISM AND CLASS CONFLICT IN LATIN AMERICA
A Comparative Perspective on the Political Economy of Structural Adjustment

Henry Veltmeyer, James Petras
THE DYNAMICS OF SOCIAL CHANGE IN LATIN AMERICA

**International Political Economy Series**
**Series Standing Order ISBN 0–333–71708–2 hardcover**
**Series Standing Order ISBN 0–333–71110–6 paperback**
(*outside North America only*)

You can receive future titles in this series as they are published by placing a standing order. Please contact your bookseller or, in case of difficulty, write to us at the address below with your name and address, the title of the series and one of the ISBNs quoted above.

Customer Services Department, Macmillan Distribution Ltd, Houndmills, Basingstoke, Hampshire RG21 6XS, England

# The Political Economy of Drugs in the Caribbean

Edited by

Ivelaw L. Griffith
*Professor of Political Science and*
*Associate Dean of the College of Arts and Sciences*
*Florida International University*
*Miami*
*Florida*

palgrave

Published by PALGRAVE
Houndmills, Basingstoke, Hampshire RG21 6XS and
175 Fifth Avenue, New York, N. Y. 10010
Companies and representatives throughout the world

PALGRAVE is the new global academic imprint of
St. Martin's Press LLC Scholarly and Reference Division and
Palgrave Publishers Ltd (formerly Macmillan Press Ltd).

*Outside North America*
ISBN 0–333–71072–X

*In North America*
ISBN 0–312–23258–6

This book is printed on paper suitable for recycling and
made from fully managed and sustained forest sources.

A catalogue record for this book is available from the British Library.

Library of Congress Catalog Card Number: 99–087197

10   9   8   7   6   5   4   3   2
09  08  07  06  05  04  03  02  01

Printed and bound in Great Britain by
Antony Rowe Ltd, Eastbourne

1005437664

# Contents

## Part I   Regional and International Contexts

## Part II   Connections and Consequences

## Part III   Coping Strategies and Countermeasures

# List of Tables and Figure

## Tables

# Figure

# List of Abbreviations

| | |
|---|---|
| ABA | American Bar Association |
| ACCP | Association of Caribbean Commissioners of Police |
| ALP | Antigua Labour Party |
| ATF | (US) Bureau of Alcohol, Tobacco and Firearms |
| BANAICO | Banco Agro Industrial y Comercial de Panama |
| BCCI | Bank of Credit and Commerce International |
| BIS | Bank for International Settlements |
| CACPA | Central American Chiefs of Police Association |
| CARIAD | Caribbean Institute on Alcoholism and Other Drugs |
| CARICOM | Caribbean Community and Common Market |
| CBI | Caribbean Basin Initiative |
| CCLEC | Caribbean Customs Law Enforcement Council |
| CDB | Caribbean Development Bank |
| CFATF | Caribbean Financial Action Task Force |
| CICAD | Inter-American Drug Abuse Control Commission |
| CIFAD | Inter-Ministeral Drug Control Training Center |
| CINSEC | Caribbean Island Nations Security Conference |
| DARE | Drug Abuse Resistance Education |
| DEA | (US) Drug Enforcement Administration |
| DFI | Direct Foreign Investment |
| DLO | Drug Liaison Officers |
| ECLAC | Economic Commission for Latin America and the Caribbean (UN) |
| ECU | European Currency Unit |
| EPIC | El Paso Intelligence Center |
| EPZ | Export Processing Zone |
| ERP | Economic Recovery Program |
| ESM | European Single Market |
| EU | European Union |
| FATF | Financial Action Task Force |
| FBI | (US) Federal Bureau of Investigation |
| FDI | Foreign Direct Investment |
| FMF | Forward Military Financing |
| FMU | Fertility Management Unit |
| FOB | Forward Operating Base |
| FRAPH | Front for the Advancement and Progress of Haiti |

| | |
|---|---|
| FTAA | Free Trade Area of the Americas |
| FURA | Fuerzas Unidas de Rapida Accion |
| GAC | Guyana Airways Corporation |
| GANTSEC | (US Coast Guard) Greater Antilles Section |
| GAO | (US) General Accounting Office |
| GATS | General Agreements on Trade and Services |
| GATT | General Agreement on Trade and Tariffs |
| GDP | Gross Domestic Product |
| GNP | Gross National Product |
| GSP | Generalized System of Preferences |
| HFLE | Health and Family Life Education |
| HIDTA | High-Intensity Drug-Trafficking Area |
| HNP | Haitian National Police |
| IBC | International Business Company |
| IBF | International Banking Facilities |
| IBRD | International Bank for Reconstruction and Development |
| ICIC | International Credit and Investment Company |
| ICITAP | International Criminal Investigative Training Assistance Programme |
| ICSID | International Center for Settlement of Investment Disputes |
| INS | Immigration and Naturalization Service |
| IDER | Integrated Demand Reduction Program |
| IFC | International Financial Company |
| IGTF | Inter-Governmental Task Force |
| IMF | International Monetary Fund |
| I-MP | Innovation-Mediated Production |
| INCSR | *International Narcotics Control Strategy Report* |
| JDF | Jamaica Defense Force |
| JIATF | Joint Inter-Agency Task Force |
| JIO | Joint Intelligence Office |
| JLP | Jamaican Labour Party |
| LAC | Latin America and the Caribbean |
| LDC | Less Developed Countries |
| LEDET | (US Coast Guard) Law Enforcement Detachment |
| MIGA | Multilateral Investment Guarantee Agency |
| MLAT | Mutual Legal Assistance Treaty |
| NA | Netherlands Antilles |
| NADAPP | National Alcohol and Drug Abuse Prevention Program |
| NAFTA | North American Free Trade Agreement |
| NBP | National Bank of Panama |

| | |
|---|---|
| NDACC | National Drug Abuse Control Council |
| NEF | Net External Flows |
| NGO | Non-Governmental Organization |
| NJM | New Jewel Movement |
| OAS | Organization of American States |
| OBC | Offshore Business Company |
| ODA | Official Development Assistance |
| OECD | Organization for Economic Cooperation and Development |
| OFC | Offshore Financial Center |
| OPBAT | Operation Bahamas and Turks and Caicos |
| OPVISTA | Operations Visits in Support of Training Assistance |
| PAHO | Pan American Health Organization |
| PARDAC | Parish Drug Awareness Committees |
| PNC | People's National Congress |
| PNP | People's National Party |
| PRD | Revolutionary Democratic Party |
| RCMP | Royal Canadian Mounted Police |
| REDTRAC | Regional Drug Training Center |
| RICO | Racketeer Influence and Corrupt Organizations Act |
| ROTHR | Relocatable Over-the-Horizon Radar |
| RSS | Regional Security System |
| SAP | Structural Adjustment Program |
| SICA | Central American Integration System |
| SIMAP | Social Impact Amelioration Program |
| SOUTHCOM | United States Southern Command |
| TCO | Transnational Criminal Organizations |
| TIEA | Tax Information Exchange Agreement |
| TOC | Tactical Operations Center |
| UN | United Nations |
| UNAIDS | UN Programme on AIDS |
| UNAIS | UN Association for International Service |
| UNCTAD | UN Conference on Trade and Development |
| UNDCP | UN International Drugs Control Program |
| UNESCO | UN Educational, Scientific and Cultural Organization |
| UNFDAC | UN Fund for Drug Abuse Control |
| UNICEF | UN Children's Fund |
| UNIFEM | UN Development Fund for Women |
| USACOM | United States Atlantic Command |
| USAID | United States Agency for International Development |
| USCS | United States Customs Service |

| | |
|---|---|
| UWI | University of the West Indies |
| VSN | National Security Volunteers |
| WB | World Bank |
| WCO | World Customs Organization |
| WTO | World Trade Organization |

# Preface: Global to Local Empirical and Conceptual Contexts and Challenges

This informed and balanced volume is very timely as issues concerning the political economy of drugs in this as in other regions are not about to disappear. Meanwhile, the analytical and policy fields on which it touches – from global politics to local development – are in need of new directions, especially as we enter a new century. In this overview, I concentrate on this volume's innovations and its contributions to emerging analyses and debates, anticipating its second edition.

The drugs nexus/industry has become big business, amounting to 10 per cent of the global political economy, even without counting the multiplier effects of money laundering, drug houses, etc. Yet its direct presence and ripple effects have all too infrequently been noticed in major studies of contemporary International Relations, Foreign Policy and Global Political Economy, etc. But 'Hot money'[1] and illegal as well as informal sectors are lifelines for marginal communities and countries; hence the anthropology of drug families and networks from Colombia to Chicago.

While there have been drug issues and controversies for centuries, the global incidence and impact of the drug nexus are relatively recent. While the ubiquity of the drugs trade cannot be blamed on globalization processes, it does coincide with post-war technological and social change; in particular the combination of the following events: (i) the Vietnam War; (ii) neo-liberalism and structural adjustment; and (iii) the end of state socialism and bipolarity. Moreover, it is inseparable from exponential inequalities and the privatization of many state functions, including security.

Curiously, in part because academic attention – empirical and conceptual – has been limited, there are minimal debates about the conceptualization, explanation, projection and reaction to the drugs nexus, being particularly absent in International Relations, Foreign Policy, International Political Economy and Development. This is especially strange as the industry/culture is so global and the embryonic field so interdisciplinary. While the present collection is hardly controversial in its treatment of such a high profile issue in the Caribbean region, it should advance alternative emphases, assumptions and expectations, a tribute to the judiciousless of its editor. Indeed, this volume may serve to help ignite debate about this covert global industry in both the North and South, especially as they are so interconnected through such exchanges.

This set of comparative chapters and cases is particularly welcome as it draws attention to: (i) the characteristic involvement of not just entre-preneurs/dealers/consumers but also the 'troika' or 'triad' of state, cor-porations and civil societies, i.e. not just the informal market; and (ii) the meso or regional as well as local, national and global levels of interaction and reaction. Such features further ensure the curiosity of many scholars and students in interrelated fields.

One element in particular may excite interest: the drugs trade is itself highly transnational (i.e. across borders with at least some non-state involvement): global networks, communications, impacts. So to contain or regulate, let alone reduce or eliminate it, requires an equally inter-state, inter-agency, inter-actor response at the international level. How-ever, the debate about how to characterize the nexus is already contro-versial. Is it indeed a 'war against drugs' – i.e. another 'holy war' for the Americans – or just a further instance of the high price for not allowing market forces to define the trade: another rationale for a robust response or an emerging 'threat' best contained through notions of human devel-opment/security?

Until there is a more agreed – identified and defined – set of alternate approaches to the Political Economy of drugs in the Caribbean as other regions, there is likely to be a certain amount of mis-communication and mis-perception. Thus there may be a consensus about the issues that should and do inform and determine policy, such as the 11 indicated below, notwithstanding any disagreement over their rank order:

1. *apparent incompatabilities between economic and political liberalizations* leading to growing internal and external inequalities so that some regimes may come to advocate more authoritarian responses to mar-ket pressures rather than parliamentary procedures, given the impera-tive of decisive responses;
2. *emerging tensions between different sectors*, e.g. are the drug trade and related new economy sectors compatible, such as the tourist industry including cruise liners, call centres, Export Processing Zones (EPZs) and just-in-time manufacturing, etc?;
3. *incompatabilities among market signals*: the World Trade Organization (WTO) and US authorities are harassing the labour-intensive banana and textiles industries yet, without them, drug production and dis-tribution constitute one of the few 'industries' left;

4. *controversial forms of Direct Foreign Investment (DFI)* including money-laundering, which may lead to bizarre cost–benefit analyses; i.e. not all foreign investment is to be welcomed uncritically;
5. *the organic linkages among diasporic communities* from the Caribbean, which can facilitate the transnational trade in major North American (now European and Asian as well) cities, with the unfortunate and expensive side-effect of northern regimes expelling (sometimes long-term) residents with criminal records;
6. *the emergence of a range of 'new' security issues,* from small arms' proliferation to money-laundering requiring more appropriate and tailored solutions rather than heavy-handed responses to attack root causes rather than mere symptoms;
7. *the distinctive place of each Caribbean island in the transnational drugs production and supply chain,* even as far as consumption is concerned – from more to less integrated and compliant, etc – leading to novel typologies reflective of the location in central networks;
8. the role of *new technologies,* such as cellular telephones and global positioning by satellite, available both to the producers and dealers as well as the states' response teams, so there is a high-tech dimension to some of the more basic features of this industry's culture and structure;
9. issues of *sovereignty* even if it's a tenuous legal fiction at the start of the new millennium, especially given US unilateral extra-territorial involvements and interventions such as directly supervising payments' facilities, hosting shipriders on its patrol vessels from Caribbean regimes with high compliance rates, imposing sanctions on non-compliant governments, etc;
10. in turn, these have led towards *new regionalisms* in addition to *the North American Free Trade Agreement* (NAFTA) and the Caribbean Community and Common Market (CARICOM) in which neighbouring islands, often facilitated by the presence of a modest US fleet, work together on interdiction operations in a new form of post-Cold War national/collective security, etc; and finally,
11. such analyses/discoveries/discourses have generated their own distinctive *set of terms* such as narco-democracy, narco-diplomacy, and narco-criminality and narco-corruption, etc. which might feature more regularly in discourses around International Relations, Foreign Policy, International Political Economy and Development?

Finally, this book offers a set of informed commentaries on the current state of overlapping fields, such as International Relations, Foreign

Policy, International Political Economy and Development. It suggests how to recast these, taking the above 11 points into account, something that could be replicated in many other regions of the world by the end of the 21st century. The wide appreciation of this volume's insights will advance crucial policy and theoretical discourse relevant to the new millennium.

## Note

1   For a useful discussion on the 'other side' of global economics and finance, see R. T. Naylor, *Hot Money & the Politics of Debt* (Montreal: Black Rose, 1987); *Dominion of Debt* (Montreal: Black Rose, 1996) and *Bankers, Bagmen & Bandits* (Montreal: Black Rose, 1996).

TIMOTHY M. SHAW

# Notes on the Contributors

**Sonita Morin Abrahams** is Executive Director of Addiction Alert Organization, Jamaica. She holds a BA in Psychology from Florida International University, a Master's in Health Science from the Johns Hopkins University, and has done graduate work in clinical psychology at the University of the West Indies (UWI), Jamaica. Mrs Abrahams has conducted drug-abuse training for the UNDCP and delivered papers at UNDCP conferences in Barbados, Thailand, Guyana and the United States. A 1993–94 Hubert Humphrey Fellow at the Johns Hopkins University, Mrs Abrahams serves in several professional anti-drug organizations, including as Vice Chair of Jamaica's National Council on Drug Abuse, and as a Committee Member of Drug Prevention Network of the Americas.

**Gabriel Aguilera Peralta**, whose doctorate in political science is from the University of Freiberg, Germany, is the Vice Foreign Minister of Foreign Affairs of Guatemala. A Professor of Political Science at the San Carlos National University, he was previously Director of the Central American Social Science Program of the Central American University Confederation in Costa Rica, Director of the Central American Institute for Political Studies in Guatemala, and Senior Researcher at the Latin American Faculty for the Social Sciences. Dr Aguilera has written numerous journal articles, special monographs, and books on civil–military relations, security, foreign policy and drugs, including *Belice y Centroamerica: una nueva etapa, Centroamerica ante las nuevas relaciones internacionales*, and *E1 fusil or olivo: la cuestion militar en Centroamerica*.

**Captain Richard R. Beardsworth** (US Coast Guard) is Director of Defense Policy at the National Security Council and was the Coast Guard Fellow at the Center for Strategic and International Studies during 1999–2000. For the previous three years he was Chief of Law Enforcement for the Coast Guard Seventh District, based in Miami, responsible for all Coast Guard narcotics and migrant interdiction in southeast United States and the Caribbean. Beardsworth, who went to Miami after a year at Harvard University's JFK School of Government as a National Security Fellow, holds a BSc from the Coast Guard Academy, an MBA from the University of Colorado and a US Coast Guard unlimited Masters licence. He also has extensive background in Coast Guard surface operations, including command of four cutters.

**Richard L. Bernal**, PhD (Economics), has been Jamaica's Ambassador to the US and Permanent Representative to the OAS since 1991. Before becoming a diplomat he was a commercial banker, a lecturer at UWI, and the holder of various positions in the Jamaican Central Bank, the Planning Institute of Jamaica, and the country's Ministry of Finance. Dr Bernal has authored several policy studies for the Jamaica government and for corporate agencies, and is Chairman of the Working Group on Smaller Economies in the Free Trade Area of the Americas Process. He has published over 75 articles in scholarly journals and books on the debt problem, development economics, regional integration, foreign policy and other subjects.

**Gary Brana-Shute**, who secured his PhD in anthropology from the University of Florida, is a former Professor of Caribbean and Central American Studies at the Foreign Service Institute and Professor of Anthropology at George Washington University. He is author of *On the Corner: Male Social Life in a Paramaribo Creole Neighborhood, Resistance and Rebellion in Suriname*, and coedited *Crime and Punishment in the Caribbean*. He also has published articles in numerous scholarly journals, including *Caribbean Review, Caribbean Studies, Caribbean Affairs, Hemisphere, Journal of Interamerican Studies and World Affairs, New West Indian Guide, Urban Sociology, Journal of Small Wars and Insurgencies* and *Armed Forces and Society*. He has been an elections monitor for the OAS and the Carter Center, and a consultant to USAID, the Pentagon and other agencies.

**Clifford E. Griffin**, Associate Professor of Political Science and Director of the Graduate Program in International Studies at North Carolina State University, is a specialist in comparative and international politics. Author of *Democracy and Neoliberalism in the Developing World*, he also has published in several journals, including *Third World Quarterly, The Round Table, Journal of Democracy, Caribbean Affairs, Social and Economic Studies*, and *Journal of Commonwealth and Comparative Politics*. Professor Griffin, a former National Fellow at the Hoover Institution on War, Revolution, and Peace at Stanford University, has also contributed to several anthologies, among them *Strategy and Security in the Caribbean* and *Democracy and Human Rights in the Caribbean*.

**Ivelaw L. Griffith**, Professor of Political Science and Associate Dean, College of Arts and Sciences at Florida International University, has published widely on politics, security and drugs in the Caribbean, including *Strategy and Security in the Caribbean*, *The Quest for Security in the Caribbean*, *Caribbean Security on the Eve of the 21st Century*, *Democracy and Human Rights in the Caribbean* and *Drugs and Security in the Caribbean: Sovereignty Under Siege*. He also has published in many journals, including *Caribbean Quarterly*, *Naval War College Review*, *Caribbean Studies*, *Conflict Quarterly*, *International Journal*, *Journal of Commonwealth and Comparative Politics*, *Journal of Interamerican Studies and World Affairs*, *Latin American Research Review*, *Low Intensity Conflict and Law Enforcement* and *Third World Quarterly*.

**Stephen E. Lamar**, who has consulted with various Caribbean governments on narcotics issues, is Director of Government Relations at the American Apparel Manufacturers Association, based in Virginia. Previously he served as a Vice-President at Jefferson Waterman International, where he advised corporate and government leaders on relations with the legislative and executive branches, a trade specialist at the International Trade Administration in the US Department of Commerce, and a Peace Corps volunteer in Botswana. Mr Lamar is a term member of the Council on Foreign Relations, a board member of the Washington International Trade Association, and is active in the National Association of Manufacturers and the National Foreign Trade Council.

**Winsome J. Leslie**, Economic Attaché at the Jamaican Embassy in Washington, holds a BA from Barnard College and an MA and a PhD from Columbia University. She taught previously at the School of Advanced International Studies at Johns Hopkins University and The American University, worked with a major New York bank, and as a consultant with Merrill Lynch, the African Development Foundation and the Social Science Research Council. Dr Leslie's regional focus is Africa and the Caribbean, with special reference to macro-economic reform, trade, structural adjustment, and debt. She is author of two books: *The World Bank and Structural Transformation in Developing Countries: the Case of Zaire* and *Zaire: Continuity and Political Change in an Oppressive State*.

**Trevor Munroe** is Professor of Government and Politics at the University of the West Indies (Jamaica). His doctorate in political science is from

Oxford University, which he attended as a Jamaica Rhodes Scholar. Dr Munroe is a longstanding activist-scholar and leader in Jamaica's labor movement. An expert on international and comparative politics, he specializes in political change in developing countries, notably the Caribbean. He has published extensively on Jamaican and Caribbean politics. His recent books include *Jamaican Politics: a Marxist Perspective in Transition*, *The Cold War and the Jamaican Left* and *Renewing Democracy into the Millennium: the Jamaican Experience in Perspective*.

**Orlando J. Perez**, PhD in political science from the University of Pittsburgh, is Assistant Professor of Political Science at Central Michigan University. His areas of research are electoral politics, democratization, political culture and United States–Latin American relations. A specialist on Central American politics, Professor Perez has conducted field work on public opinion in Panama, Guatemala, and E1 Salvador. He is editor of *Post Invasion Panama: the Challenges of Democratization in the New World Order* and has published articles in scholarly journals, including the *Journal of Interamerican Studies and World Affairs*.

**Jorge Rodríguez Beruff** is Professor of Political Science at the Rio Piedras campus of the University of Puerto Rico. He specializes in Puerto Rican politics, regional security and US policy in the Caribbean. Author of *Los Militares y el poder, Politica militar y dominacion*, co-editor of *Conflict, Peace, and Development in the Caribbean* and of *Security Problems and Policies in the Post Cold War Caribbean*, and editor of *Cuba en crisis: perspectivas económicas y politicas*, his research has also been published in a variety of professional journals. Professor Rodriguez is currently writing a book on the impact of the Second World War on Puerto Rico.

**John F. Stack, Jr**, Professor of Political Science and Director of the Institute for Public Policy and Citizenship Studies at Florida International University, received his PhD from the Graduate School of International Studies, University of Denver and the JD from the University of Miami School of Law. His research deals mainly with ethnicity in world politics and supranational institutions. Dr Stack is author of *International Conflict in an American City: Boston's Irish, Italians, and Jews, 1935–1944*, and editor of *Ethnic Identities in a Transnational World, Policy Choices: Critical Issues in American Foreign Policy, The Primordial Challenge: Ethnicity in the Modern World*, and *The Ethnic Entanglement: Conflict and Intervention in World Politics*.

**Hilbourne A. Watson** is Professor of International Relations at Bucknell University prior to which he taught for two decades at Howard University. A specialist on Caribbean politics and international political economy, Dr Watson has published extensively on a variety of topics, including Caribbean political economy, US–Caribbean relations, international migration, and global restructuring. Author of numerous scholarly articles, book chapters and monographs, he is editor of *The Caribbean in the Global Political Economy*. A former president of the Caribbean Studies Association, he is currently working on two books, one dealing with Caribbean international relations theory and the other with the crisis of modernity in the Caribbean.

**Tim Wren** joined the Northamptonshire police force in 1975 and specialized in criminal investigation. In 1987 he was assigned responsibility for the introduction of the Drug Trafficking Offences Act, and in 1989 he was seconded to the National Drugs Intelligence Unit in London to oversee the Financial Intelligence Unit, now part of Britain's National Criminal Intelligence Service. A former British representative on the Financial Action Task Force, an international anti-money laundering body, Mr Wren has been a consultant to several governments. He was Executive Director of the Caribbean Financial Action Task Force between 1993 and 1997.

# Acknowledgements

Several people in North America, the Caribbean and Europe played roles in the production of this work. Although I cannot name them all here, I would like to acknowledge those who played key roles in seeing this work during its three-and-a-half years gestation. Thanks first to Tim Shaw for inviting me to add this work to Macmillan's well-respected International Political Economy Series, of which he is General Editor, and for general guidance of the project. I really appreciate the consideration by Aruna Vasedevan, then Commissioning Editor, for accepting a final manuscript much larger than specified in the book contract, and for patience as the work progressed. Ann Marangos must be commended for her copy-editing and other editorial professionalism. A note of appreciation is due also to John Smith, Senior Book Editor, Lucy Qureshi, Editorial Assistant and the rest of the editorial and production staff at Macmillan.

Thanks also to the following individuals for a variety of roles played in the preparation of this work: Benjamin Nash, my former graduate assistant and current doctoral student; Diane Dick, my former graduate assistant and a graduate of the Masters Program in Political Science; Darlene Choy-Yuen, my former student and a graduate of the Masters Program in Political Science; Michele Atkinson, my former student and a graduate of the Masters Program in International Relations; and Lee Companioni, my secretary. My thanks, too, to the contributors for accommodating my requests for revisions to their chapters, several in some cases. Each of the contributors secured the assistance of several people in researching and writing their chapters. My appreciation is extended to them also.

IVELAW L. GRIFFITH
*Miami, Florida, USA*

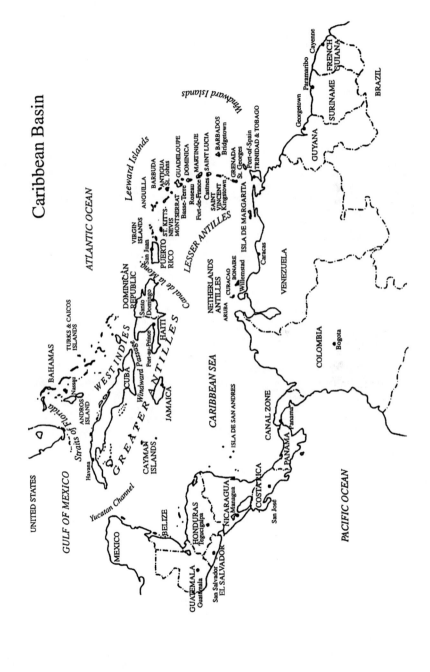

Caribbean Basin

# Introduction: Drugs and Political Economy

*Ivelaw L. Griffith*

Political scientist Peter Lupsha, a long-time scholar of narcotics issues, once asserted: 'The political economy *of drug trafficking* can be described as a dynamic, non-linear, nested, non-zero sum game.'[1] But insofar as the political economy *of the drug phenomenon* is concerned, although Lupsha's proposition is indisputable and necessary, it is not sufficient. Several corollaries need to be offered.

First, the drug phenomenon, whether viewed in global, regional or national terms, is not a one-dimensional matter; it is not simply about trafficking. Secondly it is multidimensional both in character and consequences; production, trafficking, consumption-abuse, money laundering being the main problem areas, with myriad consequences including corruption, economic resource depletion, and crime. Moreover, the characterization of the political economy of trafficking also holds true for the three other problem areas. And fourthly, appreciating the political economy dynamics of drugs warrants taking a holistic approach to the issue; understanding how production, trafficking, use, and money laundering are linked directly and indirectly; and investigating how their pursuit as well as their prevention have direct and indirect implications for economic governance, political governance and the nexus between the two.

Scholars and statesmen alike are able to condemn without compunction the drug phenomenon's precipitation or aggravation of socio-political effects such as crime, corruption, and moral degradation. But they have to temper their inclination to level wholesale condemnation when it comes to the socio-economic areas, for they are forced to recognize that drugs do have positive-sum aspects – income generation, employment creation, and resource distribution, no matter how skewed, among them. Indeed, this is at the heart of the global narcotics dilemma.[2] The

1

dilemma character becomes more readily apparent when the issue is viewed in the context of global trade and economics. As one United Nations report quite rightly states:

> The illicit drug phenomenon cannot be viewed outside the context of contemporary economic, social, and political development. Changes in the world political economy and advances in technology over the past three decades have had a significant impact on the scope and nature of the illicit drug problem. It is now recognized that rapid growth in the trade of goods and services has resulted in a more interdependent world. Yet, despite the positive implications which the increase in world trade has for prosperity and efficiency, sustained growth in international trade can complicate efforts to control the illicit problem.[3]

A few examples of this aspect of the dilemma will suffice:

> The electronic highway now links banks and non-bank financial institutions worldwide to facilitate expanding word trade and financial services, placing ever greater priority on banks of origin to establish the identity of beneficial owners and their sources of funds. There are few controls on electronic transfers, and, compounding the problem, the bank or non-bank of origin is increasingly based outside major financial centers in jurisdictions which do not adequately control money laundering and other financial crimes.[4]

> In one instance, financial 'fraudsters' obtained the secret telex codes which banks use for bank-to-bank transactions and were able to take $42 million in cash out of Hong Kong and Shanghai Bank in Jakarta [Indonesia].[5]

> One attempted transfer confirms that the world of banking is truly a world without horizons. We learned that a group proposed to transfer $1.3 billion from a bank in the Caribbean to Indonesia, heightening our concern. These and other attempts are notable, not only for their variation, but because of their higher probability of success.[6]

> Vladimir Levin, a 30–year old Russian, has attained folklore status as the hacker who engineered the 1994 heist of $10 million from Citibank by funneling the money from Citibank branches worldwide to this accomplices' accounts in the United States, Israel, Finland, Germany, the Netherlands, and Switzerland without ever leaving his

computer keyboard in St. Petersburg, Russia. The case is extraordinary not only for the amount stolen and the method by which it was accomplished but also for the furor it has stirred within the financial community and the Internet security industry.[7]

More than a dozen casinos have opened in Antigua, but most Antiguans do not know they exist. That is because the are 'virtual casinos'. Under legislation passed during early 1997, the Antigua government has been charging a mere US$100,000 a year for an Internet casino license. To play at an Internet casino, gamblers access a casino site on the World Wide Web through their personal computers, establish an account with a credit card or money order and collect their virtual 'chips'. The computer program ushers them into a full-color, multi-dimensional casino that looks remarkably similar to those in Las Vegas, and they can gamble at the table of their choice.[8]

There is a political economy truism about the narcotics phenomenon that both scholars and statesmen have to accept: the drug market is fundamentally no different from any other commodity trade since it is driven by the basic economic forces of demand and supply. Where it does differ significantly, however, is in its legal status, which influences the market dynamics involved. Price, for example, is affected significantly. Paul Stares explains that supply is artificially constricted by the rules affecting which drugs can be legally produced, medically prescribed, and sold commercially, and by the many law enforcement barriers against illicit manufacturers and distributors. He notes: 'As the availability of a commodity in demand diminishes, its price generally rises, all else being equal. The illegality of the market, moreover, allows illicit suppliers to set prices at a level that compensates them for the risk they take and the additional costs they incur in supplying the market.'[9]

Leaving aside price and other demand–supply dynamics, perhaps the other single most important political economy concern of policy-makers is about 'cost'. For instance, the cost factor is highlighted on the first page of the first chapter of the 1997 national drug strategy of the United States: 'Drug induced deaths increased 47 percent between 1990 and 1994 and number approximately 14,000 a year. Illegal drugs also burden our society with approximately $67 billion in social, health, and criminal costs each year.'[10] But while critical, cost estimates are often imprecise partly because of the lack of empirical data, partly because the costs involved are not all economic costs, but include social costs not subject to easy economic estimation, and partly because there are both private and public costs involved. According to the United Nations International Drug Control Program (UNDCP), analysts have bypassed some of the cost estimation challenges by applying the concept of opportunity cost – calculating the benefits which would be derived from the best alternative use of a particular resource – which is based on the assumption that resources always have alternative uses.[11]

Understandably, irrespective of whether one looks at the political economy of drugs globally or in one region, much more than price and costs are involved. This book probes some of the aspects and areas involved in and for the Caribbean. It is to an explanation of how this is done that attention is turned next.

## About the book

Prospective readers of a book often have three questions which they pose, either silently to themselves or openly to the author/editor of the book, or to whomever is encouraging them to read it: Why should I read – or, if it is a student, be made to read – this book? What is it all about? How does it accomplish what the author/editor has in mind? This Introduction, therefore, needs to answer these three questions.

As regards the first question, this work aims to do four things: examine the nexus between drugs as a social phenomenon and political economy as a scholarly issue area; explore the regional and global contexts of the political economy of drugs in the Caribbean; assess some of the political economy connections and consequences of drugs in the Caribbean; and discuss some of the measures undertaken to contend with drugs in the region. The answer to the second question lies in the dearth of scholarly analysis on the political economy of drugs in the Caribbean. Although the Caribbean has been examined fairly closely, the critical political economy dimension has commanded neither substantive nor sufficient attention.[12] Prior to this work, for example, there was no single-authored or edited book on the subject.

This neglect of the political economy aspects of drugs in the Caribbean is the result of the combined effect of several factors, notably:

- the preoccupation by scholars with analysis of the nature, scope and implications of drug trafficking, and resulting problems such as corruption and crime, and mainly from the political governance vantage point;
- the failure by writers to appreciate the intellectual and policy value of probing the political economy dynamics of even trafficking, not to

mention of areas such as drug production, consumption and money laundering;
- the neglect by Caribbean scholars and statesmen of the total drugs matrix and the implications of the dynamics of that matrix for economic governance as well as for political governance.

As to the third question – How? – it is important to state that although this volume focuses on the Caribbean region it is important to understand the Caribbean dynamics in global comparative terms, and for at least two reasons. First, global interdependence is an increasing reality of contemporary life, such that developments in one region have impacts which extend beyond the particular region. Secondly, the political economy connections and consequences of drugs are not being experienced only in the Caribbean; Latin American, Southeast Asia, Central and Western Europe, and Eastern and Western Africa are among regions experiencing them.[13] Thus, Part I of this work will explore elements of the regional and global contexts.

The political economy ramifications of drugs are numerous. They range from things that are 'strictly' economic, such as resource (re)allocation and trade and finance, to things that are socio-political such as democracy and criminal justice. Although all the possible ramifications in the Caribbean cannot be examined in this work, those considered critical to the region will be addressed in Part II of the volume. It is also crucial to discuss measures being adopted to cope with the various political economy challenges, and some of the implications of these countermeasures for political and economic governance. We are obliged to appreciate the multidimensional nature of responses – that several different kinds of actors are involved – by necessity, and not by choice: governments, non-governmental organizations (NGOs), and international agencies; that countermeasures have to be adopted at the national, regional and international levels; and that efforts have also to be simultaneous, not sequential, with a view to rehabilitation, law enforcement, interdiction, and other areas. Part III of the volume pays attention to these matters.

The multidimensional nature of the narcotics phenomenon and its political economy connections and consequences force us to recognize that the issues involved have an importance that extends beyond theory and empiricism to policy making and policy execution. Consequently, meaningful discussion of the various aspects of the subject would best be served by having contributions to the discussion from academic experts, policy makers and advisers, and people involved in policy execution.

With this in mind, this volume brings together academics, policy-makers, and policy implementers who are eminently qualified to contribute to the analysis. Moreover, partly because of the kinds of issues examined and the combination of experts examining them, the volume profits more from eclecticism in its theoretical and conceptual aspects than from a single theoretical paradigm.

## Conclusion

The business of drugs and of aspects of the nexus between drugs and political economy examined in this book should necessarily be of interest to students and scholars of the Caribbean, especially those in the fields of political economy, foreign policy, and international politics. However, because the academic community is not the only one with a constituency concerned with the subject, the makers and executors of policy in and for the Caribbean can be expected to have some interest in this work. Moreover, the interest should come from practitioners not only in government, but also in NGOs and international agencies, such as the Inter-American Drug Abuse Control Commission (CICAD), UNDCP, the Caribbean Development Bank (CDB) and the Caribbean Financial Action Task Force (CFATF).

## Notes

1   Peter A. Lupsha, 'Nets of Affiliation in the Political Economy of Drug Trafficking and Transnational Crime", in *Economics of the Narcotics Industry*, report of a conference held by the US Department of State and the Central Intelligence Agency, Washington, DC, 21–22 November 1994, n.p. Emphasis added.

2   See Ivelaw L. Griffith, 'From Cold War Geopolitics to Post-Cold War Geonarcotics', *International Journal*, 49 (Winter 1993–94), pp. 1–36 for an examination of the global narcotics dilemma and some of its positive-sum aspects.

3   UNDCP, *World Drug Report* (New York: Oxford University Press, 1997), p. 17.

4   US Department of State, *International Narcotics Control Strategy Report*, March 1996, p. 498.

5   US Department of State, *International Narcotics Control Strategy Report*, March 1997, p. 514.

6   Ibid.

7   M.J. Zuckerman, 'Security on Trial in Case of On-line Citibank Heist', *USA Today*, 19 September 1997, p. 12A.

8   Mark Fineman, 'Antigua Cyber-Casinos Raking in Cash', *Miami Herald*, 22 September 1997, p. 6A.

9   Paul B. Stares, *Global Habit: the Drug Problem in a Borderless World*, (Washington, DC: Brookings Institution, 1996), p. 47.

10  Office of the President, *The National Drug Control Strategy, 1997*, February 1997, p. 3.

11  UNDCP, *World Drug Report*, p. 103.

12  Among the few scholarly works on the political economy of drugs in the region have been Anthony P. Maingot, 'Laundering the Gains of the Drug Trade: Miami and Caribbean Tax Havens', *Journal of Interamerican Studies and World Affairs*, 30 (summer–autumn 1988), pp. 167–87; Scott B. MacDonald, *Dancing on a Volcano* (New York: Praeger, 1988), pp. 89–103; Faye V. Harrison, 'Drug Trafficking in World Capitalism: a Perspective on Jamaica Posses in the US', *Social Justice*, 16 (No. 4, 1989), pp. 115–31; Scott B. MacDonald and Bruce Zagaris (eds), *International Handbook on Drug Control* (Westport, CT: Greenwood Press, 1992), pp. 137–56; Anthony P. Maingot, *The United States and the Caribbean* (Boulder, Colo. Westview Press, 1994), pp. 163–82; Ivelaw L. Griffith, '*The Money Laundering Dilemma in the Caribbean*', Working Paper No. 4, Institute of Caribbean Studies, University of Puerto Rico, September 1995; Ivelaw Lloyd Griffith, *Drugs and Security in the Caribbean: Sovereignty Under Siege* (University Park: Penn State University Press, 1997), chs 3, 6, 7.

13  See, for example, James Mills, *The Underground Empire* (New York: Doubleday, 1986); Jo Ann Kawell, 'The Addict Economies', *NACLA Report on the Americas*, 22 (March 1989), pp. 33–43; MacDonald and Zagaris, *International Handbook on Drug Control*; Rensselaer W. Lee, III and Scott B. MacDonald, 'Drugs in the East', *Foreign Policy*, 90 (Spring 1993), pp. 89–107; Francisco E. Thoumi, *Political Economy and Illegal Drugs in Colombia* (Boulder, Colo.: Lynne Rienner, 1995); Stares, *Global Habit*; Roger Kaplan (ed.), *Drugs and Dollars: a Global Challenge* (New York: Freedom House, 1996); UNDCP, *World Drug Report*; and K.I. Douglas, 'War and the Global Opium Supply', *The Fletcher Forum on World Affairs*, 21 (summer/autumn 1997), pp. 121–31.

# Part I

# Regional and International Contexts

# 1

# Drugs and Political Economy in a Global Village

*Ivelaw L. Griffith*

There are four main drug or drug-related operations in the Caribbean: (i) marijuana production; (ii) consumption and abuse of marijuana, cocaine and heroin; (iii) trafficking of all three substances; and (iv) the laundering of money derived from the three other areas. These operations have numerous effects on Caribbean societies, including corruption, crime, arms trafficking, productivity loss, and economic resource reallocation.[1] The operations and effects do not exist uniformly throughout the Caribbean, but they are sufficiently widespread in the region as to constitute a regional dilemma, for they have implications for several aspects of political and socioeconomic life in the entire area. This chapter examines some of the political economy implications involved.

The Caribbean is merely a global village in terms of the drug phenomenon, as the work of several scholars and international agencies show clearly that the drugs phenomenon is truly a global interdependence issue.[2] A strict economic cost–benefit analysis of drugs in the Caribbean global village would require, at the barest minimum, measurement of the opportunity costs of the factors of production used in the drugs industry, and the income received by producers and traffickers, by money launderers and by other economic activities that derive from narcotics industry operations.[3] For a variety of understandable methodological and data-related reasons, this is infeasible, and not only for the Caribbean.

Yet it is useful to examine some of the economic positive-sum and negative-sum variables involved. This permits an appreciation of at least three things: (1) some of the economic positives and negatives of drugs; (2) some of the linkages between political governance and economic management; and (3) some of the reasons why, consequently, policy management of the drug dilemma is intractable. I offer a positive-sum–negative-sum analysis here fully conscious that drugs also carry indirect economic costs and social costs not amenable to easy economic estimation. And although by itself this assessment would reveal some of the political economy connections of the Caribbean drugs business, the connections are best appreciated if explored in the context of an economic portrait of the Caribbean global village.

## Portrait of an economic village

A survey of the Caribbean economic landscape finds that there are some important natural resources in the region, including oil, bauxite, gold, diamonds, and nickel. However, very few countries have these resources. Only Trinidad and Tobago, and Barbados and Suriname, to a much lesser extent, have oil industries, although exploration is underway in Cuba and Guyana, and there are refining and transshipment operations in many countries. Bauxite is produced only in the Dominican Republic, Guyana, Jamaica and Suriname. Diamond is mined only in Guyana, and only Cuba, the Dominican Republic and Guyana produce gold, although there is evidence that Belize also has this mineral. As for nickel, it is found only in Cuba and the Dominican Republic. This limited mineral resource availability partly explains why the region's Gross Domestic Product (GDP) revolves around a narrow economic base: (i) agriculture – mainly sugar and bananas; (ii) mining and manufacturing – notably of bauxite, oil, nickel, and gold; and (iii) services.[4]

Off-shore banking and tourism are the two most critical industries in the service sector. Off-shore banking has long been important to Aruba, the Bahamas, Curaçao, and most of the British dependencies in the region, and it is becoming increasingly so to Antigua–Barbuda, Barbados, and Belize. But more important than this industry, both to these countries and the region as a whole, is tourism. Dennis Gayle has explained that tourism is the only industry in the Caribbean Basin that has grown progressively since 1973, generating some US$96 billion in gross expenditure annually. Indeed, 'tourism generates more foreign exchange and tax revenues per dollar of investment than any other industry'.[5] The World Bank (WB) also reports that tourism is the largest export earner for the region, and one country – Cuba – where tourism had been playing second place to other economic sectors, notably agriculture, reported in September 1997 that tourism had surpassed sugar as the single largest foreign exchange earner.[6]

Table 1.1  Key Economic Indicators for Caribbean Countries[a]

| Country | Size (km)$^2$ | Population | GNP per capita | GDP growth rate | Foreign inflation rate | Foreign debt ($m) | Debt as % of GDP |
|---|---|---|---|---|---|---|---|
| Antigua–Barbuda | 440 | 66,500 | 2,330 | –3.8 | –0.6 | 234.7 | 157 |
| Aruba | 193 | 83,651 | 16,380 | 9.1 | 3.4 | 206.4 | 15 |
| Bahamas | 13,942 | 276,000 | 11,059 | 0.8 | 2.0 | 392.0 | 12 |
| Barbados | 432 | 264,000 | 6,580 | 2.5 | 1.8 | 562.0 | 30 |
| Belize | 22,960 | 217,000 | 2,264 | 3.8 | 3.2 | 183 | 32 |
| Cuba | 110,860 | 11,005,000 | 1,185 | 2.5 | NA | 9.1** | 71 |
| Dominica | 750 | 73,500 | 2,654 | 1.8 | NA | 100 | 48 |
| Dominican Republic | 48,442 | 7,921,000 | 927 | 4.8 | 9.2 | 4.1** | 35 |
| Grenada | 345 | 98,000 | 1,970 | 2.8 | 2.1 | 84.7 | 44 |
| Guyana | 214,970 | 834,000 | 772 | 6.3 | NA | 2.1** | 433 |
| Haiti | 27,750 | 7,180,000 | 229 | 4.5 | 27.1 | 778 | 35 |
| Jamaica | 11,424 | 2,547,000 | 1,637 | 0.5 | 19.9 | 4.2** | 129 |
| St Kitts-Nevis | 269 | 43,530 | 1,530 | 3.4 | 2.6 | 52.4 | 81 |
| St Lucia | 616 | 145,325 | 2,790 | 4.0 | 4.6 | 112 | 28 |
| St Vincent & Grenadines | 388 | 110,724 | 740 | 7.4 | 3.2 | 87 | 107 |
| Suriname | 163,270 | 405,000 | 817 | 5.2 | 50 | 193 | 58 |
| Trinidad–Tobago | 5,128 | 1,306,000 | 4,369 | 3.2 | 5.3 | 2.2 | 36 |

Notes:
[a] All figures are for 1995; ** billion; NA – not available.
Sources: Caribbean–Latin American Action, Caribbean Basin Profile (Grand Cayman: Island Caribbean Publishing, 1996); Caribbean Development Bank, Annual Report 1996, March 1997.

Caribbean countries also have to carry an economic albatross in the form of huge foreign debts, as Table 1.1 indicates. The 6 million people of the English-speaking Caribbean alone had a 1995 foreign debt of some US$9 billion. Cuba's debt was over US$9 billion; Haiti's was some US$800 million. However, as Table 1.1 also makes clear, it is not merely the size of the debt that is problematic, but also its servicing. Guyana, with its US$2 billion debt and 433 per cent debt-service-to-GDP ratio, provides dramatic evidence of this. In his 6 February 1995 budget speech finance minister Asgar Ally (who resigned in May 1995 over policy disputes with President Cheddie Jagan) indicated: 'During 1994, total debt service payments stood at US$99.2 million, a 16.6 per cent increase on 1993 levels.... Even with debt relief of over US$300 million between 1990 and 1994, the ratio of our existing loan portfolio to GDP is still uncomfortably high at over 400 per cent with no new borrowing, and the ratio of debt service to merchandise exports is still above what is considered to be the critical level.'[7] Ally's successor, Bharrat Jagdeo, told parliament in January 1996 that 'At the end of 1995, Guyana's external debt stock amounted to US$2.06 billion, or a 3 per cent rise over the previous year.'[8]

It is not being suggested here that no progress has been made in the region. Indeed, there is notable progress in life expectancy, general health care, education, and in GDP growth, among other things. One WB study points out, for example, that 'Most Caribbean countries have made substantial progress on macroeconomic stability in the 1990s. Inflation rates in 1994 and 1995 were below 20 per cent annually in all countries except Jamaica and Suriname.... Exports as a share of GDP have increased in the last decade.'[9] Yet, as one Trinidadian economist has observed, the achievements do not mask the reality, which is that the region is in crisis; that poverty is rising in several states; and that Caribbean economies remain fragile and vulnerable.[10] Moreover, my 1993 characterization of Caribbean economic vulnerability in *The Quest for Security in the Caribbean* is still accurate: the vulnerability is not only functional, but also structural, in that economies suffer from heavy reliance on foreign trade, limited production and export diversification, low savings, heavy dependence on foreign capital, and a dearth of capable economic and management skills, among other things. Furthermore, as is shown in Chapters 2 and 4 of this volume, much of this vulnerability has been highlighted recently as some Caribbean countries experienced setbacks in the garment and tourism industries and as others face a threat to their banana market guarantees.

Migration itself affects the economic landscape. Not only are many Caribbean migration rates very high but also the majority of those who migrate are skilled workers. In her 1997 study Judy Baker reveals that 'In the Dominican Republic, Guyana, and Jamaica, about half of the skilled people graduating from local institutions emigrated between 1980 and 1986. Of emigrants from St. Lucia, and Guyana, 47 and 76 per cent, respectively, had secondary education or higher. Although individuals who emigrate vacate jobs in labor markets with generally high employments rates these positions are usually for highly skilled workers and are difficult to fill. This drain on skills has likely reduced the pace of economic growth and thus slowed the process of overall job creation and affected the long-run development potential in the region.'[11] Aaron Segal noted that migration will continue to be a mostly positive factor for receiving countries, adding to their music, arts, and human [and economic] resources the talents of several million productive persons and their offspring.[12] This observation, while probably correct, is no consolation for sending countries.

All of these circumstances make credible the statement by one Economic Commission for Latin America and the Caribbean (ECLAC) analyst, that people in Cuba, the Dominican Republic, Haiti, Jamaica, Suriname (and I would add Guyana) – the biggest Caribbean countries – have become poorer over the last decade.[13] Indeed, according to one report, 'Approximately 38 per cent of the total population in the Caribbean or more than 7 million people can be classified as poor.... The incidence of poverty is highest in Belize, Dominica, Guyana, Haiti, Jamaica, and Suriname.... Poverty levels are lowest in Antigua-Barbuda, the Bahamas, Barbados, and St. Kitts-Nevis.'[14] The Baker study identifies two broad poverty groups: the chronic poor, and the new poor. The former traditionally is comprised of groups that are not labor market active – children, senior citizens, and indigenous populations such as the Caribs in Dominica, various Amerindians groups in Guyana and Suriname, and the Maroons in Suriname. As regards the new poor, which includes the unemployed, the underemployed and school leavers without labor market skills, this group is said to be the consequence of the extended economic decline and concomitant employment contraction.

Several academic and policy analysts have shown that the decline in the countries concerned has also been affected by reduced government services – the result of coping with budgetary difficulties generally but also necessary for debt servicing. Currency depreciation in some places has also aggravated the situation, affecting prices, purchasing power, savings, and investment. Reduced production and exports, economic mismanagement, and adverse global economic and financial conditions are also relevant factors.[15]

The circumstances described above have led to several developments. For one thing, they have increased the importance of foreign remittances, both cash and in-kind, and both for the survival of individual families and the buoyancy of economies. According to Jamaica's Minister of State for Finance, Errol Ennis, between January and November 1994, Jamaicans resident in the United States alone remitted some US$278 million to the Jamaican economy.[16] And, said Deputy Prime Minister and Minister of Foreign Trade Seymour Mullings, the two-and-a-half million Jamaicans living in New York, Miami, Hartford, Washington, DC, Toronto, London, and Philadelphia remitted US$600 million to Jamaica during 1994.[17] The 27 September–2 October 1996 edition of the *Santo Domingo News* reported that remittances to the Dominican Republic by Dominicans living abroad reach US$1.2 billion per year, the second largest source of foreign exchange after tourism. And, on average for the region, says *Poverty Reduction and Human Development in the Caribbean*, remittances account for some 6 per cent of the region's Gross National Product (GNP), with about 36 per cent of the households in Guyana, 11 per cent in Jamaica, 13 per cent in Trinidad and Tobago, and 17 per cent in St Lucia receiving remittances.

The combined effect of the debt crisis, depressed exports, mismanagement, and other factors has been such that Caribbean countries have been forced to seek foreign economic and financial support. One consequence of this has been the prescription by the WB and the International Monetary Fund (IMF) of strong doses of structural adjustment, central to which are privatization and deregulation. Structural adjustment programs have been presented as beneficial to Caribbean countries in the long term, but they have some deleterious short-term social and economic effects. One study of the Jamaica situation with region-wide relevance shows that the state's role in providing welfare has diminished as social justice becomes subordinated to market considerations. Both the quantity and quality of social services have been affected by cuts in public sector spending, and reduced or removed subsidies for food, education, and health services, among other areas, has increased economic deprivation. Wages have lost the battle with persistent inflation, and prices have risen continually, partly because of the free market emphasis.[18]

In addition, and because of circumstances described above, the growth and importance of the informal economy have been stimulated, such that in places like the Dominican Republic, Guyana, Haiti, and Suriname it has become relatively more important to most citizens than the formal economy. All of this makes the engagement in illegal activities more palatable for some people and justifiable for others. It also makes some citizens both more susceptible and vulnerable to corruption, to corruption by acts of commission and by acts of omission. In other words, the economic condition of the Caribbean global village itself makes the region hospitable to the conduct of drug operations. What, then, given this economic portrait, are some of the political economy dynamics of drugs in the contemporary Caribbean global village?

## Positive-sum variables

Drug production, trafficking, and money laundering provide at least three areas of actual and potential economic positives: employment, income regeneration, and revenue enhancement.

For obvious reasons, it is impossible to quantify the benefits from employment – or from any of the other areas for that matter – in terms of number of people doing direct and indirect, and full-time and part-time work related to drugs. Categories and numbers of people employed vary from place to place and operation to operation, but, generally, several different occupational areas are involved, including farmers, pilots, laborers, engineers, drivers, accountants, look-outs, and guards. This list does not include the variety of people in different public and private sector roles who are bribed to facilitate production, trafficking, and other operations. Moreover, in thinking of employment, account must be taken of the fact that narcotics countermeasures by governments also often boost employment in police, customs, coast guard, judicial and other agencies.

A look at one area of operation – production – suggests that, given marijuana production and eradication levels in the Caribbean, especially in Jamaica, Guyana, Belize, and the Eastern Caribbean, the number of people throughout the region 'employed' directly and indirectly in this area would run into the tens of thousands. As regards Jamaica, production is said to have generated employment and income for small farmers and wage workers in the context of declining jobs and income from traditional agricultural exports such as sugar and bananas.[19] Some 6,000 Jamaican farmers alone are said to have been involved in marijuana production during the 1980s.[20]

As regards income generation, production, trafficking, sale, and money laundering transactions do generate income. For some of the people involved, the income is primary income; for others it is supplementary earnings. One Jamaican government study established clear linkages between marijuana production and income generation: 'The

Government's anti-drug eradication program has succeeded in destroying vast areas planted in marijuana, but the socio-economic problems remain. The small growers in these target communities have been experiencing a worsened situation in generating income or finding suitable employment.... The average disposable income was 84 per cent above the national level, but since the [eradication] program it fell to 18 per cent above the per capita disposable income.'[21]

For many people the relative economic deprivation and poverty in the region are justification for engagement in drug activities. Paul Stares makes an observation that certainly is applicable to the Caribbean: 'For most people involved in cultivating drugs, the motivation derives less from the promise of economic gain and more from the pressure of economic necessity.'[22] As a matter of fact, some analysts see clear linkages between drug activities and contributors to the deprivation, particularly debt and structural adjustment. Jamaican economist and diplomat Richard Bernal, for instance, asserts: 'The debt burden serves to encourage indulgence in the illicit drug industry...'.[23] University of the West Indies (UWI) Professor of Economics Dennis Pantin argues: 'Amelioration of the drug trade is, [however,] impossible without a reduced burden of the so-called structural adjustment, which creates the fertile environment for drug activity.'[24] Apart from poverty and deprivation, people are motivated by greed and acquisitive materialism. And given the 'big money' involved in drugs and the poor salaries for a wide cross-section of jobs in most places, one can understand the susceptibility to corruption, which itself generates income.

While it is true that drug operators do not pay income, corporate, or other taxes into the formal economy, some of the income they generate does interface with the formal economy, contributing to government revenue. One way this happens is when income generated by drug transactions is used in a legal context where value added, property, sales, and other taxes are paid. Moreover, Caribbean countries that place a premium on off-shore banking and financial services do benefit from licensing and relicensing fees for companies created either expressly to launder drug money, or that undertake legitimate business but are also used for narcotics money laundering. Revenue enhancement is also a function of seizures of drug-related assets, fines levied by courts against people convicted of drug offenses, and fines imposed by regulatory agencies, such as central banks and customs departments, against companies that violate anti-trafficking and anti-money laundering regulations.

Understandably, much of the economic activity generated by drug operations becomes a part of the informal economy. However, as noted above, the informal economy is crucial to economic survival in some countries. Moreover, there is always some interface between formal and informal economies in all countries, which means that formal economies in the Caribbean benefit from drug operations. Undoubtedly, then, employment, income generation, and revenue enhancement due to drugs affect the formal economy, and in positive (as well as negative) ways.

The impact of drugs is also felt in more indirect ways. One area pertains to savings. Although there is conspicuous consumption by many people who profit from drug operations, money is also saved and invested, and in and through formal financial institutions. This not only adds to the stock of savings, but it also affects, often positively, such things as investment capital and interest rates.[25] As Stares has said in a general context, 'Money gained from the drug business also makes its way into the local economy with the purchase of goods and services, the capitalization of banks and investment in real estate and legitimate businesses.'[26] In relation to Jamaica, Carl Stone once noted: 'The drug trade provided access to capital and capital accumulation in an economy dominated by a closely knit network of local white, Jewish, Lebanese, and brown entrepreneurs, and [by] foreign capital. [It] served to open up opportunities for wealth accumulation for black middle class interests who found themselves unable to break into the big business sector dominated by the ethnic minorities.'[27]

Another area of impact is the availability of foreign currency. The stark reality is that given demand–supply dynamics and the strength of the currency of the world's most significant narcotics market – the United States – drug operations generate US dollars, and these are used in both the formal and informal economies. In Guyana, for example, drug operations are said to have so influenced foreign currency dealings as to affect not only the quantity of US dollars available but also the official exchange rate with the local currency. In Jamaica, Stone remarked that in their highly dependent economy imports represent some 50 per cent of GDP. However, the foreign exchange crisis of the 1970s reduced the formal economy's ability to pay for imports, affecting negatively both production and consumption. The government's response to the crisis involved tight foreign exchange controls and import restrictions. According to Stone, 'Drug production and trafficking were, however, immensely helpful to Jamaica. The illegal marijuana trade emerged as the way business interests attempted to fill the growing gaps between their demand for foreign exchange and the declining supply through legitimate channels. In other words, the marijuana trade helped to sustain the flow of imports into this highly import dependent economy by providing a supplementary source of foreign exchange to importers, by way of a rapidly growing black market in US dollars which was supplied mainly from the drug trade.'[28]

Over and above all this, as is done in Latin America and elsewhere, Caribbean drug operators often engage in a form of social investment – Robin Hoodism – by doing what governments are sometimes unable to do: they fulfill social welfare needs, either on an individual or a communal basis. They provide medical and school supplies or funds for people to secure specialist medical care, sporting equipment and facilities, and church relief, among other things. They also bring business and work to some areas, and sometimes in a noticeable way. Understandably, the beneficiaries of this benevolence do not see the drug operators as moral or legal reprobates; often they see them as heroes. This partly explains why some communities not only fail to aid in the apprehension or conviction of drug operators but also sometimes they actually protect those operators from the law.

## Negative-sum variables

Like the positive-sum entries, the negative-sum ones defy quantification. But they can be identified as including the impact on certain industries, fines imposed by foreign countries, and resource utilization.

Tourism, which, as seen above, is critical to several countries, is vulnerable to drug operations. The impact is largely indirect, and relates to crime. As a matter of fact, Gordon "Butch" Stewart, one of the region's leading tourism entrepreneurs, has called crime 'the evil of tourism'.[29] The negative effect results from (a) media reports that scare potential tourists away, and (b) the high incidence of drug-related crime in some places. Caribbean observers have known for some time what the *New York Times* reported in April 1994: that drug-related crime has transformed the 'paradise' character of the United States Virgin Islands and other Caribbean vacation spots, driving fear into locals and tourists alike, and depressing tourism.[30]

In the case of Jamaica, where tourism accounts for about 45 per cent of the foreign exchange earnings, in July 1994 the Jamaica Tourist Board reported a decline in tourist arrivals of 5.8 per cent in April 1994 and 15.1 per cent the following month. Carlyle Dunkley, then the tourism minister, attributed the decline to Jamaica's 'image problem', caused by the alarmingly high rate of violent crime. There were over 653 murders in Jamaica in 1993 alone. By June 1994 some 360 people had been killed, and by the end of the year the figure had risen to 690, many of the cases involving drug-related issues. Indeed, crime is said to be a major factor in the three per cent decline in tourism in 1994 – US$30 million less than the US$ 943 million earned in 1993.[31] The impact of drugs-driven crime on tourism is also of concern in Belize, Puerto Rico, Trinidad and Tobago and elsewhere in the region. It is also a matter of concern in the Bahamas where the 1994 crime rate was the highest in five years, in Puerto Rico which had 868 homicides in 1996, and Jamaica, which had 921 murders during that year. In both Puerto Rico and Jamaica, most of the murders were drug-related. Indeed, 495 murders were committed in Jamaica up to mid-July 1999, triggering both alarm and crisis reaction by the government and corporate bodies, including the deployment of troops to tourist areas.[32]

The garment industry, which is used for trafficking, especially in Jamaica, the Dominican Republic, and the Eastern Caribbean, is also affected. In one Jamaican situation, Hanes, the country's largest garment manufacturer, suspended for many months all shipments of cut goods for assembly in Jamaica following the discovery in June 1994 in a Florida warehouse of 200 pounds of marijuana in a shipment of clothing from Jamaica. One could well imagine the potential impact on Jamaica's economy when it is recognized that directly and through subcontracting Hanes produces about US$200 million worth of garments annually.[33] In November 1998, Cupid Foundations, a US-owned garment company that had been operating in Jamaica for 22 years announced the closure of operations and relocation to Nicaragua. According to General Manager Ronald Josephs, the company could no longer afford the losses incurred with the seizure by US Customs of its merchandise because of attempts to smuggle drugs into the United States among its clothing. Moreover, Jamaican law enforcement authorities could not provide assurance of drug-free shipping. The closure of the company placed 550 people out of work.[34]

The industry is critical to Jamaica's economy. It generated US$570 million in exports in 1995, with a net value added of 20 per cent. It is estimated to have provided direct employment for some 50,000 people, 14,000 working for the domestic market, and 36,000 for the export market. There are 221 apparel plants, 110 of which are registered exporters. Garment manufacturers employ 35 per cent of the workers in Jamaica's manufacturing sector. In some parishes, such as Hanover and St Mary, it employs between 70 and 80 per cent of the labor force.[35] The industry is even more crucial to the economic buoyancy of the Dominican Republic, where in 1995 it employed over 170,000 people in 436 firms and generated exports of close to US$2 billion. Indeed, the Dominican Republic has been described as 'the largest textile exporter to the US in the Western Hemisphere and the fifth in the world'.[36]

In addressing the implications of drugs for the industry, Lucien Rattray, president of the Jamaica Promotions Corporation, noted that for the period 1993–94 drugs were found in the shipments of 18 garment companies. Such finds not only affect the integrity of products but they also result in prohibitive fines against local and foreign contractors,[37] thereby affecting the solvency of companies and the performance of the industry overall. Ambassador Peter King explained to this writer that security measures by the apparel industry add 8 per cent to its operating costs. As a result of the drug situation, some shipping companies that transport garments or garment material have threatened to withdraw their service from Jamaica.

The second minus-side entry relates to fines. It is related to the impact on the tourism and garment industries, but the effect goes beyond these areas. Heavy fines are often levied by US. Customs against the owners of carriers on which drugs are found. Under US legislation – 19 U.S.C. 1584, amended by PL 99-570 – if a vessel found with drugs is not seized, there is a fine of $1,000 per ounce for cocaine, heroin, morphine, and opiate. The fine for marijuana or opium used for smoking is $500 per ounce.[38]

In recent times, for example, a US$1.2 million fine was imposed on the Guyana Airways Corporation (GAC) after a GAC flight arrived in New York with about 100 pounds of marijuana. That was in January 1992. On 7 November of the same year another GAC plane arrived in New York with 17 pounds of cocaine in an unaddressed mailbag, triggering a fine of US$273,600 by US Customs.[39] The most dramatic episode for GAC was on 15 March 1993, when flight GY714 arrived in New York from Guyana with 117 pounds of cocaine in the plane's paneling. There was a US$1.8 million fine for this infraction, which led the GAC to offer a $1 million (Guyana) reward for information that would lead to the arrest and successful prosecution of the people involved in the affair.[40] That was the first time a Caribbean airline was forced to resort to such desperate and dramatic action to deal with air trafficking. The case is yet to be solved.

Of all the countries affected by fines, notably Guyana, the Dominican Republic, Haiti, the Bahamas, Trinidad and Tobago, the Cayman Islands, and Jamaica, the last named country has suffered the heaviest toll. The fines have been devastating to Air Jamaica, a state-owned corporation until November 1994, when it was acquired by Gordon 'Butch' Stewart and a consortium of private businessmen. The fines contributed to Air Jamaica's 1988–89 losses of US$14 million, which was 20 per cent above the previous year's loss. In all, between 1989 and 1991, Air Jamaica was fined about US$37 million for illegal drugs found on its planes entering the United States. The fines were however reduced to US$3 million, with agreement that the remaining money be used to upgrade security at Jamaica's international airports.[41] Hence, both state and commercial enterprises have felt the full effect of fines. For private companies they affect directly the viability of companies, and indirectly the economies concerned. In the case of state corporations, both the solvency of the companies and the impact on economies concerned are direct. Hence, whether the fines are against private or public companies their net effect is to exact a toll against already weak Caribbean economies.

As Chapters 6, 8, 9 and those in Part III of this volume show, government (and non-governmental agencies) have been forced to adopt a wide range of narcotics countermeasures. Generally, the measures are costly, and even where there is external support, countermeasures have multiple economic–financial effects. First, they require governments to devote considerable portions of already scarce financial resources to combat drugs. For example, in recent times, most of the Bahamas Defense Force expenditure has been devoted to counternarcotics measures. In 1990 it was 85 per cent. The seriousness of the situation is more readily appreciated when it is realized that counternarcotics measures are not only undertaken by defense and police forces; they extend beyond interdiction and law enforcement, to education, rehabilitation and legislation, among other areas..

As a result of economic difficulties generally and budgetary constraints specifically, governments are obliged to reallocate resources, taking funds away from health, education, housing, and other areas to channel them to meet the drug threat. Jamaica is one dramatic case in point. For several years, Jamaica's budgetary allocations to national security have been the second largest, after education and ahead of health, housing, and other critical social areas. For the 1994–97 budgets, the top three allocations have been as follows (figures in Jamaica dollars):

- 1994–95: education, $5.6 billion, national security, $3.92 billion, health, $3.24 billion;
- 1995–96: education, $8.2 billion, national security, $4.6 billion, health, $3.2 billion;
- 1996–97: education, $10.18 billion, national security, $4.71 billion, health 4.42 billion.[42]

In Barbados, to cite another example, defense expenditure – a major part of it going to fight drugs – have climbed progressively between 1995 and 1998. The allocations have been as follows (in Barbados dollars): 1995–96: $4.6 million; 1996–97: $4.9 million; 1997–98: 5.3 million.[43]

Apart from the three main economic costs of drugs discussed above, other, less significant but noteworthy, implications exist. One relates to foreign aid. Although the gravity of the global drug threat offers the prospect of increasing certain bilateral and multilateral aid flows into the region, the potential for the denial of more significant aid is real. At the bilateral level, US foreign aid, which is important to many Caribbean countries for substantive and symbolic reasons, has often been jeopardized by drug operations. One example will suffice.

Under the 1986 US Anti-Drug Abuse Act (PL 99–570), the US President is allowed to impose sanctions, including duties, cancellation of visas, loss of tariff benefits, a 50 per cent withholding of bilateral aid, and suspension of air services against 'offending countries' – countries that the US considers to be taking insufficient action to combat drug production, trafficking, or money laundering that affects it. The Congress can reverse presidential action to grant aid or impose sanctions by passing a joint resolution within 45 days of the President's determination on the matter, which is due on 1 March each year.[44] Ever since the passage of PL 99–570 Caribbean countries concerned have managed to receive certification. But Congress has not always agreed with the President's assessment and certification. In both 1988 and 1989, for example, Congress attempted to overturn the certification for the Bahamas. In the 1989 case, Senator John Kerry (Democrat from Massachusetts), then Chairman of the powerful Subcommittee on Terrorism, Narcotics, and International Operations, led the decertification effort. However, the President (and the Bahamas) won by a 57–40 vote.

The debit-side entries discussed above are largely direct economic costs. But as noted earlier, drugs also carry indirect economic costs, and social costs not amenable to easy economic estimation. For instance, providing public and private health care for drug users, for children exposed to drugs before and after birth, and for victims of drug-related crime also exact high social and economic costs. Moreover, there is lost or lower labor productivity (a) due to absenteeism, (b) because of the use of illegal drugs, (c) because of imprisonment for drug crimes, and (d) because of death from drug crime victimization, or drug-related work place or traffic accidents. Further, there is also a cost attached to having legitimate industrial production diverted to the production and distribution of illegal drugs. In addition, one has to factor into this social and economic matrix the diminished quality of life caused by illegal drug use, such as pain and suffering of families, friends and crime victims.

The 1997 *World Drug Report* points to an additional negative-sum variable: large scale movements of illegal capital, particularly in small economies, can disable a government's ability to plan and control monetary policy. According to the report, a traditional tool of macroeconomic stabilization is a central bank's ability to make credit – and therefore consumption and investment – more or less expensive by increasing or decreasing the money supply. However, 'when the underground economy is large in relation to the legitimate one, these conditions no longer apply. Similarly, the two most important data sets governments use for planning – the balance of payments and national income accounts – become worthless when large international flows of liquidity, goods and services are unaccounted for'. The report adds, 'decreased financial control undercuts financial credibility and as a result the benefits to a given country can be more than offset by reduced access to legitimate sources of finance. Small economies are more vulnerable to large amounts of illicitly derived capital flowing through the system because the relative proportion of illicit to licit capital is greater and, it could be argued, because small economies are more in need of accurate planning and policy'.[45]

Beyond all this there is what Paul Stares calls 'the most pernicious effect' of the drug phenomenon: undermining the economic integrity and political legitimacy of the state. He argues:

> Successful drug traffickers not only encourage others to imitate them, but they also contribute to the growth of an underground economy by visibly demonstrating the impotence of government authorities. Their ability to operate with impunity and avoid taxation infects other business practices, further corroding public confidence in the ability of state authorities to regulate economic activity equally for the common good. They deprive the government of revenues from untaxed business activity and makes its management of the economy more difficult. Moreover, traffickers erode the state's traditional functions in providing for public safety and the security of property. This in turn stimulates the growth in private protection services, which add to the expense of doing business and further undermine public trust in the effectiveness of law enforcement agencies and the justice system in general. It also promotes the private

resolution of disputes, usually by intimidation and armed force. As law and order begin to fray, local capital takes flight, and potential investment goes elsewhere.[46]

## Conclusion

This chapter validates for drugs in the Caribbean an assertion made elsewhere about drugs internationally: they constitute a dilemma partly because there are both negative and positive aspects involved.[47] Settling the balance sheet is not an easy task, partly because of the non-quantifiable nature of this rough positive-sum–negative-sum assessment, the fact that economic costs are both direct and indirect, and the existence of social costs. Yet, it is difficult not to sense that, in national and regional terms, although not always in individual terms, the costs involved far outweigh the benefits.

## Notes

1   For a comprehensive examination of these problems and some of the effects, see Ivelaw Lloyd Griffith, *Drugs and Security in the Caribbean: Sovereignty Under Siege* (University Park: Penn State University Press, 1997).

2   See, for example, Paul B. Stares, *Global Habit* (Washington, DC: Brookings Institution, 1996); Roger Kaplan (ed.), *Drugs and Dollars: a Global Challenge* (New York: Freedom House, 1996); United Nations International Drug Control Program, *World Drug Report* (New York: Oxford University Press, 1997), and US Department of State, *International Narcotics Control Strategy Report*, March 1999.

3   For more on these and other cost–benefit analysis challenges, see Francisco E. Thoumi, 'The Economic Impact of Narcotics in Colombia', in Peter H. Smith (ed.), *Drug Policy in the Americas* (Boulder, Colo.: Westview Press, 1992), pp. 57–8.

4   Ivelaw L. Griffith, *The Quest for Security in the Caribbean* (Armonk, NY: M.E. Sharpe, 1993), pp. 56–8.

5   Dennis J. Gayle, 'The Evolving Caribbean Business Environment', in Anthony T. Bryan (ed.), *The Caribbean: New Dynamics in Trade and Political Economy* (Miami, Fla: North–South Center, University of Miami, 1995), p. 144.

6   For the WB statement, see WB, *Caribbean Countries: Caribbean Economic Overview 1996*, Report No. 15471–LAC, May 1996, p. 12, and for the report on Cuba, see 'Tourism Overtakes Sugar as Hard Currency Earner', *CanaNews*, available at http://207.234.177.34/cgi-bin/supersite.exe?news, 2 September 1997, p. 3.

7   Government of Guyana, Parliament, *Budget Speech*, Sessional Paper No. 1, 6 February 1995, p. 38.

8   Government of Guyana, Parliament, *Budget Speech*, Sessional Paper No. 1, 19 January 1996, p. 25.

 9  WB, op. cit., p. 4.
10  Ramesh Ramsaran, 'Challenges to Caribbean Economic Development in the 1990s', in *The Caribbean: New Dynamics Trade and Political Economy*, pp. 123, 125.
11  Judy L. Baker, *Poverty Reduction and Human Development in the Caribbean*, WB Discussion Paper No. 366, July 1997, p. 25.
12  See Aaron Segal, 'The Political Economy of Contemporary Migration', in Thomas Klak (ed.), *Globalization and Neoliberalism: The Caribbean Context* (London: Rowman and Littlefield, 1998), p. 225.
13  Trevor Harker, 'Caribbean Economic Performance in the 1990s', in Hilbourne A. Watson (ed.), *The Caribbean in the Global Political Economy* (Boulder, Colo.: Lynne Rienner, 1994), pp. 10–12.
14  Baker, op. cit., p. 3.
15  See John La Guerre, (ed.), *Structural Adjustment: Public Policy and Administration in the Caribbean* (St Augustine, Trinidad: University of the West Indies, 1994); Baker, op. cit., Harker, op. cit.; WB, op. cit.; and Caribbean Development Bank, *Annual Report 1996*, Bridgetown, March 1997.
16  'US$278 Million to Local Economy', *New York Carib News*, 28 November 1994, p. 7.
17  'Jamaicans Remitted US$600 Million', *New York Carib News*, 7 November 1995, p. 13.
18  See Dorith Grant-Wisdom, 'Globalization, Structural Adjustment, and Democracy in Jamaica', in Ivelaw L. Griffith and Betty N. Sedoc-Dahlberg (eds), *Democracy and Human Rights in the Caribbean* (Boulder, CO: Westview Press, 1997), pp. 193–211.
19  Carl Stone, 'Crime and Violence', in Peter Phillips and Judith Wedderburn (eds), *Crime and Violence: Causes and Solutions*, University of the West Indies (Jamaica) Occasional Paper No. 2, September 1988, p. 44.
20  See Scott B. MacDonald, *Dancing on a Volcano* (New York: Praeger, 1988), p.90.
21  Government of Jamaica, Ministry of Agriculture, *Alternative Systems for an Illegal Crop*, September 1994, p. 8.
22  Stares, op. cit., p. 50.
23  Richard Bernal, 'Debt, Drugs, and Development in the Caribbean', *TransAfrica Forum*, 9 (Summer 1992), p. 91.
24  Dennis Pantin, 'The Colombian Nightmare: Drugs and Structural Adjustment in the Caribbean', *Caribbean Affairs*, 2 (October–November 1989), p. 145.
25  Some of these relationships were noted by a Trinidad and Tobago central bank official, who requested anonymity, in an interview in Port of Spain on 8 July 1994.
26  Stares, op. cit., p. 95.
27  Stone, 'Crime and Violence', p. 45.
28  Ibid., p. 44.
29  Don Bohning, 'For Resorts, Crime=Crisis', *Miami Herald*, 10 April 1995, pp. BM43, BM44.
30  Larry Rohter, 'Slaying in St. Thomas Stains Image', *New York Times*, 19 April 1994, p. A17.
31  'Alarm at Downturn in Jamaican Tourism', *Trinidad Guardian* 4 July 1994, p. 9; Richard Browne, 'Multinationals Have no Plans to Leave', *Sunday Gleaner*

(Jamaica), 18 December 1994, p. 1F; and 'Jamaica Tourism Declines', *Miami Herald*, 17 January 1995, p. 3C.

32   See 'Jamaica: Crime Triggers Alarm', *New York Carib News*, 20 July 1999, p. 3. For reports on the impact of crime on tourism during 1999 in the Caribbean, see and Leslie Casimir and Corky Siemaszko, 'Sand, Sun and Siege: Rising tide of Violence hits Isles of Caribbean', *New York Daily News*, 17 July 1999, at http://www.nydailynews.com/, and Paula Szuchman, 'Caribbean Cops Make Waves Against Crime', *Condé Nast Traveler*, August 1999, pp. 25–30.

33   'Ganja Found in Clothing Shipment', *New York Carib News*, 12 July 1994, p. 7.

34   *Miami Herald*, 'Firm closes factory over drug smuggling', 6 November 1998, p. 6A

35   Interview with Ambassador Peter King, Kingston, Jamaica, 12 August 1996; and Caribbean Textile and Apparel Institute, *The Jamaica Garment Industry*, Kingston, Jamaica, 7 August 1996.

36   'The Dominican Republic: The Western Hemisphere's Largest Textile Exporter to the United States', *Caribbean Week*, 19 July–1 August 1997, p. 37.

37   'Hats, Blouses, – and a Few Kilos', *Virgin Islands Daily News*, 25 November 1994; and *New York Carib News*, 'Drug Traffickers Targeting Garment Exports', 6 December 1994, p. 7.

38   I am grateful to LCDR J. Chris Sinnett of the US Coast Guard for this information, provided in September 1996.

39   'GAC Fined 1.2M (US) for Transporting Ganja', *Guyana Chronicle*, 29 January 1992, p. 3; and 'GAC Faces Further US\$ 273,600 Fine for Cocaine Mail Bag', *Stabroek News*, 8 December 1992, p. 20.

40   See Gitanjali Persaud, '117 Pounds of Cocaine Found on GAC Plane', *Stabroek News*, 15 March 1992, p. 1; and 'GAC G1M Reward for Cocaine Find Leads', *Stabroek News*, 19 March 1993, p. 1.

41   US Congress. House, *Drugs and Latin America: Economic and Political Impact and U.S. Policy Options*, Select Committee on Narcotics Abuse and Control. 101st. Cong., 1st Sess., 26 April 1989, pp. 12–13; Janice A. Cumberbatch and Neville C. Duncan, 'Illegal Drugs, USA Policies, and Caribbean Responses', *Caribbean Affairs*, 3 (October–December 1990), p. 168; and 'US Customs, Air Jamaica Sign Anti-Drug Pact', *Jamaican Weekly Gleaner*, 23 December 1991, p. 5.

42   Interview with Dr Carlton Davies, Secretary to the Cabinet, Jamaica, Kingston, Jamaica, 12 August 1996.

43   See *Barbados Advocate*, 'Big \$\$ for Defense', 4 March 1997, p. 1.

44   US Congress. Senate. Committee on Foreign Relations, *International Narcotics Control and Foreign Assistance Certification: Requirements, Procedures, Timetables, and Guidelines*, 100th Cong., 2nd sess., March 1988, pp. 1–2.

45   United Nations International Drug Control Program, *World Drug Report*, p. 144.

46   Stares, *Global Habit*, p. 96.

47   See Ivelaw L. Griffith, 'From Cold War Geopolitics to Post-Cold War Geonarcotics', *International Journal*, 49 (Winter 1993–94), esp pp. 26–9.

# 2
# The Globalization of Finance: Role and Status of the Caribbean[1]

*Hilbourne A. Watson*

This chapter contains two main parts. In the first part I raise several philosophical and theoretical issues and problems that help to put global financialization in an appropriate context. I then analyse Caribbean phenomena, arguing that the Caribbean is integral to the global totality, which is fragmented and heterogeneous. The Caribbean and the global totality are not seen as constituting discrete spaces or geographies, but as interrelated, asymmetrically interdependent components of a heterogeneous unity. I emphasize a number of issues around global neoliberalism and the tendencies of financialization in the Caribbean, including the dialectic of financialization, the rise of offshore financial centers (OFCs) and the context of competition in OFCs and the role of structural adjustment programs (SAPs) and foreign direct investment (FDI).

The terms global finance, globalization of finance and global financialization are used interchangeably for convenience, partly because they pertain to a trend where very large amounts of productive capital have been 'liquefied' because there are more profitable returns to money capital than investments in productive activity like bricks and mortar. Financialization also refers to the emergence of new financial instruments and mechanisms like global custody and securitization that are enhanced by the new information technology; it is a tendency within global capitalism that intensifies commodification to broaden the scope of capital accumulation. Capital accumulation is central to historical capitalism's *raison d'être*. It is inappropriate to limit the definition of capitalism to a system of private property in the means of production, economic exploitation, markets and so-called individual initiative, because all these have predated capitalism to one degree or another. The definition of capitalism must extend to the generalization and intensification of commodification and private capital accumulation, around the deepening of the socialization of production for private appropriation. While portions of capital are transformed into social capital under state ownership, state ownership of capital does not negate market process, commodification, the operation of the law of value (exploitation) and/or private accumulation.

In examining the role and status of the Caribbean in global finance, my point of departure is that the real economy is the global market economy. I argue that national political and economic space are not coterminous, because capitalism is a global system, as opposed to a haphazard interaction of groupings of national states. States use their territorial space as sites where capital transacts business activities for the ends of capital accumulation which is a global process They claim sovereignty over population, territory and resources, and they confer national citizenship identity on individuals. Capital is always more or less restless and is prone to change its forms, always prowling the earth in search of more profitable environments, including those activities that may require planting roots and making large financial and techno- logical commitments with long gestation periods. The anarchy that characterizes the competition that states enter to attract capital and capital's own restlessness and accumulation imperative make it impos- sible for any state to design a strategy that can bring capital any definit- ive satisfaction.

Global finance includes three flows: from outside the Caribbean into it; within the region; and from the region into different investment activities. In the post-Cold War period the Caribbean has experienced a net decline in all categories of capital inflows. Concessional flows have shifted in large measure to countries of the former Soviet Bloc. The emerging stock markets of Asia and Latin America are attracting FDI and portfolio capital, and the better part of capital flows exists as lique- fied capital. The Caribbean will find it extremely difficult to reverse this trend.[2]

## Deciphering the global problematic

### Information technology, social relations of production and the enigma of money

Information technologies accentuate the slippery, elusive and enigmatic features of the money capital, but these features are not independent of the social relations of production. It is in the production of commodities and exchange value, and the alienation of surplus value that money is separated from its social nature in the relations of production, always seeming to acquire a relative autonomy, and epitomizing social aliena- tion in the process. When separated and alienated from labor and commodities – but linked to the market, circulation and accumulation – money acquires the fantastic appearance of a 'thing', moving through the other circuits of capital as the universal equivalent, transforming actors and agents alike into commodities (e.g. labor power), expressing the value of all other commodities and giving social relations their 'thinghood' in market symbols. Credit money plays a central role in capitalism as the link to future production, exploitation and capital accumulation. Credit money engenders the institutions of regulation, control, accountability, obligation, financial discipline and punishment. The base metal and paper that stand for money as a medium of exchange and a measure of value mask the social class relations. Herein lies the great enigma of money in capitalism.[3]

Global finance expresses social relations of production in spatial terms via offshore and international financial centers. Global finance/finan- cialization requires locations that are sensitive to the requirements of market spaces that contain the mix of enterprises, expertise and scale. Technological requirements like information technology intensify glo- bal financialization. Capital insists on juridicolegal institutions specific to its interests and rights. Factors like economic and political stability are also important to make risk and secrecy tolerable. Some Caribbean countries participate in global financialization in activities that range from legitimate financial services, like banking and insurance, to money laundering and secrecy services, such as tax evasion and sheltering.[4] No matter how asystemic money laundering and tax evasion activities may seem, they still are directly tied to the fundamental process of capitalist reproduction and capital accumulation. I view global financialization as an aspect of the relationship between capital and national states and as a property relation around state sovereignty where the latter masks global property relations. Sovereignty is foremost a juridical principle that evolved with capitalism to meet a variety of domestic and inter- national imperatives of the global system of states. This makes it histor- ical and contingent. Hence, it is unacceptable to treat sovereignty as a kind of timeless category that has evolved as an extension of attributes of prenational states.[5]

Understanding sovereignty as a property relation takes the analysis of sovereignty beyond the static nationalist discourse that reduces capital and sovereignty to two opposing things, one defined by its foreign character and the other by its domestic identity. It is important to find

out how and where the state enters the foreign capital-national sovereignty picture. Since the 1970s–1980s, global technoindustrial restructuring has aggravated the inability and/or unwillingness of many Less
Developed Countries (LDCs) to meet external debt obligations to other
states, commercial banks and multilateral institutions such as the WB.
The management of the debt crisis has served to strengthen the involvement of global actors in the domestic affairs of indebted states, in order
to shift key aspects of national decision-making toward the global level,
where capital accumulation is primary. The multilateral institutions play
a key role in this process, in conjunction with the US Federal Reserve
System.[6]

With reference to the Caribbean the WB asserts that 'partly as a result
of past government efforts, the growth of the middle class and the
diversification of the private sector and NGOs over recent decades *the
state* can now reduce its role in many areas...'[7] Neoliberalism wants
repressed (leaner) states that will consume smaller portions of social
resources, so as to give advantage to the 'private sector'. Leaner states
strengthen public order, limit economic regulation and provide necessary infrastructural services like educational and technical skills the
private sector cannot make profit from providing while global neoliberalism wants leaner states and demobilized, detached and depoliticized
polities. Global financialization works through the market to unleash
the power of liquefied capital upon the world.[8] In reality, financialization displaces some of capitalism's contradictions: crisis management in
contemporary financialization also employs debt and credit as manage-
rial tools for displacing the turbulent effects of market anarchy and
crises.[9]

### Global financialization, the nation-state and social class relations

It has been difficult to see globalization in its complexity due to the
reproduction of geography and nation as fetishized objects, around
which social relations between people are reduced to technical relations
between things. One effect is that various forms of competition in the
global arena tends to be reduced to competition between states. In fact,
what states practice as coercion in their national jurisdictions and what
constitutes the appropriation of surplus value at the global level are
integrally connected. States are never autonomous of the economy
because the state is an 'integral aspect of the set of social relations
whose overall form is determined by the extraction of the surplus from
the immediate producer'.[10] Thus, the global market constitutes a 'single
system in which state power is allocated between territorial entities'; the

national state has a 'national political constitution' while accumulation has a 'global character'.[11] The state, therefore, is not an autonomous actor affected by globalization; rather, it is integral to the process of globalization.

Innovation-mediated production (l-MP) technologies aggravate over-accumulation of capital and intensify the tendency of capital to flow out of productive activity into speculative activity through the medium of global money. Global financializtion lends capital an overdetermined monetary character, when money appears to shed its social character in the market where money assumes the form of a 'thing' and blends in with the market. Money as national currency provides a strategic link between the national state and the global economy, for each state rules over a portion of the global economy where we observe the global character of capital accumulation, the national character of currency and the politics of money in the national state. It holds a special place in the social construction of power in capitalist societies. Money and the market work through the rule of law to equate the abstract universality with formal political equality – the fictive equality capitalism engenders.

Money facilitates the expansion and deepening of social relations, while it masks class and power relations by reducing participants in the market to 'competition subjects'. The effect is the production of a market and 'monetary fetishism' that reinforce the fiction of the market as a self-regulating 'thing' with technical relations shaped by the calculus of predetermined rational self-interests. In reality, the market is the site where condensed social class relations are mediated, even when money masks the real nature and forms of existence of those very social relations.[12] These very elements are designed to displace capitalism's insoluble contradictions. In fact, 'the power of the state in its liberal capitalist form is embodied in the rule of law and money which are at the same time its own presupposition. This is the most appropriate form to serve the expansion of capitalist social relations since the social power of the bourgeoisie is embodied in the abstract form of money'.[13] Global financialization facilitates the projection of the terroristic power of capital in the market economy, where capital masks its real political intentions. Cleaver notes that the 'victories of monetary terrorism, in the central capitalist countries as in the Third World, have not been matched by a redirection of money into a restructuring of class relationships capable of reestabilizing capitalist power and relaunching a new cycle of accumulation'.[14]

As part of the global crisis, the Mexican financial crisis and the challenge to the status quo posed by the insurrectionary movement in

Chiapas show that the 'moves to regionalism across the globe...repres-
ent an attenuation of the tension between national states and the global
economy as the crisis of the class relation is simultaneously expressed as
a crisis of the international states system'.[15] Financialization deepens
certain social, political, economic, and ideological contradictions. In
fact, 'the absolute contingency of space is epitomized in the existence
of capital as money. Whenever money capital moves...the spatial pattern of the relations between capital and labor changes'.[16] Several centuries ago, capital, coercion and the modern European national state
embarked on a journey, where globalization became integral to the
nature of capitalist relations of exploitation, mediated through money,
a relation freed from spatial constraint. The aspatial, global nature of
capitalist social relations has been a central feature of capitalist development since its bloody birth in conquest and piracy.[17] It has taken a while
'to decompose global society into national states'.[18] Intellectually, ideas
that restrict the state to national space block the development of theoretical consciousness, for 'the state and its relation to capital...can be
understood only in a global context'.[19]

What International Relations treats as conflict or competition among
national states are the forms and processes of competition among ruling
classes under the rubric of their national political and cultural identities.
States' membership in multilateral institutions, their adoption and
rationalization of global neoliberalism, and their accommodation to
global financial swarming by setting up OFCs and other vehicles of
financial terrorism provide ample evidence of the state's own complicity
in the ways of capital and in the exploitation of workers. The state is
adept at distancing itself from its own oppressive and terroristic norms
and practices, while capital is schizophrenic about its own political
character, which explains why capital relies on separation to imbue the
market with objectivity in order to mask its own political nature.

States are never neutral about capital accumulation strategies such as
global financialization, because they develop partly through and around
capitalist social reproduction and capital accumulation. Money publi-
cizes its arrogant dissatisfaction with the relations of exploitation by
concentrating on the short term. The more attractive states make the
terms for attracting capital, the more insubordinate and demanding
money capital becomes. Central banks become sentinels of global
money and the enforcers of the 'discipline' of the market, while pre-
tending to secure national currency. Demystified, the discipline of the
market is the terroristic rule of money where the social class identity of
capital is hidden from sight through market automatism. The shift of

national financial decision-making to the global level has been afoot for some time, and now, more so as the borders of states are being rolled back while states and economies undergo decapitalization via liberalization and privatization. Decapitalization and indebtedness are folded into a new psychology of subordinated determinism. Financialization works alongside structural adjustment with the effect of eroding the productive base. The WB Group marginalizes all but the most powerful states and imposes Mafia norms of financial terrorism to manage world debt and maintain capitalist hegemony, as the preferred way to impose discipline on the wayward who resist the consequences of the inability of productive activity to sustain global capital accumulation. Financial terrorism is the logic of world money.

The nationalist notion that global financial power and national sovereignty are inversely related is plausible but very illusory. First, national sovereignty is an historically constructed, nationalized property relation. In addition, one very serious consequence of the location of national states within the global system is the on-going decomposition of national states and societies. In this process the prevailing spatial class dynamics no longer hold. Space, place and time dynamics shift, thereby producing serious implications for international relations as a whole: not that there is no center as poststructuralists assert rather naively; rather, the center is like a moving target in the nanosecond age of the new technological paradigms. Poststructuralism confirms the lag between the motion of the paradigm shift and the social relations of production. Holloway notes that swarming is common to bees and global financialization: bees swarm when there is an insufficiency of honey in their hive, and capital swarms because there is not enough productive activity to sustain profit-making in productive activities. Financial swarming confirms that there is an accumulation crisis in which 'production has ceased to be so attractive for capital' and yet it is real productive activity that is the life line of 'capital's self-expansion'.[20] Global I-MP and financial swarming are the latest attempts by capital to achieve this most elusive end.

## The Caribbean problematic

Caribbean Community and Common Market (CARICOM) countries have joined other Commonwealth countries in registering their concerns about how recent global financial, economic and trade developments, with reference to globalization, market integration, and protectionism in industrialized economies are affecting them. They stress the likely impact of the World Trade Organization (WTO) on global trade, due to the erosion of preferences. They are nervous about the prospect of the industrialized economies using trade, environmental issues and labor standards to promote protectionism and impede global trade liberalization, and they point to the steady decline of official development assistance (ODA) by the Organization for Economic Co-operation and Development (OECD) countries: in 1995, it (ODA) declined to 0.27 per cent of the GNP of OECD economies. This was in conjunction with the stagnation of International Bank for Reconstruction and Development (IBRD) lending and the increase in net negative transfers. Other concerns extend to how shocks in capital flows could worsen their macroeconomic management difficulties. These countries also encourage speeding up the flow of 'long-term commercial investments' into their countries. They have reservations about how the European Union (EU) and the North American Free Trade Agreement (NAFTA) may shape national monetary policies, global banking, and capital flows. In particular, they have serious concerns about 'deflational fiscal policies to meet the Maastricht Treaty's convergence criteria'.[21]

## Global neoliberalism and OFCs in the Caribbean

By its very nature national money is political with its base in the social relations of production, even in relation to its technical functions in an economy. Hence the notion of the depoliticization of national currency is a technical one that fetishizes market automatism and grounds fictive sovereignty in ways that mask alienated labor.[22] Global neoliberalism does not seem like the complex, multidimensional political economy agenda it constitutes, because its veneer is the automatism of the market, where capital hides its political interests and strategies with the effect of seeming to externalize the social relations of production by reducing them to 'things'. The only evident connecting thread is a putative individualist humanism through which the market works its supposedly disinterested, subjectless magic.[23] This putative humanism masks the real character of social labor in individualism, money, and the separation of coercion from the economy via the market.

In the context of the Caribbean, SAPs compromise the state's sensitivity to national, gender, trade union and other struggles. Global capitalism demands shifting strategic elements of state power to the global level in order to improve the coordination of bilateral, multilateral and global decision-making. Caribbean states consistently embrace global neoliberalism,[24] despite their frustrations over problems of international liquidity in relation to world trade and Special Drawing Rights. Adjustment and exchange rate stability, in relation to the asymmetry between countries in surplus and those in deficit, aggravates differences between the countries with appreciating currencies and those with depreciating currencies. Financial swarming aggravates the net transfer of real resources with respect to stabilizing the perverse effects on LDCs from the gyrations of private capital markets and the destructive effects of the debt crisis. Moreover, it contributes to their marginalization in the global monetary system. A level playing field with transparent rules is a necessary legitimatizing principle under capitalism; yet, competition, uneven development, the law of value and market anarchy negate this.

Global financialization is changing the character of banking, as banks are under increasing pressure to move into asset management and corporate finance. Bank loans were 49.5 per cent of 'cross-border capital flows from the rich countries private sector', but the impact of bad loans in many LDCs has caused banks to reduce their exposure to the point where, in spite of the fact that 'loans outstanding have tripled in the past decade, to $4 trillion...bank lending's share of capital outflows has declined to 9.2 percent'.[25] In a world where major banks have to control vast sums of custody assets, sometimes as much as US$1 trillion, to exploit advantages of scale and scope, it is difficult to imagine Caribbean stock markets defining their own autonomy in the global financial arena. Investment innovation to secure and sustain market share has now become a mantra of the market. It seems that foreign equities trading will concentrate in a handful of large regional money and financial centers, with New York likely to become the 'hub for Latin American shares'.[26]

Farrell calls for a 'supranational organization with the capacity to address the special financing needs of small states'.[27] His argument about the problems and constraints small states face does not reflect the core contradictions in global neoliberalism: that the neoliberal offensive is designed to transform how national states deal with the imperatives of a global economy under the rule of global capital that consistently reconfigures interstate relations by shifting national power to the global level. The formal control states may have over 'policy instruments' is secondary because considerable national power has already shifted to the global level where the real base of capitalism lies. As such, the issues go beyond small state-big state or North–South dichotomies, though the two factors are made plausible by the sway of the territorial trap.

Girvan takes issue with Farrell's pessimism about the 'possibilities for reform of the international monetary system and of the Bretton Woods institutions...'. He wants to build consensus and cooperation for collective global ends, and he opines that it would be 'more logical to organize constituencies according to common interests derived from similarities of size and economic structures, and to reflect these groupings in the structure of regional offices. By this criterion...the countries of CARICOM and the Central American Common Market might be better served by having their own constituency and office either separately or jointly'.[28] This very plausible but problematic argument shows that Girvan is yet to come to terms with the issue in the relationship between global capital and national states. He relies on plausibility to fold size into a shared experience, and his ideas seem to be conditioned by geographical determinism to the point that he ignores the real bases of global intercapitalist competition. Girvan continues to treat capital as a thing that can be made definitively accountable to the idea of national sovereignty.

Clearly, capital and national sovereignty do not coincide. Girvan reverses the historical process by making the imagery of the national economy the real economy to the point that he is in danger of making things the way they never were. He must be reminded that OFCs attest to the 'explosion of fictitious capital formation in the Euromarkets in the 1960s and 1970s', where a 'series of little places-islands and micro-states have been transformed by exploiting niches in the circuits of fictitious capital. The Bahamas and the Cayman Islands...are...part of a worldwide network of...marginal places which have come to assume a crucial position in the global circuits of fungible, fast-moving, furtive money and fictitious capital. These offshore financial centres are sites that dramatically evince the contrary and complex melding of offshore and onshore, of national and international, and of local and global'.[29]

OFCs point to the deepening of financialization, partly through credit capital. They accommodate the process in which furtive money transforms itself into legitimate activities, and they mirror the aspatiality of capital accumulation. Caribbean OFCs are sites where credit liabilities accumulate and mediate via electronic financial data flows often as entries 'in a computer system', 'a nameplate in a lobby of another bank', 'a folder in a filing cabinet', the signifiers of fictitious capital and fictitious spaces.[30] These OFCs signal the swarming of money capital as extreme overaccumulation that finds no outlets in productive activity. They allow for the temporary displacement of space and crisis by speeding up the process, intensifying flows, and working the latest technologies within the neoliberal dispensation. This is where we may grasp the legal, administrative and political arrangements by Caribbean OFCs like Barbados to attract liquefied capital via offshore business companies (OBCs) and international financial companies (IFCs). As extensions of the Eurocurrency markets, Caribbean OFCs are facilitating thrust points in the power dynamics of supranational finance capital.

## Competition, OFCs, and the dialectics of financialization in the Caribbean

The defunct Bank of Credit and Commerce International (BCCI) became a major player in global financialization, with offices and interests in Europe – mainly the UK and Luxembourg – the US and LDCs, including Caribbean countries. In 1991, when BCCI was closed, it had US$20 billion of assets in 69 countries. BCCI integrated the laundering of illegal money into the global financial network.[31] The Cayman Islands became one of BCCI's core money laundering centers. As one of its unregulated havens, the Caymans became BCCI's 'bank within the bank' with three entities – BCCI Foundation, International Credit and Investment Company (ICIC) Staff Benefit Trust, and ICIC Business Promotions – which owned 41 per cent of BCCI itself. It was here, within the untraceable labyrinth of shares and accounts, that the dirtiest of BCCI's financial dealings occured. Among the Caymans' main commodity services were 'money evading taxes, money from drug sales and other criminal activities, and illegal capital-flight money zooming out of the Third World'.[32]

Apart from being a first-order tax haven, the Caymans are a key registered center for international shipping, trading, insurance, real estate, banking and finance. Most major banks registered in the Caymans do not conduct normal business there. BCCI activities in the Caymans typified the extremes of the aspatial liquefaction of capital. Global money works against spatiality to accommodate the need for secrecy, since those who engage in illegal financial transactions will devise ways and means to protect their assets from discovery, taxation or seizure. Aspatiality feeds evasive measures and complex arrangements through which to fold more and more secret assets into other secret activities. Global finance and swarming, especially in the shady zones of furtive money – tax evasion and money-laundering from drug trafficking – encourage measures by some states and certain types of capitalist enterprises to strengthen secrecy in liquefied money markets.[33] Even OECD states are concerned about the annual outflow of upward of $50 billion, and they have considered imposing capital controls to stem that tide, while other states have been thinking of ways to limit the inflow of portfolio investment to encourage higher inflows of FDI to boost productive activity.[34]

The technological revolution in communications and telecommunications has accelerated the offshore financial activities of financial MNCs, thereby contributing, along with the development of 'interbank and Eurocurrency markets and the growth of worldwide financial branching networks', to the restructuring of global capital.[35] The transformation of 'tax haven economies' into new sites for global business is a part of the global techno-financial restructuring.[36] Former UK colonies with financial ties to the City of London have tended to exploit development potential from London's own expanded financial exposure. The Bahamas and the Caymans emerged as the largest offshore haven centers during the 1980s,[37] and the keen competition for global market share of OFC services helped to push the Caymans to become the 'fifth biggest financial center with over 550 registered banks' by the middle of 1996.[38] In 1996, the global offshore banking 'sector' managed about US$2.1 trillion in assets. Global offshore business has been growing at about 15 per cent per year: Swiss banks manage over 30 per cent of the total; UK and the US hold about $300 billion each, with the Bahamas and Caymans accounting for a 'smaller amount'.[39] The needs of large companies to reduce their taxes, expand the scope and complexity of their global activities, reduce barriers to the movement of their commodities, enhance the competitiveness of their products and improve their profitability contributed to the growth of both onshore financial centers and OFCs.

Commonwealth Caribbean states faced a number of problems preparing themselves to become OFCs. They have been stymied by economic nationalism in their development planning, tensions developed around issues such as zero tax or low tax, with or without double taxation treaties with other states, and special tax provisions were developed for particular international businesses such as banking, shipping, insurance, and export processing zones (EPZs). By the early 1980s, neither Jamaica nor Trinidad and Tobago had developed as financial centers due partly to bank localization and spates of 'political instability'. By 1990, Antigua–Barbuda, the Bahamas, Barbados, Belize, Bermuda, the British Virgin Islands, the Caymans,[40] Grenada, Montserrat, Anguilla, Netherlands Antilles (NA), Nevis, St Kitts, St Lucia, St Vincent, and the Turks and Caicos Islands were listed among the world's tax havens.[41] By 1996, Bermuda, which became an offshore center as early as World War Two to provide tax-exempt services for foreign companies, had become the biggest offshore center for insurance companies in the world. More than 8,600 tax-exempt companies have incorporated in Bermuda, including more than 1,350 insurance companies with over US$18 billion in premiums and US$76 billion in assets. The insurance industry is one of Bermuda's economic mainstays.[42]

Caribbean tax havens and OFCs exploit their proximity to North American financial and regional capital markets and to Central and South American states in politically unstable conditions; both factors enhanced their appeal for flight capital and other furtive money. Easy communication with the rest of the world, convenience for moving flight capital out of Latin America, and strategic location for the Latin American drug route add to the region's appeal.[43] Eastern Caribbean tax haven centers such as Antigua–Barbuda, Dominica, Grenada, Montserrat, St Kitts, St Lucia and St Vincent and the Grenadines, which did not develop into OFCs, became attractive because of US and UK tax treaties that extended 'interoffshore provisions...to colonial areas, thereby permitting their use as a base for holding companies'.[44] By the early 1980s, a complex of factors-political and constitutional status, tax treaties, reputation gained from dealing with 'shell banks' and shady operators, low level of economic and social infrastructure, long-standing inter-territorial rivalries, and the expansion of OFC infrastructures in other parts of the world, including the Middle East and Asia – had worked against prospects for most Caribbean islands developing into OFCs.[45]

By the end of the 1980s, there were four primary regional OFCs in the world: the Caribbean and Central America; European enclaves such as the British Isle centers, Switzerland and Luxembourg; the Persian Gulf; and Hong Kong, Singapore and the Oceania (see Table 2.1). The dollarization of currency bonds in the 1970s, and the massive expansion of petrodollar surpluses strengthened the role of the US dollar as a world currency. Worsening terms of trade, difficulty attracting directly productive capital and constraints arising from servicing the external debt exacerbated the structural problems Caribbean countries faced. In severely indebted countries such as Guyana and Jamaica,[46] the crisis of the state is aggravated by very difficult fiscal problems linked to inflation, devaluation and debt service requirements. The limited and insecure tax base of Caribbean states produces consequences for state 'provisioning and financing', a reality that is worsened by capital flight, a general decline in all types of capital inflows and debt service and other imperatives.

Table 2.1   *Global Distribution of Small Island Tax Havens and OFCs*

| Caribbean and South Atlantic | Europe & Middle East |
|---|---|
| Anguilla, Antigua, Bahamas | Bahrain, Cyprus, Guernsey |
| Barbados, Bermuda, British | Isle of Man, Jersey, Malta |
| Virgin Islands, Cayman Islands, | |
| Antilles, Nevis & St Kitts | **Asia-Pacific** |
| St Lucia, St Vincent | Cook Islands, Marshall Islands, |
| Turks & Caicos | Vanuatu, Western Samoa |

*Source*: Mark Hampton, 'Treasure Islands of Fool's Gold: Can and Should Small Island Economies Copy Jersey?', *World Development*, Vol. 22, No. 2, 1994, pp. 237–50.

The narcotics industry uses the latest information technologies, such as computer networks, to improve its trading activities.[47] Drug money is money always in the process of becoming speculative capital and/or productive capital; it will operate according to the limits of the market, finance bricks and mortar and/or launder itself via financial swarming around OFCs. The major economic effects and implications of international financial secrecy work through production, national income and income distribution, savings and investment, fiscal and monetary policies, balance of payments, exchange rates and the terms of trade. Weak states that specialize in the export of international financial secrecy services incur political costs such as bribery, corruption, dependence on such services for employment and pressure from powerful foreign states to choose between strengthening niches in the global financial system and adjusting to externally generated geopolitical impositions. Criminal activity such as involvement by politicians, technocrats, and security officials in illegal drug activity, the social and health consequences of drug trafficking, drug use and dependence, and pressures for disclosure of secret financial transactions produce an array of negatives for the security of states and societies.[48]

Walter estimated the 'annual gross revenues generated by all narcotics sales in the US... somewhere between $60 and $120 billion in 1988, of which between $40–$100 billion... was believed to be transferred out of the US for investment elsewhere, with the other half remaining in the country for investment in a range of legitimate instruments and businesses'.[49] The illegal drug business is vast in its global scope and organization; it produces very large amounts of money that has to reproduce itself as capital.[50] Drug producers and money launderers are specialists who rely on connections to globally integrated strategies to promote their own links to capital accumulation. The drug business survives by corporatizing its operations to make it easier to deal in various currencies in order to move money around the globe and work the OFCs in the four regions of the globe. This strategy derives from the vast amount of money the industry turns over annually, and from other conflicts with states.

Uprimny theorizes for 'a political economy of drug trafficking' that sees drug trafficking as a form of market accumulation, bearing in mind that the illegal and often violent trade of drug trafficking is still without an acceptable way to transform the guilt of money-making as capital accumulation into a peaceful market passion.[51] I share Uprimny's sentiment that 'drug trafficking is an illegal market and not a parallel one' on the grounds that the 'illegal market comes from repression and the prohibition of certain goods and services so that, in principle, only illegal markets for those goods and services exist'. But I question his assertion that 'illicit commercial production cannot be considered capitalist because it does not employ paid labourers'.[52] I argue that wage labor is necessary but not sufficient for capitalist production. In the history of capitalism, capitalists have created many ways to use non-wage labor techniques, including slavery, indenture, peasant labor, household labor units, coupled with extra-economic strategies to pump surplus value out of laboring populations. Producers of narcotic drugs transform means of production into capital and commodify their inputs and outputs and accumulate capital.

The narcotics industry is not alien to market capitalism, though the commodity, its trade and proceeds are subject to generalized and absolute prohibition by the state. The illegality of the narcotics industry does not negate its productive existence as value-creating activity: legalism and methodological atomism merely mask the objective value-creating process that the production of illegal drugs represents under capitalism. Those who produce the crops in response to market calculus find it to be more economically fruitful and stable than legal agrarian production, due to contradictory impacts of the debt crisis, structural adjustment, protectionism, the export of inflation by the US and the other consequences of the global swarming of money capital. Uprimny is correct to argue that drug production is neither a form of transfer of money between individuals nor a parasitic activity.

Several Caribbean countries have signed bilateral agreements with the US to share information on criminal, currency and customs matters within the norms of the evolving institutions for global economic and financial management. There is no comprehensive agreement on how to combat and/or eliminate money laundering of drug proceeds and activities related to tax evasion and fraud, for states have to compete in a variety of ways to attract capital for development. The US relies on numerous laws, policy initiatives, institutional mechanisms, and international structures to counter money-laundering activities at home and overseas.[53] The US has worked through the Organization of American States (OAS) to create uniform 'model money laundering and asset forfeiture legislation which could be used as a blueprint for OAS member countries to adopt'. In addition to the OAS, the US used the 1994 Summit of the Americas to streamline a 'coordinated strategy and response to combat money laundering' on a hemispheric basis.[54]

Laundering the proceeds of illegal drug deals has developed into one of the leading financial industries in the world.[55] State coercion, violence and monetary terrorism have been integral to the growth of historical capitalism, so illegal drugs and money-laundering are not such aberrations after all. Small states are no more capable of limiting and/or stopping drug trafficking and money-laundering than they are capable of stopping the flow of supranational finance capital; the narcotics industry has had to rely on the money form of value as the main vehicle of its accumulation, but it can never be satisfied with this situation. This money is an integral part of global money capital, a fact that reinforces drug trafficking as an integral part of the globalized market economy; drug money is subject to the rhythm of the political economy of capitalism in its economic, market and extra-economic dimensions such as political and military action to limit the production, export and/or exchange and distribution of drugs in consumer societies. The illegal drugs industry cannot be reduced to a pathological condition among producers or consumers: the capitalist market gives narcotics its pathway through the legal economy.[56]

British and Dutch dependencies in the Caribbean were encouraged to develop as OFCs as a way to reduce their colonial dependency and their financial dependence and grant-in-aid status.[57] OFCs may be on-shore (within a city), like a 'region-state',[58] or offshore (on an island). Many contemporary OFCs are ex-British colonies with British common law traditions that stress the confidential relationship between banker and client. OFCs tend to be tax free or low-tax zones that normally make special concessions to nonresident businesses. Several OFCs are dependencies of onshore states that have no central bank. Most Caribbean countries are politically stable, with high profiles in banking stability, excellent communications in close proximity to the US, and they compete with one another and with other regions to attract OFC business. (See Table 2.1.)

Table 2.2   *Caribbean Ranking among Major Money-laundering Countries in 1995*

| Priority | Location |
|---|---|
| High[a] | Aruba, Cayman Islands |
| Medium–high[a] | Netherlands Antilles |
| Medium[b] | Antigua, Bahamas, Montserrat, St Vincent |
| Low–medium[c] | Cuba, Dominican Republic, Trinidad |
| Low[c] | Anguilla, Barbados, Bermuda, British Virgin Islands, French West Indies, Haiti, Jamaica, St Kitts, St Lucia, Suriname |
| No priority[d] | Dominica, Grenada, Guyana, Turks & Caicos Islands, US Virgin Islands |

*Notes:*
[a] Locations in which action is needed to stem and prevent money laundering in order to make headway into the international money-laundering problem.
[b] Locations in which a significant volume of money laundering is occurring, but action to stem and prevent money laundering is not needed as much as it is needed for high-priority countries.
[c] Locations in which a moderate amount of money laundering occurs, but the situation is not expected to worsen.
[d] Locations in which the Department of State is unaware of any money laundering or where the problem is considered too insignificant to be a factor in the international drug money-laundering market.
*Source*: General Accounting Office, *Money Laundering: A Framework for Understanding U.S. Efforts Overseas*, 1996, pp. 29–30.

Many of the elements that enhance the prospects for OFC status – tourism, regulation, low taxes or no taxes – also accelerate the spread of financial markets. OFCs are not a special case; to treat them as such is to ignore the recent technological revolution in the production of goods and services. The benefits of hosting an OFC may outweigh the costs, and the expanding global offshore markets indicate potential income generation for some OFCs that are located close to emerging supra-regional blocs. Table 2.2 depicts the profiles of Caribbean countries in relation to money-laundering activities in 1995. With the exception of Aruba, Caymans, and the Netherlands Antilles, the other Caribbean countries were not considered to be high profile money-laundering countries.

## Competition in Caribbean OFCs

Bermuda, the Caymans, and the Netherlands Antilles have shown that sovereignty is not a prerequisite for becoming important OFCs. All Caribbean OFCs use self-promotion and image as part of their competitive strategy. The Barbados 1993–2000 Development Plan stresses the country's bid to become 'the' international financial center of the Caribbean. Jamaica too has set its sights on this coveted position.[59]

Caribbean states compete among each other for a share of the regional OFC market, and the region competes with other regional OFCs for a share of the global OFC business. For example, the NA stress several advantages, such as their Dutch legal system, geographical location at the crossroads of the Caribbean/Latin America trade routes, sophisticated financial institutions and management that favor international business profitability, political and social stability, preferential trade arrangements under EPZ status, tax holiday facilities, duty free importation of materials for constructing new facilities, Caribbean Basin Initiative (CBI) beneficiary status, access to EU markets via ties with the Netherlands, stable oil refining and transshipment facilities, ship repair service, a very strong tourism sector and the availability of expatriate middle management labor from which to supplement local labor. The main offshore business operations in the NA include holding and finance companies, offshore banks, mutual funds, offshore trading (reinvoicing) companies, shipping/air transportation companies, patent and royalty companies, real estate and holding companies and reinsurance companies.[60]

The global OFC market is heterogeneous and competitive. Caribbean countries do not produce the technologies that are commonly used in OFC activities, so that they rely on the OFC institutions to provide the technology, which is part of the global strategy of those institutions to gain or increase market share. In some ways, then, competitive advantage in Caribbean OFCs is a derivative of competition at the broader global level. There is intense competition in global custody management that is hollowing the industry; the concentration of custody capital is centered in a handful of megabanks.[61] It would be misguided to look to global financial centers for long-term stability or security, given 'the mobility of financial institutions', the effects of the global telecommunications revolution, and the need to keep up with expensive innovation technology on a regular basis. In the 1980s, there was a spate of onshore activities to set up international banking facilities (IBFs) to take back a share of OFC business. Several US-based IBFs tried to hitch OFCs to their wagons and set them in tow to the US; the main effect is that Caribbean OFCs now service mainly the needs of US institutions.[62]

Caribbean states need productive capital but they are doing better attracting liquefied capital, including furtive money. Liquefaction and swarming are evidence that capital has already thumbed its nose at many states. There is little chance Caribbean states will succeed in immobilizing this money on the prowl. A major challenge is to exploit useful information technology, relevant education, technical skills and productive employment from OFC activities. Ironically, the leadership instability in the major economies and the perverse conditions occasioned by neoliberal SAPs in many LDCs also explain why OFCs are so popular among wealthy patrons and owners of liquefied capital. It is the same powerful states that use their own instability to export their contradictions: this very instability engenders many of the furtive tendencies of money capital.

Image is important to how Caribbean OFCs market themselves. It is part of the strategy to mediate vulnerability. These societies transgress the borders of reality to fold change into tradition.[63] But image alone will not suffice. The emphasis OFCs put on political stability, education infrastructure, labor peace, inexpensive labor, racial and ethnic harmony, social tranquillity and banking stability tends to transgress reality. To design a competitive strategy and idealize their OFC appeal, these states invent their own imaginary networks of power and other options to cement their own sense of stability, solidity, substantiality, and transparency. The invention of these imaginaries as a mode of legitimization is quite understandable considering the reality of the furtive and cowardly nature of some types of money capital. In the process the marginalization of workers is raised to new heights, because resolute states have to show they will not hesitate to depoliticize and alienate labor. Since several Caribbean OFCs depend on financialization as the main source of employment, they are predisposed to stress labor peace in the face of chronic unemployment, youth disillusionment and the crisis effects of SAPs.

Several Caribbean states have been attempting to restructure their production bases away from traditional (factor advantage) competition, given the futility of trying to compete with Asia in price and wages,[64] and in light of the major changes in production and trade that affect preferences, regionalization and competitiveness. Caribbean countries do not have complex production infrastructures, because they have never had capital goods infrastructures, nor do they have capitalists with credible records in technoindustrial innovation. More broadly, the Western Hemisphere lacks an integrated restructuring strategy grounded in a common techno-industrial base. Flexibilization, defined as a complex of heterogeneous strategies for deploying global production has become an integral part of the neoliberal paradigm for American capital:it brings together disparate elements of primitive Taylorism, neoTaylorism, and I-MP. All technoindustrial moves into Latin America and the Caribbean – for example, cars in Mexico or apparel in the Caribbean – have the effect of eroding workers power at all levels. American capital, at home and across Latin America and the Caribbean, sets out to implement a perverse restructuring strategy,[65] vigorously duplicating and realigning 'the vertical axis of increasing flexibility...in a universally Taylorist industrial paradigm' of flexibilization.[66]

## Global financialization, SAPs and FDI in the Caribbean

The WB conditionally supports 'debt restructuring...for highly indebted countries that are pursuing or sustaining structural adjustment and that are improving the efficiency of their program spending' in the Caribbean.[67] It admonishes the adjusted state in Caribbean societies to 'focus public sector activities on areas that only it can provide, such as the legal system, public health and safety, basic education, environmental protection, and macroeconomic management'. SAPs in the Caribbean become instruments of leverage to secure state compliance with the global neoliberal strategy for 'public sector modernization' which includes all the mechanisms for reinventing government for the ends of state adjustment at the national, regional and global levels.

Global financialization and SAPs come together through external debt and around bank and nonbank trade-related claims on LDCs, the growth of portfolio investment relative to the decline of FDI, and the competition LDCs enter into with one another to attract liquefied capital. Jamaica, the Dominican Republic, Trinidad and Tobago, Guyana, Barbados, Cuba, and other Caribbean states have undergone one or another version of a SAP. Jamaica is the Caribbean country with the most extensive SAP relationship with the WB Group, dating to the 1970s. SAPs help to demystify the property relational aspect of sovereignty and the social nature of alienated labor, by working through devaluation, debt service ratios, and privatization and other mechanisms that benefit debtors at the expense of workers and their standard of living. They encourage the expansion of the so-called informal sector, and an increase in the number of low-wage jobs in EPZs. Areas such as education, health, public housing, public transportation, subsistence agriculture, social services like youth and community development, and local government suffer in real terms in order to liberate capital from most of the nationally imposed social and political constraints.[68]

Caribbean economies have neither hinterlands of labor reserves nor the attractiveness to FDI which places like China offer. Nor do they boast a clear record in technoindustrial innovation or a tradition in the production of intellectual property goods. Yet intellectual property is playing a bigger role in global flows of FDI due to the broad impact of I-MP technologies. The scope and reach of global techno-industrial restructuring is so comprehensive that all economies, including a low-wage economy like China, with its vast hinterland of labor reserves and its success in attracting the lion's share of all investment flows into Asia,[69] are forced to incorporate innovation advantage strategies to reposition their competitive strategies.[70]

In the 1990s, FDI flows have grown almost 400 per cent due largely to market liberalization, fewer restrictions on FDI flows, and the ways MNCs have been restructuring and integrating their strategies with closer attention to the formation of strategic global alliances. Largely, FDI flows to LDCs 'have been ignited by privatization projects... specially in infrastructure... privatization (which) have averaged about US$2.2 billion per annum in 1990–1995'.[71] Caribbean governments are concerned about the low levels of FDI that flow into the region, and the impact of FDI on economic and social activity. The formation of global regions like the EU and NAFTA and the overlapping of trade agreements under the Generalized System of Preferences (GSP) and the WTO, and investment protocols, are strategically tied to WB Guidelines on the Treatment of FDI and the trend of establishing laws, treaties, and instruments that explicitly favor FDI and the interest and rights of capital. These measures and provisions are designed to reduce capital's sense of insecurity and speed up its mobility.[72] WB Group agencies such as the International Center for Settlement of Investment Disputes (ICSID) and the Multilateral Investment Guarantee Agency (MIGA) are playing bigger roles in restructuring the environment for global FDI flows. There is little doubt these agencies are intensifying the shift of national decision-making in many an LDC toward the global level.

Between 1990 and 1996, about US$436 billion in FDI flowed into all LDCs. In 1996 alone, about $73 billion in FDI flowed into East Asia and Latin America. The US and Japan dominate the accumulated global FDI stocks 'accounting for more than 90 per cent of recent flows and 95 per cent of the stock of FDI'.[73] In 1994, Latin America and the Caribbean (LAC) had a cumulative FDI stock of US$186 billion; in 1993, LAC received US$19 billion in new FDI and US$20 billion in 1994. In 1993 and 1994, the Caribbean attracted 4 per cent and 3 per cent, or US$570 million and US$800 million, respectively, of the FDI flows to LAC. Privatization has featured heavily in these FDI flows to LAC by increasing the number of foreign affiliates relative to the decline in the number of state enterprises.[74]

The Caribbean has not attracted any significant levels of net FDI flows in recent times; rather, there has been a shift in ownership from the state through privatization. The United Nations Conference on Trade and Development (UNCTAD) insists that – relative to development (per capita GDP), market size (GDP/population), and market growth (GDP growth rates in constant prices) and factors like natural resources, quality of infrastructure, labor cost, productivity and FDI policy and climate – Caribbean countries can be said to utilize their FDI potential.[75] While UNCTAD's view reflects the level of development of existing investment infrastructure, business culture and capital absorption capacity in CARICOM countries, it also confirms that there is very limited potential for absorbing significant quantities of FDI.[76] The very limited scope of venture capitalism in the Caribbean also points to the strong mercantile and commercial character of the business culture and the limited scope of directly productive activity. CARICOM capitalists have achieved only a superficial level of financial, industrial and production integration.[77] Many Caribbean capitalists recognize the need to compete for market share outside a region in which it is increasingly difficult for capital to reproduce itself in customary ways. Just as Caribbean states are renewing efforts to attract productive capital, some CARICOM capitalists have begun to join the contemporary global swarming process.

From 1974 to 1988, CARICOM countries and the Dominican Republic attracted US$4,661.4 million or 2.3 per cent of the global total of net FDI flows. For the CARICOM economies (excluding the Bahamas the bulk of whose capital inflows go into OFC activities), the 1988 inflow of net FDI was only 25.3 per cent of the 1981 level of US$575.9 million. About 50 per cent of the net FDI inflows to CARICOM economies between 1974 and 1988 went into Trinidad's petroleum and petrochemical industries. Global restructuring of investment under the new technologies have weakened the export of traditional goods from the region.[78] Between 1989 and 1993, FDI inflows by country were as follows (in US$ millions): Bahamas (−$8.9), Barbados ($41.4), Dominica ($49.6), Grenada ($61.2 [1989–92]), NA ($102.3), Haiti ($30.6 [1989–91]), Jamaica ($498.5), the Dominican Republic ($940.3 [1989–94]), Suriname (−$231.2 [1989–92]), and Trinidad and Tobago ($605.5 [1989–92]).

In 1994, FDI flows to the region were about US$1,235 million, divided (in US millions) as follows: Antigua/Barbuda ($13.9), the Bahamas ($118.9), Barbados ($43.9), Belize ($13.7), Dominica ($9.0), Dominican Republic ($190.1), Grenada ($11.5), Guyana ($24.0), Jamaica ($349.3), St Kitts/Nevis ($12.6), St Lucia ($18.5), St Vincent and the Grenadines ($49.5), Suriname (−$35.0), and Trinidad and Tobago ($415).[79] For most of the largest Caribbean economies in 1993–95, FDI inflows averaged 4.4 per cent of GDP in Barbados, the Dominican Republic, Guyana, Jamaica, Suriname, and Trinidad and Tobago.[80] Since 1986–87, net external flows (NEF), as opposed to net FDI flows, to the larger Caribbean economies have shown a consistent pattern of fluctuation and a net decline of flows to the state, compared with post-1986 private sector flows.[81]

Several CARICOM states – notably Antigua–Barbuda, Barbados, Dominica, Grenada, Guyana, Jamaica, St Lucia, St Vincent and the Grenadines, and Trinidad and Tobago – have committed to the General Agreements on Trade and Services (GATS) with reference to market access in information services, offshore financial services, professional services and entertainment services. Information services cover software, data processing, and telecommunication services and market access applies to cross-border supply, consumption abroad, commercial presence, and presence of natural persons.[82] These states have not imposed any barriers to market access in information services, offshore financial services (re-insurance, banking\deposits, and banking\lending), professional services (legal, accounting, architect, engineering, and advertising), and entertainment (and sporting) services. They pledge to 'allow greater foreign access to their service markets' to the great satisfaction of the WB Group.[83]

Caribbean states are operating under greater constraints as they attempt to allocate funds between public sector investment and to repay principal on the foreign debt, without being able to draw on private sector inflows to meet debt obligations. In the 1990s, about 15 per cent of Caribbean public sector grants were given for debt forgiveness and the 'reversal of credit financing flows from multilateral and commercial sources accounts for most of the aggregate decline of the external financing'.[84] The trends in net external financing in Caribbean economies are consistent with the neoliberal strategy of multilateral institutions to repress the social side of the state to the benefit of profit-seeking capital. The multilaterals have made market liberalization and state restructuring preconditions for loan eligibility and other transfers and supports. Such a shift dovetails with the restructuring of the global business culture and environments and deepens the integration of the region into the global political economy, beyond any concern with improving the quality of life for the vast majority. Social human dumping is partly a function of tendencies toward market hegemony. Clearly, any useful analysis of the place, role and status of the Caribbean in global finance must address several factors beyond mere capital flows and self-serving and obfuscating rhetoric about free markets.

## Conclusion

The laws of motion of capital – competition, uneven and unequal development, the anarchy of market production, commodification and the law of value – are at work in contemporary global restructuring. Global financialization is integral to restructuring, which also signals a major transition in the historical composition of global capital. This shift takes place at the level of the real economy, which is the global market economy. Hence the proper starting point for discourse has to be the global level as opposed to the national one. The shift has two broad dimensions: the flight of important amounts of global capital out of bricks and mortar and into a swarming mode because of the inadequacy of profitable activities in productive processes, and the emergence of new financial and market instruments like electronic money and 'fictitious capital' that are occasioned by the new information technologies.

The Caribbean is an integral part of global capitalism and Caribbean states are sites for processing complex global relations. All Caribbean states, societies, classes, ethnic groups, and gender groups feel the impacts of restructuring through industry, financialization, regionalization and SAPs. OFCs are a sign of the important developments in restructuring: no Caribbean state is attracting significant quantities of productive capital for development and accumulation, and the transition to OFCs coincide with SAP strategies that jointly erode the space in which national states claim to exercise sovereignty. State sovereignty, which is by nature historically contingent and spatial, is best seen as the expression of a nationalized property relation that presupposes a global environment for its exercise and validation.

The crisis of capital, as expressed in financialization, is a crisis of the entire spectrum of the social relations of production around international relations, the nation-state, ethnic, class, and gender relations, and how we imagine and write about space-time dynamics. It signals transitions that are paradigmatic in scope and converge at the intersection of national and postnational processes. The world is experiencing the trauma of the collapse of postwar Keynesian arrangements and bourgeois national projects in the LDCs, and the disintegration of Sovietism. These three shifts are indicative of a much deeper crisis of capital accumulation, in capitalism's institutions of legitimization that are grounded in the imaginaries of universalism, and the reformism that served as the glue of the system. Financialization is one way capital is responding to this disintegration, and Caribbean academics would do well to investigate and theorize the broad implications of these ruptures rather than try to hide behind the imaginaries of nationalist sensibilities about autonomous nations and economies.

## Notes

1 Support for this project was provided by a research grant from Bucknell University.
2 See Blackman Associates, *Comprehensive Review of CARICOM Investment Climate* (Georgetown: Caribbean Community Secretariat, February 1996).
3 Susan Roberts, 'Fictitious Capital, Fictitious Spaces: The Geography of Offshore Financial Flows', in S. Corbridge, R. Martin and N. Thrift (eds), *Money, Power and Space* (Oxford: Blackwell, 1994), p. 91.
4 See Ingo Walter, *The Secret Money Market: Inside the Dark World of Tax Evasion, Financial Fraud, Insider Trading, Money Laundering, and Capital Flight.* (New York: Harper and Row, 1990).
5 See Etienne Balibar, 'The Nation Form: History and Ideology', *Review*, XIII, 3 (Summer 1990).
6 Ethan Kapstein, *Managing the Global Economy: International Finance and the State.* (Cambridge, Mass: Harvard University Press, 1994), p. 90.
7 See WB, *Caribbean Countries: Public Sector Modernization in the Caribbean.* Report No. 15185–CRG, 1996a.
8 Samir Amin, 'The Challenge of Globalization', *Review of International Political Economy*, Vol. 3, No. 2 (Summer 1996).
9 S. Corbridge and N. Thrift, 'Money, Power and Space: Introduction and Overview', in S. Corbridge, R. Martin and N. Thrift (eds), *Money, Power and Space*, (Oxford: Blackwell, 1994), p. 11.
10 Peter Burnham, 'Capital, Crisis and the International State System', in Werner Bonefeld and John Holloway (eds), *Global Capital, National State and the Politics of Money* (New York: St Martin's Press, 1995), p. 93.
11 Ibid., 94.
12 See Amin, op.cit., p. 231.
13 Burnham, op.cit., p. 102.
14 Harry Cleaver, 'The Subversion of Money-as-Command in the Current Crisis', in Werner Bonefeld and John Holloway (eds), *Global Capital, National State and the Politics of Money* (New York: St Martin's Press, 1995), p. 168.
15 See Burnham, op.cit., p. 95.
16 John Holloway, 'Global Capital and the National State',in Werner Bonefeld and John Holloway (eds), *Global Capital, National State and the Politics of Money*, (New York: St Martin's Press, 1995), p. 123.
17 Ibid., p. 123.
18 Ibid., p. 124.
19 Ibid., p. 116. Also see Sol Picciotto, 'The Internationalization of the State', *Capital and Class*, No. 43 (Spring 1991); and David Ruccio, S. Resnick and R. Wolff, 'Class Beyond the Nation-State', *Capital and Class*, No. 43 (Spring 1991).

20   See Holloway, op.cit., p. 135.
21   Commonwealth Secretariat, *International Development Policies: Review of the Activities of International Organizations* (London: Commonwealth Secretariat. 1996), p. 4.
22   See Blackman Associates, *Comprehensive Review of Caricom Investment Climate* for a discussion about the depoliticization of national currency.
23   Jon Mulberg, *Social Limits to Economic Theory* (London: Routledge, 1995), p. 1.
24   See Robin Rosenberg and Steve Stein, (eds), *Advancing the Miami Process: Civil Society and the Summit of the Americas* (Miami, FL: North-South Center Press, 1995).
25   G. McTigue, Ellen Leander and Iain Jenkins, 'The Globalization of Finance: Why We Need to be Plugged In', *Global Finance*, Vol. 9 (November 1995, pp. 35–36.
26   Ibid., 35–6.
27   Terrence W. Farrell, 'Back to the Future: Small Developing Countries in the International Monetary System', in G.K. Helleiner (ed.), *The International Monetary and Financial System: Developing-Country Perspectives* (London and New York: Macmillan Press 1996), p. 468.
28   Norman Girvan, 'Comments on Terrence Farrell's, 'Back to the Future: Small Developing Countries in the International Monetary System''' in G.K. Helleiner (ed.), *The International Monetary and Financial System: Developing-Country Perspectives* (London and New York: Macmillan Press, 1996), p. 475.
29   See Roberts, op.cit., p. 92.
30   Ibid., p. 92.
31   See Ethan Kapstein, *Managing the Global Economy: International Finance and the State.* (Cambridge, Mass.: Harvard University Press, 1994), pp. 110–11, 155–76; Jonathan Beaty and S.C. Gwynne, *The Outlaw Bank: A Wild Ride into the Secret Heart of BCCI* (New York: Random House, 1993), pp. xxvi, 278–319.
32   See Beaty and Gwynne, op.cit., pp. 113, 325–328. Also see Roberts, op.cit.
33   Adam Courtenay, 'Buck Never Stops', *Banker*, 144 (November 1994), pp.88–9; Rodrigo Uprimny, 'In Search of a "Narco" Theory: Elements Towards a Political Economy of Drug Trafficking as a Particular Form of Market Accumulation', *Beyond Law*, Vol.4, No.10 (July 1994), p. 21.
34   McTigue, *et al.*, op.cit., p. 33.
35   Richard A. Johns, *Tax Havens and Offsore Finance: A Study of Transnational Economic Development* (New York: St Martin's Press, 1983), p. 185.
36   Hazel Johnson, *Global Banking Today: The Markets, Players and Issues*, (Chicago: Probus Publishing Company, 1994), pp.118–19.
37   See Richard A. Johns, *Tax Havens and Offshore Finance: A Study of Transnational Economic Development* (New York: St Martin's Press, 1983), pp. 186, 187.
38   Jules Stewart, 'Cleaning Up Offshore', *Euromoney*, No. 324 (April 1996), p. 128. Also, see Johns, op.cit., p. 189.
39   Stewart, op.cit., p. 128.
40   'By 1980, there were 320 international banks, dealing mainly in offshore activities, 6000 exempt trusts and more than 12,000 companies in the Caymans', says Johns, op.cit., p. 197.
41   See Walter, op.cit., pp. 187, 210–19.
42   Stewart, op.cit., p. 130.
43   Walter, op.cit., p. 210; and Stewart, op.cit., p. 128.

44  Johns, op.cit., p. 191.
45  Johns, op.cit., pp. 191–2; pp. Walter, op.cit., p. 210.
46  See WB, *Trends in Developing Economies 1995.* (Washington, DC: WB, 1995).
47  Ellen Leander, 'How Money Launderers are Fighting Back', *Global Finance*, Vol. 10, No. 2, (February 1996), pp. 55–8.
48  See Ivelaw Griffith, *The Quest for Security in the Caribbean: Problems and Promises in Subordinate States,* (Armonk, NY: M.E. Sharpe, 1993).
49  Walter, op.cit., p. 151.
50  Henry Harington points out that, after cleaning up US$122 billion of drug profits in the US and Europe in 1992, money launderers had set out to target Europe, the Middle East and Southeast Asia. See Harrington, 'Go East or Bust', *Banker*, Vol. 143 (15–17 January 1993), p. 143.
51  Uprimny, op.cit., p. 11.
52  Ibid., p. 12.
53  According to the General Accounting Office, the: 'US works with other countries through multilateral and bilateral treaties and arrangements to establish global anti-money-laundering policies, enhance cooperation, and facilitate the exchange of information on money-laundering investigations. The U.S.'s multilateral efforts to establish global anti-money-laundering policies occur mainly through the Financial Action Task Force (FATF) established in 1989.' Working with other countries involves mainly trying to get its way since the US finds it extremely difficult to accept direction from others. This grows out of the myth that the US has a right to lead as the world's only invincible state. See US General Accounting Office, *Money Laundering: A Framework for Understanding U.S. Efforts Overseas,* GAO/GGD-96–195, 1996, p. 3. Also, see Johannes Dumbacher, 'The Fight Against Money Laundering', *Intereconomics: Review of International Trade and Development,* Vol. 30 (July–August 1995), pp. 177–86.
54  Ibid., pp. 44–7.
55  Rowan Bosworth-Davies, 'Money Laundering: Cleaning Up', *Banking World*, 11 (March 1993), pp.28–9.
56  See Uprimny, op.cit., pp. 14–19; and Johns, op.cit., pp. 75–148.
57  Mark P. Hampton, 'Treasure Islands or Fool's Gold: Can and Should Small Island Economies Copy Jersey?', *World Development,* Vol.22, No.2 (1994), pp. 241–2.
58  Kenichi Ohmae, 'Putting Global Logic First', *Harvard Business Review*, Vol. 73, No.1 (January–February 1995), pp.119–25.
59  Richard Bernal, *Strategic Global Repositioning and Future Economic Development in Jamaica,* North–South Agenda Papers, No. 19, 1996.
60  *Netherlands Antilles Central Bank Report 1995,* Table 2.7; pp. 73–82; and Price Waterhouse, *Doing Business in the Netherlands Antilles* (Willemstad, Curaçao: Price Waterhouse, 1992), pp. 3, 28–34.
61  McTigue, *et al.,* op.cit.
62  Roberts, op.cit., p. 100.
63  Ibid., pp. 105–7.
64  Havelock Brewster, 'Increasing International Competitiveness: A Caribbean Community Program', in Yin-Kann Wen and J. Segupta (eds), *Increasing the International Competitiveness of Exports from Caribbean Countries.* (Washington, DC: WB, 1991).

65   For details about the impact of NAFTA on trade investment and technology diversion from the Caribbean, see Bernal, op.cit., p. 3; WB, *Caribbean Countries: Caribbean Economic Overview 1996.*, Report No. 15471–LAC, 1996b, pp.8–11; and *Jamaican Weekly Gleaner*, North American edn, 6–12, February 1997, p. 1.

66   For a discussion of a set of proposals for a 'global repositioning strategy' for Jamaica in the contemporary global context see Bernal, op.cit.; *Jamaica Weekly Gleaner*, North American edn, 24–30, January 1997, p. 19; and WB, 1995, op.cit., p. 255. In particular, Bernal's proposals stress the divide between national political space end economic space. Bernal appreciates the role of the scientific and technological revolution in restructuring the global division of labor. He calls on Jamaica to shift from low-wage light industry, and he sees a future in 'services' like 'financial services in the new dynamic sectors in the global economy such as microelectronics, biotechnology, telecommunications, robotics, and information' (p. 7). While Bernal offers a number of imaginative proposals he does not sufficiently consider the contradictions raised by the flexibilization and global financialization that inform the US global accumulation strategy, given his suggestion that Jamaica has an opportunity to become a 'Western Hemisphere techno-pole'.

67   WB, 1996a, op.cit., p. xv; WB, *Caribbean Countries: Caribbean Economic Overview 1996c*, pp. 3–4.

68   See *The Jamaican Weakly Gleaner*, 6–12 February 1997, p. 1.

69   Joan Ogden, 'How the Overseas Chinese Are Financing Asia's Growth', *Global Finance*, Vol. 9, No. 11 (November 1995), pp. 49–51.

70   In 1994, Asians contributed US$30 billion of the $76 billion that was invested in Asia. Overseas Chinese were the major source of capital that was invested in China (People's Republic of China) and East Asia. Between 1985 and 1994, US$70 billion flowed from 'Overseas Chinese' in Hong Kong to the PRC, and US$15 billion moved from 'Overseas Chinese' in Taiwan, Macau, Singapore, and Thailand into the PRC. Overseas Chinese number about 50 million; but they a vast amount to regional GDP. Some of the largest overseas Chinese-conglomerates account for up to 5 per cent of the GDP of the countries where they're based, and they dominate financial and investment markets way out of proportion to their share of the population. See Ogden, op.cit., pp. 49–50.

71   WB, *Global Development Finance 1997*, (formerly called *World Debt Tables*). (Washington, DC: WB, 1997), pp.3–4. See also United Nations Conference on Trade and Development (UNCTAD), *World Investment Report 1995: Transnational Corporations and Competitiveness.* (New York and Geneva: United Nations, 1995), pp. 69–84.

72   WB, op.cit., pp. 3–16.

73   Ibid., pp. 3–7.

74   UNCTAD, op.cit., pp. 69–84.

75   Ibid., pp. 86–7.

76   See Blackman Associates, *Comprehensive Review of CARICOM Investment Climate*, pp. 71–73 for more on the relationship between financialization and foreign exchange reserves, liberalization and the restructuring of commercial banking, and developments in non-bank financial activities in the CARICOM countries.

77   See Blackman Associates, op.cit., pp. 82–86 for a discussion of recent financial and investment strategies of CARICOM firms with reference to competitiveness initiatives.

78   Hilbourne A. Watson, 'Global Restructuring and the Prospects for Caribbean Competitiveness: With a Case Study from Jamaica', in Hilbourne A. Watson (ed.), *The Caribbean in the Global Political Economy*, (Boulder, Colo.: Lynne Rienner Publishers, 1994), p. 76.

79   WB, 1996b, op.cit., Table 3.2.

80   Ibid., p. 3.

81   Ibid, Table 3.2.

82   Natural persons refers to services that may require temporary movement of natural persons where a complex service may require specialized skilled persons from originating country in conditions where such high-tech labor is not available in the destination country.

83   WB, *Caribbean Countries: Prospects for Service Exports from the English speaking Caribbean*. Report No. 15342–LAC, 1996d, pp. 59–71.

84   WB, 1996b, op.cit., p. 19.

# 3
# Drugs, Debt and Structural Adjustment in the Caribbean

*Richard L. Bernal, Winsome J. Leslie and Stephen E. Lamar*

In the late 1990s, the economies of the Caribbean are confronted with the challenge of undertaking structural adjustment while being constrained by the use of resources for servicing debts and fighting drugs. On one hand, because of recent developments in the international economic environment, the countries in the region must be preoccupied with the imperatives of structural adjustment to pursue economic development. On the other hand, the persistence of the debt burden coupled with the corrosive effects of the international drug trade divert resources and attention from important development priorities. Thus, there is a vicious circle. Under these circumstances, the best defense against the penetration of drugs is economic development. However, such development is retarded by the debt burden, especially in Jamaica and Guyana.

In order to address these challenges, the countries of the region are having to pursue policies that essentially work at cross purposes with each other. Structural adjustment, for example, requires governments to restrain expenditures, leaving less resources for fighting drugs and servicing debt. Structural reforms in many instances results in increased poverty, making illicit forms of activity such as narcotics trafficking more attractive. High levels of domestic and international debt service in the midst of an economic reform effort can limit a government's room for maneuver in terms of effectively waging the war against drugs. The dilemma may only get worse in the years to come as Caribbean governments respond to the changing composition of external resources flows. In the late 1990s, Caribbean governments are finding themselves increasingly squeezed for resources as bilateral development assistance, particularly from the United States, had been sharply reduced.

This chapter argues that there are connections between drug trafficking, debt, and structural adjustment in the Caribbean context. The predicament which confronts countries in the region is how to sustain the fight against drugs while effectively servicing debt and undergoing structural adjustment, the costs of which are felt in the short term, and far ahead of the benefits. Furthermore, the accumulation of both external and internal debt has contributed to the immiseration of lower-income groups, because governments have been constrained in their ability to lessen the deflationary effects and distortions inherent in structural adjustment. One of the adverse impacts is the increase in poverty which is occurring as the same time as a reduction in the capacity of governments to alleviate it through fiscal expenditure and social programs.

First, this chapter outlines the context in which structural adjustment is taking place. In particular, it highlights aspects of the current international environment within which Caribbean countries must operate. Secondly, it describes the structural adjustment process and its implications for poverty and Caribbean development. It then examines the debt situation and the constraint of debt servicing on governments' ability to alleviate poverty and fight drug trafficking. Next, it indicates that drug production, consumption and trafficking have not been contained, and, indeed, may have increased. Finally, we point out that the Caribbean dilemma is that highly indebted countries experience impoverishment during structural adjustment. This increases the likelihood of a drug problem, which cannot be effectively addressed because heavy debt service deprives the government of resources which could be devoted to poverty alleviation and fighting drugs. This situation requires a holistic approach linking debt, drugs and economic development in the Caribbean. The immediate imperative is debt management schemes, which reduce debt servicing, freeing resources to promote development and counter-narcotics programs.

## The present context

As was shown in Chapter 1, there are significant differences in population, income levels, and natural resources within the Caribbean. There are, however, similarities, the most notable being the economic vulnerability of these countries, which derives from their small size, poverty, and economic fragility. Trade is large in relation to GDP, and there is a high import content in production and consumption. Moreover, there is a concentration on a narrow range of products for foreign exchange earnings, usually tourism or primary commodities, such as bananas, bauxite, and sugar. As a result, these countries are particularly vulnerable to external shocks attributable either to natural disasters, such as periodic hurricanes, or to abrupt changes in the international trading system. In this type of economy, the process of growth depends on the amount of foreign exchange reserves. This in turn depends on capital inflows (aid, loans, investment and export earnings). Given the limited sources of export earnings and the fact that primary commodity exports are vulnerable to price and demand changes, the growth process is fragile.

It is against this background that the efforts of Caribbean countries to adapt to the global environment must be seen. Several international trends have highlighted the need for rapid structural changes in Caribbean economies: (a) the progressive globalization of production and finance and at the same time, the erosion of national barriers to the international movement of goods, services and capital; (b) shifts in international labor markets favoring services and knowledge-based employment, and against low-wage labor-intensive manufacturing; (c) weak long-term prospects for primary products; and (d) erosion of preferential trading arrangements such as the Lomé Convention with the EU.[1]

Recent developments in the United States, which is the principal trading partner of Caribbean countries, have also had adverse implications for the region. The CBI, which provides preferential entry into the United States for the majority of Caribbean exports has been undermined in recent years by the NAFTA. The most glaring example is apparel exports. The NAFTA provides to Mexico duty and quota free access for textile and apparel products in excess of that which is accorded to the Caribbean. As a result, Mexican apparel exports to the US are now growing at a rate three times that of the Caribbean. The Caribbean Textiles and Apparel Institute estimates that the NAFTA has been a factor in the loss of roughly 123,000 Caribbean jobs and the closure of some 150 apparel factories throughout the region.[2]

This is compounded by recent US actions which have challenged or changed existing trading arrangements for important Caribbean exports such as rum and bananas. In the case of bananas, a US-led coalition of Latin American countries successfully challenged the EU banana regime before the WTO. If this regime is dismantled, it could have devastating implications for Caribbean banana exports, and destroy the banana industry in the Windward Islands where it accounts for on average, 16.5 per cent of GDP and between 40 to 80 per cent of total export earnings, employing 33 to 70 per cent of the labor force.[3] Collectively, these developments in apparel and bananas have raised serious questions about the prospects for long-term economic growth in the Caribbean.

In addition, official capital inflows to the region have declined substantially since the early 1980s. WB figures reveal that net financing for the public sector in selected Caribbean countries declined from a US$1.646 billion in 1982 to less than US$100 million in 1994, as governments repaid official and private loans.[4] As a result, Caribbean countries have not been able to rely on previously high levels of external funding to ease expenditure constraints, and therefore there are added pressures on government budgets. Although net financing from the private sector increased from US$538 million in 1982 to US$1,424 million in 1994, it did not fully compensate for this shortfall. Private sector flows are under pressure as well. In 1996, for example, the US Congress closed a private sector financing mechanism that supported the investment of more than US$2000 million worth of foreign direct investment in CBI countries from 1986 to 1995.[5] This follows a significant reduction in US aid to the region.

Many countries are responding to these challenges by attempting to diversify their export base, deepening the process of economic reform, and forging trading relationships with new partners. These policies are being implemented within an overall framework of structural adjustment. The pressures on the economy caused by adjustment, however, are further complicated as governments work to address two other issues – servicing the debt incurred during the 1970s and 1980s and fighting the narco-traffickers of the 1990s.

## The impact of structural adjustment

Structural adjustment is a process involving the implementation of a range of medium-term macro-economic measures with the objective of promoting structural changes in response to international economic developments and internal supply bottlenecks. These measures are typically preceded or accompanied by short-term economic stabilization measures involving monetary and fiscal policies to deflate demand, and exchange rate adjustment, usually a devaluation. Structural adjustment programs themselves focus on 'deeper' supply-side reforms such as trade liberalization, privatization, liberalization of financial markets, deregulation, public sector 'down-sizing' and tax reform.[6]

Beginning in the mid-1970s, several Caribbean economies experienced severe balance of payments difficulties, due to a combination of internal and external factors. These included:

1. a series of substantial increases in the price of oil;
2. reductions in price and demand for certain primary product exports, e.g. bauxite;
3. stagflation in industrialized countries; and
4. reductions in domestic production, because of natural disasters (hurricanes) and state intervention.

In response, some governments sought to compensate for the loss of momentum in these economies by increased fiscal expenditure, regulation and government ownership. Much of the additional expenditure was financed by external borrowing, including, in the case of Jamaica, commercial bank loans. By the late 1970s, these countries had accumulated levels of indebtedness which were difficult to service. As a result, Jamaica, Guyana and Grenada, reluctantly resorted to using IMF facilities. These facilities involved conditionality which took the form of deflationary stabilization programs. By the mid-1980s, the multilateral financial institutions and bilateral assistance agencies were advocating a more comprehensive approach to economic reform, via structural adjustment and sector adjustment programs. The economic situation was particularly acute in Guyana and Jamaica, which had to undertake comprehensive adjustment strategies, with harsh austerity measures, supported by borrowing from the IMF and WB. Levels of debt had

Table 3.1  World Bank Structural Adjustment Loans to Caribbean Countries, 1980–95

| Country | Date |
|---------|------|
| Guyana | 1981 |
| Jamaica | 1982 |
| Jamaica | 1983 |
| Jamaica | 1984 |
| Jamaica (Trade and Financial Sector Adjustment) | 1987 |
| Jamaica (Public Enterprise Sector Adjustment) | 1987 |
| Dominica | 1988 |
| Jamaica (Agricultural Sector Adjustment) | 1990 |
| Guyana | 1990 |
| Trinidad & Tobago | 1990 |
| Jamaica (Trade and Finance Adjustment) | 1991 |
| Jamaica (Private Sector Development Adjustment) | 1993 |
| Guyana (Private Sector Development Adjustment) | 1995 |

*Source*: World Bank, *List of Active and Completed Projects in the Caribbean Region, 1991–1996* (World Bank, Management Information Systems, 1997).

Table 3.2  IMF Agreements with Caribbean Countries, 1977–97

| Country | Standby Agreements | Extended Fund Facilities |
|---------|-------------------|--------------------------|
| Barbados | 1982, 1992 | – |
| Belize | 1984 | – |
| Dominica | 1984 | 1981, 1986[a] |
| Dominican Republic | 1985, 1991, 1993 | 1983 |
| Grenada | 1975, 1976, 1979, 1981 | 1983 |
| Guyana | – | 1979, 1980, 1990[b], 1994[b] |
| Haiti | 1977,1982, 1983, 1989, 1995 | 1978, 1986[a], 1996[b] |
| Jamaica | 1977, 1984, 1985, 1987, 1988, 1990, 1991 | 1978, 1979, 1981, 1992 |
| Trinidad & Tobago | 1989, 1990 | – |

*Notes*
[a] Structural Adjustment Facility.
[b] Enhanced Structural Adjustment Facility.
*Source*: IMF.

become unsustainable by this time, and therefore countries also embarked on successive rounds of debt rescheduling. By the early 1990s, many of the countries in the Caribbean were pursuing various structural adjustment regimes. Some governments, such as those in Jamaica and Guyana, opted for a formal IMF/WB program. Others, such as those in Grenada and Suriname, designed their own structural adjustment strategies.[7]

One unintended consequence of many structural adjustment policies is that lower income groups are adversely affected. The poor in particular are least able to absorb severe deteriorations in their standard of living, and have fewer options for coping with economic crisis.[8] A 1987 WB study on the social costs of adjustment, points out that adjustment measures designed to balance aggregate demand and supply tend to depress output, employment and consumption.[9] Structural adjustment essentially involves shifts in resource allocation, and studies have shown that these shifts, in combination with privatization and economic restructuring, which frequently lead to higher levels of unemployment and underemployment, increase poverty levels. The extent of the impact on the poor often depends on the time horizon over which structural adjustment policies are applied, with short programs having the severest effects on these social groups.[10] Furthermore, as Anderson and Witter maintain, structural adjustment is a social process, not just an economic one. As such, adjustment policies affect the entire society, with some social groups 'winning' at the expense of others. 'Losers' are often the working non-poor, who frequently slip into poverty because of restructuring and austerity measures.[11] The extent to which adjustment policies are applied by the IMF and WB varies from case to case. However, the fact remains that the standard 'menu'of economic reform measures includes devaluation and reductions in public expenditure to achieve fiscal and monetary targets.

Devaluation is a central policy measure in stabilization/adjustment programs and is undertaken to correct balance of payments deficits by discouraging imports and making export more competitive. Guyana, for example, embarked in 1988 on an Economic Recovery Program (ERP), which included a series of devaluations of the Guyanese dollar. The benefits of depreciation of the exchange rate and the removal of price controls went to large farmers whose supply response was stronger due to prior investments in infrastructure and technology. The increased output could also be readily sold, as Guyana had fallen well below its quotas in preferential markets.[12]

Nevertheless, regardless of the benefits, in the small open economies of the Caribbean with their heavy reliance on imports (for both production and consumption), the negative impact of devaluation on poverty and the distribution of goods can be dramatic. In terms of production, devaluation increases the cost of raw material and intermediate inputs, increasing the prices of final products. On the consumer side, devaluation often results in large and sudden price increases for consumer goods on the local market and subsequent increases in the cost of living. In Guyana, exchange rate depreciation under the structural adjustment program was passed on when price controls were removed on essential consumer items such as cooking gas, flour, kerosine and rice. As a result, prices for these items rose by as much as 244 per cent, putting them beyond the reach of the poor.[13]

In order to maintain moderate levels of public sector expenditure, governments embark on austerity programs, typically making spending cuts in vital areas such as education, health, housing, infrastructure and public sector wages. A WB assessment admits that in 1984 and 1985, the period of harshest adjustment in Jamaica, government expenditures on social services declined in real terms.[14] Real per capita expenditures on education declined from US$84 in 1981/82 to US$58 in 1986/87, while expenditures on health declined from US$44 in 1982/83 to US$25.6 in 1986/87.[15] Cuts in education, coupled with large increases in the standard of living, resulted in increasing teacher/pupil ratios, low school attendance and a decline in academic performance, particularly at the secondary level. Reductions in health expenditures aggravated manpower shortages in hospitals and health clinics. The health status of the population also declined. Incidents of infectious diseases such as gastroenteritis increased during this period and the per capital caloric intake fell from 119.4 in 1978 to 112.7 in 1982.[16]

Stabilization also involves the elimination of subsidies, replacing them with user fees, as well as the removal of price controls on essential food items. Reduced expenditures in the social sectors, coupled with the removal of subsidies effectively removes the social safety net for large segments of the population, and the burden of adjustment in this regard falls on the poor. Trinidad and Tobago began an adjustment program in 1988, and while GDP growth moved from −2.3 per cent in 1981–90 to 3.3 per cent in 1995, a 1995 study found increasing levels of malnutrition among children in the early 1990s.[17]

Reductions in public sector wages or the lack of wage increases, particularly in the face of the high levels of inflation, result in an increase in poverty and lower standards of living, even for the middle class. In Jamaica, for example, the per centage of the population below the poverty line increased from 29.8 per cent in 1988 to 38.9 per cent in 1991.[18] In Guyana, between 1980 and 1990, real per capita GDP declined by approximately 29 per cent, and it is estimated that the incidence of poverty increased from approximately 26 per cent to 43 per cent in that same period.[19]

Public sector reform measures frequently include significant reductions in civil service employment. Jamaica for example, reduced the public sector workforce by 10 per cent in the 1992/93 fiscal year alone. Privatization of public entities also results in job displacement, as the new privatized entity is often restructured for more efficient operations.[20] When such retrenchments take place, employees at the lower end of the public sector hierarchy tend to be disproportionately affected. Furthermore, with their relatively low level of skills, these workers experience difficulties gaining new employment. Restructuring of the agricultural sector in Jamaica, while improving labor productivity, resulted in a loss of 29,200 jobs between 1992 and 1994, due in part to the divestment of government-owned entities such as Victoria Bananas.[21] As in the case of Guyana's ERP, these labor market shifts can be somewhat mitigated by expanded informal sector activities, and new employment opportunities in agriculture and small-scale service industries. However, these jobs are low-wage, are unstable and require low skills.

The cumulative impact of all these structural reform measures is that increasing numbers of people join the ranks of the poor, aggravating the competition for access to scarce government resources.[22] In addition, adjustment tends to widen existing income inequalities. The study by Anderson and Witter of adjustment in Jamaica between 1977 and 1989 shows a dramatic shift in the distribution of the national income away from those earning wages and salaries. For example, in 1977, 35 per cent of workers reporting their income earned no more than half the minimum family income. By 1985, this figure had risen to 61 per cent. Subsequent wage adjustments by the Jamaican Government provided some relief. However in 1989, the proportion of workers earning less than half the minimum family requirement still stood at 46 per cent.[23]

Poverty in the Caribbean is now extensive, and presents a major challenge for the countries in the region. Poverty levels within the Eastern Caribbean has been estimated at 25 per cent, approximately 13 per cent below the average in the wider Caribbean. In Trinidad 22.5 per cent of all households lived below the poverty line in the period 1988–1992, while in Jamaica, the figure was 37.7 per cent in 1992 and 28.3 per cent in 1993.[24] According to calculations by the Institute of Jamaica, the poverty level still remains at 28 per cent in 1997. In practical terms, this means that nearly one in three Jamaicans are living on J$37 or just about US$1 a day. Vulnerable groups include children, the youth and women. Several studies have shown the extent to which the burden of adjustment falls on poor urban women.[25] In Jamaica, for example, women comprise 53 per cent of the poor in Kingston, and 50 per cent of the poor in rural areas.[26] The gender distribution of poverty is all the more significant in the wider Caribbean context because of the pivotal role women play in poor families in meeting survival needs.

Early structural adjustment programs in the 1980s in the Caribbean and elsewhere were based on the premise that restoring growth in adjusting countries would be most effective way of alleviating poverty. However, by the end of that decade, the adverse effects of structural adjustment on social welfare, were clearly apparent, even to the WB itself.[27] In recognition of the need for 'adjustment with a human face', Caribbean governments in the late 1980s began to implement a number of programs with funding assistance from the WB and other multilateral agencies, to provide a 'social safety net' and protect vulnerable groups. Jamaica began a School Feeding Program and a Food Stamp Program to improve the nutritional status of those classified as poor or vulnerable. While the Program currently targets benefits to 320,000 individuals island-wide, coverage is inadequate, in terms of the number of people in need. Furthermore, the program has fallen short of targets, because of low rates of application by vulnerable groups, difficulties with registration, inadequate staff and administrative systems due to government expenditure constraints. At the present time, the Food Stamp Program is being phased out, and replaced by Skills 2000, a program to promote self-reliance through skills training for food stamp recipients and their dependents.

The School Feeding Program provides at least one meal or snack a day to students in Basic Schools, infant, primary, All Age and New Secondary Schools. In recent years, government research has shown that increasing numbers of children from households above the poverty line are benefiting from the program, thereby compromising attempts to target those children in need. A Social and Economic Support program was also introduced in 1990, to cushion the effects of adjustment on youth, the poor and the aged, especially in inner city communities and rural areas. The program supports community-based infrastructure projects, employment and training. Finally, a Social Investment Fund was launched in 1996, with funding from the WB and Inter-American Development Bank to put in place social infrastructure to facilitate self-reliance for low-income groups.

In 1991, the Guyana government initiated a Social Impact Amelioration Program (SIMAP) as a short-term strategy to mitigate the economic effects of the Recovery Program on the most vulnerable social groups. Funded by the WB and the Inter-American Development Bank, the program includes public infrastructure projects, social services projects, short-term cash payments to supplement basic needs and skills training to promote self-reliance. While the program has had a positive impact, the WB has expressed concerns about the program's inability to target and reach the most vulnerable and poorest segments of the population.[28] It is, thus, clear that the impoverishment that accompanies structural adjustment can be alleviated in some measure by government intervention with social programs. However, governments' ability to assist can be sharply constrained by heavy debt servicing.

## Debt as a constraint

Many Caribbean economies became heavily indebted in the 1980s, due to high levels of external borrowing in the previous decade to offset high public sector deficits. Whereas during the 1970s external debt for the region was 35 per cent to 40 per cent of GDP, by 1987–88 this had risen to 70 per cent of GDP. [29] The largest debtors in absolute terms were

Table 3.3 External Debt of Selected Caribbean Countries, 1980–1995 (US$m)

| Countries | 1980 | 1988 | 1989 | 1990 | 1991 | 1992 | 1993 | 1994 | 1995 |
|---|---|---|---|---|---|---|---|---|---|
| **Barbados** | | | | | | | | | |
| Total debt | 165.7 | 702.9 | 643.6 | 683.0 | 652.1 | 609.6 | 569.9 | 614.7 | 597.0 |
| Use of IMF credit | 2.9 | 10.4 | 4.3 | 0.7 | 0.0 | 50.7 | 50.6 | 53.8 | 37.1 |
| Total debt/exports (%) | 28.9 | 89.8 | 72.5 | 81.7 | 78.4 | 74.1 | 64.9 | – | – |
| Total debt service/exports (%) | 4.4 | 12.0 | 11.5 | 16.8 | 16.8 | 12.3 | 12.9 | – | – |
| Net transfers on debt | 13.1 | 91.3 | –76.2 | –28.8 | –79.9 | –47.0 | –85.5 | –7.8 | –63.3 |
| **Guyana** | | | | | | | | | |
| Total debt | 811 | 1,866 | 1,633 | 1,945 | 1,960 | 1,897 | 1,954 | 2,038 | 2,105 |
| Use of IMF credit | 86 | 110 | 106 | 113 | 149 | 168 | 177 | 179 | 172 |
| Total debt/exports (%) | 197.4 | – | – | – | – | 385.1 | 364.7 | 343.8 | 328.1 |
| Total debt service/exports (%) | 21.6 | – | – | – | – | 20.7 | 17.2 | 16.4 | 17.0 |
| Net transfers on debt | 80 | 66 | –325 | 135 | 30 | –16 | –6 | –51 | –43 |
| **Haiti** | | | | | | | | | |
| Total debt | 302.4 | 820.0 | 806.2 | 888.9 | 758.4 | 785.1 | 803.0 | 716.9 | 806.8 |
| Use of IMF credit | 46.2 | 47.4 | 41.3 | 37.6 | 32.6 | 35.1 | 33.8 | 35.0 | 28.7 |
| Total debt/exports (%) | 72.8 | 202.4 | 221.3 | 273.6 | 289.9 | 682.1 | 672.5 | 1,118.3 | 386.8 |
| Total debt service/exports (%) | 6.2 | 14.6 | 14.4 | 10.1 | 10.2 | 4.7 | 4.2 | 2.0 | 45.2 |
| Net transfers on debt | 50.9 | –16.5 | –16.7 | 26.7 | 27.5 | –4.7 | –5.0 | –79.3 | 46.6 |
| **Trinidad & Tobago** | | | | | | | | | |
| Total debt | 829 | 2,102 | 2,138 | 2,512 | 2,488 | 2,375 | 2,131 | 2,221 | 2,556 |
| Use of IMF credit | – | 115 | 205 | 329 | 385 | 282 | 155 | 91 | 50 |
| Total debt/exports (%) | 24.6 | 119.2 | 114.5 | 107.7 | 111.4 | 109.0 | 111.5 | 101.6 | 87.9 |
| Total debt service/exports (%) | 6.8 | 19.5 | 13.2 | 19.3 | 19.2 | 26.4 | 32.4 | 24.8 | 14.8 |
| Net transfers on debt | 0.33 | –1 | –47 | –262 | –276 | –218 | –432 | –152 | 122 |

Source: World Bank, *Global Development Finance*, Vol. 2 (Washington, DC: World Bank, 1997).

Jamaica, with US$4.3 billion, Trinidad and Tobago, with US$2 billion and Guyana, with US$1.6 billion.[30] Indeed, by the mid-1980s, many countries such as Jamaica were locked into a 'vicious circle of foreign debt',[31] where new borrowing was just sufficient to match debt servicing. Since that time, external debt in the region has fallen, due to debt rescheduling, and debt swaps in the case of Jamaica. (See Tables 3.3 and 3.4.) However, debt ratios, while lower than in the 1980s, are still high. In Jamaica, the ratio of total debt to GDP in 1995 was 118.5 per cent, the ratio of total debt service to exports was 17.9 per cent. In Guyana, the ratios were 377.2 per cent and 17 per cent respectively, and in Trinidad 87 per cent and 14.8 per cent.[32] In Guyana, 38.1 per cent of central government revenue was allocated to debt service in 1996, and 47 per cent will be allocated in 1997.[33] In Jamaica, 34 per cent of Recurrent Expenditures went to debt service in the 1995/96 fiscal year, compared to 31 per cent in 1997/98.[34]

Debt constrains the structural adjustment process, retards economic growth and deprives counter-narcotics programs of funds. Resources devoted to debt servicing are not available to support structural adjustment in the form of expenditure on health, education, poverty alleviation programs and institutional reform. External debt servicing also reduces foreign exchange available for imports. Given the critical dependence of investment, production and consumption in Caribbean countries on imports, the process of economic growth is stymied. Furthermore, in the face of debt servicing and pressing social demands and development needs, governments often economize on resources for counter-narcotics programs. Drug trafficking in the Caribbean Basin is a growing security and social problem. Therefore, the effect of the debt burden on structural adjustment and economic reform is exacerbated by the need for more resources to be devoted to the drug war. Although the drug issue has long been present in Caribbean societies, its prominence in the region has been enhanced by increased demand in the United States and Europe and the aggressive tactics of the drug cartels.

## Production, consumption and trafficking of drugs

The production, trafficking and consumption of drugs have emerged as a triple threat to sustained economic development throughout the Caribbean.[35] First, domestic production imposes additional burdens in the form of expensive eradication programs and opportunity costs associated with the loss of productive resources. Secondly, domestic consumption exacts a heavy toll on Caribbean societies because of the added cost of preventing use, incarcerating users, or treating drugs addicts. Thirdly, drug trafficking by South American cartels disrupts legitimate commercial relationships throughout the region and adds a substantial cost to the external defense needs of small Caribbean security forces. An understanding of how the illicit narcotics issue retards Caribbean economic growth requires an appreciation of some of the dimensions of the issue.

### Domestic production

Unfortunately, the Caribbean countries have climate and topographic conditions that are well-suited for the cultivation of marijuana. The mountainous terrains, the small land masses and plot sizes, and the proximity to the largest consumer market make marijuana an extremely profitable crop to grow throughout the Caribbean. The 1997 *International Narcotics Control Strategy Report* give an indication of this problem. Marijuana cultivation in Jamaica in 1996, although down by about 40 per cent from 1991, still remains at some 1,000 hectares. Even when half of that hectarage is destroyed, the potential yield is still 356 tones – a figure equivalent to roughly 5 per cent of worldwide marijuana production. US government surveys of marijuana production identify Guyana, Jamaica, Trinidad and Tobago, and the countries of the Eastern Caribbean as significant producers of marijuana, both for local consumption and for export.[36]

Caribbean countries have directed considerable effort at eradicating or confiscating the supply of domestically grown marijuana. Governments throughout the region have opted for different methods of eradication. Jamaica, Trinidad and Tobago and Belize, for example, manually eradicate marijuana plants by cutting and burning plants that have been located through periodic aerial reconnaissance. In countries where such practices are not impractical for political reasons, the use of herbicides through aerial spraying or manual application plays a role in eradication efforts.

As was indicated in Chapter 1, the costs to society of domestic production are significant. Regional governments are required to maintain active security forces devoted to the identification and destruction of marijuana fields. As some marijuana strains, such as indica and sin semilla, can produce as many as four to six crops annually, eradication becomes a constant activity. Moreover, marijuana is often smuggled to the United States and markets in Europe, adding to international interdiction costs. Domestic production poses an opportunity cost as well in the form of foregone production of other cash crops. Moreover, some farmers, who intercrop marijuana with legitimate products, devote considerable energy and resources in concealing their illicit products from the routine aerial inspections. Presumably, if they directed these talents in other directions, they could enhance their own bottom line through legitimate income-generating ventures while making significant contributions to the national economy.

## Domestic consumption

The drug menace has taken a toll as Caribbean residents and visiting tourists have participated as consumers of illicit narcotics and psychotropic substances. Although some reports suggest that the United States – with only 5 per cent of the world's population – consumes 30 per cent of the world cocaine supply,[37] there is evidence that suggests that drug use in the Caribbean remains a major problem. While drug addiction rates vary widely among countries – crack cocaine use is expanding in Aruba although it seems to be on the decline in the Bahamas – the demand for illicit narcotics persists throughout the Caribbean.

In many respects, the demand for narcotics, whether in the United States or throughout the Caribbean, represents the most critical element of the international drug trade because it defines the market. If drug demand can be sufficiently suppressed, the basis for the drug trade will evaporate. With this in mind, many governments have launched campaigns to reduce the demand for drugs and to assist former addicts in recovering from their drug abuse. Again, as with interdiction and law enforcement efforts, such campaigns represent a drain on the pool of resources available for development purposes.

Part III of this volume examines many of the efforts to combat drugs. Suffice it to say here that nearly every Caribbean country has an active drug treatment and drug reduction program in operation. The Government of Belize, for example, sponsors the National Drug Abuse Control Council (NDACC), which provides anti-drug education, outreach, and rehabilitation. In Aruba, the Ministry of Education and the Health Department promote anti-drug awareness campaigns targeted at youth sporting events. Each of these programs carry an explicit cost in the form of higher health care for drug users and their dependents and increased expenses associated with treatment programs. In addition, as drug users are treated in demand reduction programs, society pays an implicit cost in the form of decreased labor productivity because of illness or imprisonment.[38]

## Narcotics trafficking

Located between the major drug producing countries in Latin America and the major drug consumers in North America, the Caribbean has the dubious distinction of being one of the major transit routes for illicit narcotics. Presently, seven of the 32 countries that the United States identifies as 'major drug-producing or drug-transit countries' are in the Caribbean Basin.[39] Drug trafficking, however, touches almost every country in the region. As drugs are produced, marketed, shipped, and consumed, the international trafficking cartels rely upon an ever-changing network of suppliers and routes to move their product from the Andean jungles to the main consumer markets in the United States and Europe. Jonathan Winer, US Deputy Assistant Secretary of State for Law Enforcement and Crime, sums up the problem: 'The Caribbean is a significant drug transit zone because there are lots of harbors, lots of airstrips, and governments without a lot of money.'[40]

US officials believe that roughly 20 per cent of the 760 tones of cocaine annually produced in South America is transhipped to the United States through the Caribbean Basin.[41] European officials suspect that close to 30 per cent of the cocaine smuggled from Latin America to Europe passes through the Caribbean as well. In fact, the State Department's annual *International Narcotics Control Strategy Report* for 1997 indicated that nearly every country in the region intercepted cocaine shipments during 1996. In many cases – such as in St Lucia, St Vincent and the Grenadines, and the NAs, where cocaine seizures increased nearly seven-fold from 1995 to 1996 – cocaine shipments appear to be on the rise.[42]

Cocaine is not the only problem. South American-produced heroin is also putting increasing pressure on Caribbean transit routes as cocaine cartels begin to diversify into heroin production and US consumers turn increasingly to this drug to satisfy their addiction. In 1996, for example, Jamaican law enforcement officials seized 300 grams of Colombian heroin, the first such seizure in over two years. Over the past few years, large heroin shipments have been intercepted in the Bahamas and the Dominican Republic as well.[43]

Such high volume drug transhipments have both direct and indirect financial impacts on the economies of many Caribbean countries and, as a result, are an added challenge to sustainable development. Regional governments now have to devote increasing resources to aerial and maritime patrols to interdict drug smugglers and to implement tighter customs procedures so as to more effectively police legitimate export and import shipments. While these activities are important functions of any national government, they divert attention and scarce human and financial resources away from other equally pressing development needs.

## Impoverishment and drugs

Structural adjustment increases poverty, which needs to be addressed by 'social' expenditure by governments. However, governments' capacity is reduced and constrained by debt servicing. Consequently, in the highly indebted countries, such as Jamaica and Guyana, there has been an immiserization of large segments of the population, creating increased economic vulnerability and leading more individuals to succumb to the temptation of involvement in drug activities.

The production, consumption and trafficking of drugs have increasingly affected most aspects of Caribbean society. This is turn has a debilitating effect on structural adjustment and development. First, there are adverse effects on economic activity. A country that develops a reputation as one that is unable or unwilling to confront its drug problem can find a chilling effect on efforts to attract new investment and promote tourism. Faced with the added costs of extra security for their shipments and potential embarrassment if their cargoes are used for drug smuggling purposes, many multinational companies may simply opt to do business in countries that are less prone to narcotics transhipment. The net effect is a diversion in investment, a decline in export revenues, and a loss of legitimate jobs.[44]

Secondly, the drug problem increases dependence on external support for counter-narcotics efforts. In cases where governments do not have adequate resources, Caribbean countries often permit the United States or the United Kingdom to patrol national waters and make arrests within those waters. While such joint efforts may reduce the financial strains, it divests much of the control of interdiction resources to US and British agencies. This situation exposes Caribbean counter-narcotics efforts to abrupt reallocation of resources. For example, when the Clinton Administration assumed power, it downgraded drug interdiction efforts and decided to reallocate resources away from the Caribbean transit zones to undertake more operations in the South American source countries. The premise was that each dollar would be more effectively spent in cutting off drugs at the supply, rather than closing the transit routes.[45] Although funding for drug interdiction declined from about US$1 billion in fiscal year 1992 to US$569 million in fiscal year 1995, increased funding for the so-called source countries never materialized.[46] The resulting drop in interdiction resources was accompanied by a surge in narcotics production in the Andes and an attendant surge in narcotics trafficking through the Caribbean. As a result, inhabitants of Caribbean countries develop a perception that they are captive to two simultaneous external forces, namely the cartels that smuggle the drugs and the foreign navies that fight to stop them.

Thirdly, the drug trade undermines the integrity of economic institutions. Several Caribbean countries, especially those which are offshore banking centers, have been compromised by an escalation of money laundering. As drug dealers seek to channel illicit profits into legitimate businesses, enterprises, and investments, they take advantage of inadequate financial controls or bank secrecy laws in a number of Caribbean countries. Virtually every Caribbean country, including Cuba, is at some risk of money laundering activities. In 1996, the United States included four Caribbean Basin countries: Aruba, Cayman Islands, NA, and Panama, among its list of the top 20 money laundering centers.[47] It is estimated that as much as US$50 billion of the US$500 billion in annual drug profits is laundered through the Caribbean Basin.[48] The problem ranges from channeling funds through offshore bank accounts and shell companies, which is a common concern in the Cayman Islands, to investing drug money in legitimate real estate and hotel ventures, which has become a growing problem in Aruba and the NA.[49]

Fourthly, the drug trade is closely associated with increased criminal activity and violence. This trend towards increased violence in a number of Caribbean localities is directly related to the proliferation of firearms and ammunition, which Jamaican Prime Minister Patterson recently labeled the 'currency of the drug trade'.[50] Aside from the increase in crime statistics and the rise in prison populations, this violence also manifests itself though the proliferation of barbed wires, burglar bars, and armed guards, which serve as visible scars of the drug trade, and which last long after the trade has moved to a new neighborhood.[51]

Fifthly, the drug trade has increased the incidence of drug-related corruption. There are growing reports of drug-related corruption among law enforcement and other government officials. In each of these instances, governments must divert attention and resources away from development needs to respond to the challenges posed by such criminals. The increased costs are measured in ways that are both tangible in terms of the loss of life, the need to build additional prisons, or train law enforcement officers, and intangible, in terms of the psychological effect of increased insecurity and fear among residents and tourists.

Increased criminal activity has been compounded by the deportation of criminals by the United States and other countries. In a effort to control spending on prison maintenance, US federal and state governments have increasingly looked to deportations of individuals of Caribbean heritage as a way of alleviating prison overcrowding and saving on incarceration costs. Florida correctional officials believe they saved US$15 million in tax money by deporting 328 illegal aliens during 1996. These savings, however, are offset by a rise in drug-related criminal activity in many parts of the Caribbean. In the Dominican Republic, officials believe rising crime statistics are the direct result of some 5,000 criminals deported to that country during 1996, up from 1,225 in 1995. Jamaica, which experienced a surge in the national murder rate during 1996, received 1,765 criminal deportees during that year, an increase of more than 100 per cent from the year before. It is interesting to note that, of that total, 902 were involved in drug related crimes while overseas.[52] Chapters 5 and 6 offer more discussion on the deportation of criminals and the impact of this practice on crime in the region.

## Conclusion

Clearly, the suffocating challenges presented by drugs in the Caribbean create a vicious cycle in which scarce funding and changing priorities prevent authorities from dedicating sufficient resources to pursue vital development programs. As important development needs go unfunded, the prevalence of drugs and the catalytic effect they have on violent criminal activity further undermine the fabric and institutions of society. As a result, many of the smaller economies of the Caribbean are faced with the real threat that their sovereignty will be undermined by the reach and greater fiscal resources of the drug cartels.

Caribbean countries are also under pressure in many traditional sectors that compete directly with narcotics. Although the Caribbean is noted for the production of other agricultural commodities, such as sugar and bananas, these products are often not as competitive as similar products grown elsewhere under more suitable conditions. As a result, Caribbean countries rely upon a series of protective mechanisms to preserve their share of key markets in the United States and Europe. As pressure grows to dismantle these mechanisms, displaced farmers may find it increasingly acceptable to engage in narcotics cultivation.

Although it is unlikely that this trend will trigger widespread cocaine or heroin cultivation in the Caribbean, it does suggest that marijuana cultivation could increase in the years to come.

As US policy-makers seek to balance the competing needs presented by debt and structural adjustment, while working to foster a credible defense to the problem of drug trafficking, they should strive to incorporate several issues in their policy decisions. First, because the economies of the region are interdependent, and because the drug menace makes no distinction in terms of national boundaries, any policy should be comprehensive to the region as a whole. The need for a holistic approach is underscored by the dispute over bananas. According to General John Sheehan, former Commander-in-Chief of the US Atlantic Command, efforts by one US agency to dismantle the EU banana regime threaten the Caribbean banana industry and expose many smaller economies to increased drug trafficking risks.[53] This, in turn, undermines the narcotics interdiction policies pursued by other US government agencies and by Caribbean governments.

Secondly, a vital component to the success of any drug prevention strategy in the Caribbean, whether undertaken by a single country or a group of countries, is adequate funding. Access to funding – to undertake interdiction and law enforcement tasks, operate drug rehabilitation and education centers, and launch economic development programs – is necessary if Caribbean countries are to combat the awesome power of the cartels. If the United States and other major consuming nations are serious about helping Caribbean countries arrest the flow of narcotics through the region, they should help ensure that the environment in the Caribbean – both in terms of interdiction capabilities and economic opportunities – are conducive to such a strategy.

The Partnership for Prosperity and Security Agreement signed at the May 1997 Caribbean/United States Summit in Barbados is potentially the beginning of this holistic approach. It is predicated on the recognition of the 'inextricable link' between economic development and resistance to the drug trade. The US has agreed to link the fight against drugs to Caribbean development by actively seeking to increase trade opportunities for Caribbean countries. Finally, serious efforts must be made to focus on debt management schemes which would reduce debt service, thereby enabling Caribbean governments to use scarce funds for development. There is every indication that Guyana will be recommended by the IMF and the WB as the third country to qualify for this new program, after Uganda and Bolivia. However, the issue of debt sustainability must be examined for other Caribbean countries, moving beyond criteria such as debt to export ratios and the fiscal burden. It is only by recognizing and, together with the countries in the region, seeking lasting solutions to the Caribbean predicament, that the United States and other bilateral and multilateral 'partners' can assist in promoting sustainable Caribbean development.

## Notes

1 Richard Bernal, 'Strategic Global Repositioning and Future Economic Development in Jamaica', *The North–South Agenda Papers*, No. 18 (May 1996) (Miami, FL: North–South Center Press, University of Miami).

2 Richard Bernal and Pamela Coke Hamilton, 'Region Seeks to Redress Apparel Issue', *Hemisfile*, Vol. 8. No.2 (March/April, 1997), p.3.

3 David Hallan and Professor the Lord Peston, 'The Political Economy of Europe's Banana Trade.' The University of Reading, Department of Agricultural and Food Economics, Occasional Paper No. 5 (January 1997), pp. 1–4, and Keith Nurse and Wayne Sandiford, 'Windward Island Bananas: Challenges and Options Under the Single European Market', (Kingston, Jamaica: Frederich Ebert Stiftung, 1995), pp. 2–5.

4 WB, *Caribbean Economic Overview*, Report No. 15471 LAC, (Washington, DC: WB, Caribbean Division, May 1996), Table 3.1, p. 14.

5 Caribbean Basin Countries eligible for this program were those who signed a Tax Information Exchange Agreement (TIEA) with the United States. These countries were as follows: Barbados, Costa Rica, Dominica, Dominican Republic, Grenada, Guyana, Honduras, Jamaica, St Lucia, Trinidad and Tobago. For a more complete discussion of the phasing of this program, see Richard Bernal and Stephen Lamar, 'Caribbean Basin Economic Development and the Section 936 Tax Credit.' *The North–South Agenda Papers*, No. 22 (Miami, FL: The North–South Center, University of Miami, December 1996).

6 For a discussion of WB structural adjustment programs, see Winsome J. Leslie, *The WB and Structural Transformation in Developing Countries: The Case of Zaire* (Boulder, CO.: Lynne Rienner Publishers, 1987).

7 Grenada began to implement a 'home-grown' adjustment program in 1992, with assistance from the Caribbean Development Bank and monitoring by the IMF and the WB. Suriname also began a structural adjustment program in 1992, designed by a London consulting firm, without the assistance of either the WB or the IMF.

8 Carol Graham, *Safety Nets, Politics and the Poor: Transitions to a Market Economy*. (Washington, DC: The Brookings Institution, 1994), p. 13.

9 Yukon Huang and Peter Nicholas, 'The Social Costs of Adjustment', *Finance and Development*, June 1987, p. 22.

10 See Tony Killick, Tony Addison and Lionel Demery, 'Poverty, Adjustment and the IMF', in Khadija Haq and Uner Kirdar (eds), *Human Development, Adjustment and Growth* (Islamabad, Pakistan: North-South Roundtable, 1987), pp. 117–18.

11 Patricia Anderson and Michael Witter, 'Crisis, Adjustment and Social Change', in Elsie Le Franc, (ed.), *Consequences of Structural Adjustment: A Review of the Jamaica Experience* (Kingston, Jamaica: Canoe Press, University of the West Indies, 1994), pp. 21–2.

12 WB, *Guyana: Strategies for Reducing Poverty*, Report No. 12861 – GUA (Washington, DC: WB, 6 May, 1994), p. 5.

13 Ibid., p. 5.

14 Jere R. Behrman and Anil B. Deolalikar, 'The Poor and the Social Sectors During a Period of Macroeconomic Adjustment: Empirical Evidence for Jamaica', *The WB Economic Review*, Vol. 5, No. 2, 1991, p. 310.

15 Kari Polanyi Levitt, 'The Origins and Consequences of Jamaica's Debt Crisis: 1970–1990' (Kingston, Jamaica: University of the West Indies, Consortium Graduate School of Social Sciences, 1991), p. 50.

16 Anderson and Witter, op.cit., pp.46–9.

17 World Bank, 1996a op.cit., p. 2; Rhoda Reddock, 'Women and Poverty in Trinidad and Tobago', *Beyond Law*, Vol. 5, No. 14 (March 1995), cited in Savitri Bisnath, 'Poverty Eradication in the Anglophone Caribbean: A Focus on Methodologies and Capacity-Building' (New York: United Nations Development Program, 1996).

18 WB, *Jamaica: Achieving Macro-Economic Stability and Removing Constraints on Growth.* Country Economic Memorandum (Washington, DC: WB, 21 May, 1996b), p. 22.

19 WB, 1994, op.cit., pp. 3–4.

20 Richard Bernal and Winsome Leslie, 'Privatization in The English-Speaking Caribbean: An Assessment.' in Jerry Haar (ed.), *Privatization in Latin America and the Caribbean* (Miami, FL: University of Miami, North-South Center, forthcoming.

21 Dorith Grant-Wilson, 'Globalization, Structural Adjustment, and Democracy in Jamaica', in Ivelaw L. Griffith and Betty N. Sedoc-Dahlberg, (eds) *Democracy and Human Rights in the Caribbean* (Boulder, CO: Westview Press, 1997), p. 204.

22 Carol Graham makes the distinction between the 'new poor', i.e. workers displaced in the economic reform process, and the 'structural poor'. (op.cit., pp. 11–15).

23 Anderson and Witter, op.cit., pp. 21, 34 and 36.

24 Selwyn Ryan, 'Democratic Governance and the Social Condition in the Anglophone Caribbean' (New York, NY: United National Development Program, Caribbean Division, December 1995), p. 27.

25 See for example, Omar Davies and Patricia Anderson, 'The Impact of the Recession and Adjustment Policies on Poor Urban Women in Jamaica', in *The Invisible Adjustment: Poor Women and the Economic Crisis* (Santiago, Chile: UNICEF, The Americas and The Caribbean Regional Office, 1989), pp. 207–36.

26 The Planning Institute of Jamaica, 'Jamaica's Poverty Eradication Policy'. July 1995, p. 5.

27 Huang and Nicholas, op.cit., p. 24; Elaine Zuckerman, 'Adjustment Programs and Social Welfare' WB Discussion Paper No. 44. (Washington, DC: WB, 1989).

28 WB 1994, op.cit., pp. 93–6.

29  Bertus J. Meins, 'Adjustment, Reform and Growth', in *Choices and Change*, p. 73.

30  Richard Bernal, 'Debt, Drugs and Development in the Caribbean', *TransAfrica Forum* Vol. 9, No. 2 (Summer 1992), p. 85.

31  Richard Bernal, 'The Vicious Circle of Foreign Indebtedness: The Case of Jamaica', in Antonio Jorge, Jorge Salazar-Carilo and Frank Diaz-Pou (eds), *External Debt and Development Strategy in Latin America* (New York: Pergamon, 1985), pp. 111–28.

32  *Global Development Finance* Vol. 2, (Washington, DC: WB, 1997) pp. 256, 284 and 528.

33  Estimates by the Inter-American Development Bank.

34  Government of Jamaica, 'Memorandum on the Budget, 1995/96' and 'Memorandum on the Budget, 1997/98' (Kingston, Jamaica: Ministry of Finance and Planning).

35  The global trade in illegal drugs has grown exponentially in recent years. According to the first World Drug Report, published by the United Nations International Drug Control Programme, illicit drugs generate US$400 billion a year, which is equivalent to 8 per cent of world trade. See Stephen Filder and Jimmy Burns, 'Illicit Drugs Trade is put at $400 billion.' *Financial Times*, 26 June 1997.

36  *International Narcotics Control Strategy Report* (Washington, DC: US Department of State, March 1997), pp. 121–24, 161–221.

37  'Rethinking International Drug Control: New Directions for US Policy', A Task Force Report by the Council on foreign Relations (New York, NY: Council on Foreign Relations, February, 1997), p. 49.

38  Ivelaw Griffith, 'Drugs in the Caribbean: An Economic Balance Sheet'. *Caribbean Studies*, Vol. 28, No. 2 (1995), p. 298.

39  Text of a letter from the President to the Chairman and Ranking Members of the House Committee on Appropriations and International Relations and the Senate Committees on Appropriations and Foreign Relations. (Washington, DC: The White House, Office of the Press Secretary, 3 December 1996).

40  Douglas Farah, 'Caribbean Key to US Drug Trade', *Washington Post*, 23 September 1996.

41  *International Narcotics Control Strategy Report*, op.cit., pp. 11 and 22.

42  Ibid., pp. 196–9, 208–21.

43  Ibid., pp. 181, 174.

44  Canute James, 'Exporters Fight Drug War On New Front'. *Journal of Commerce*, 5 August 1996.

45  Statement by Robert Wasserman, Chief of Staff, Office of National Drug Control, *Policy in Drug Interdiction: US Programs, Policy and Options for Congress*. (S. Print 104–56), Senate Caucus on International Narcotics Control. (Washington, DC: US Government Printing Office, September 1996).

46  *Drug Control: US Interdiction Efforts in the Caribbean Decline*, Report to the Chairman, Subcommittee on National Security, International Affairs, and Criminal Justice, Committee on Government Reform and Oversight, House of Representatives (GAO/NSIAD-96–119) (Washington, DC: General Accounting Office, April 1996).

47  *International Narcotics Control Strategy Report*, op.cit., p. 554.

48  John Hamilton, Testimony Before the House International Relations Western Hemisphere Subcommittee, 14 May 1997.
49  *International Narcotics Control Strategy Report*, op.cit., pp. 560–563.
50  Speech by the Rt. Hon. Prime Minister, P.J. Patterson, 30 September 1996.
51  Ivelaw Griffith, op.cit., p. 299.
52  Figures in this paragraph are taken from Michelle Faul, 'Caribbean Blames Violence on US' Associated Press, 23 April 1997.
53  Thomas Lippman, 'An Appeal for a Banana Peace'. *The Washington Post*, 6 June 1996, p. 127.

# 4
# Ethnicity, the Nation-state and Drug-related Crime in the Emerging New World Order

*John F. Stack, Jr*

## Introduction

As a study of the ubiquitous effects of drug trafficking in the Caribbean, this book illustrates the transformation of *both* the study *and* practice of contemporary international relations. In the first instance, the study of world politics *even* in the emerging international system of the 1990s has been slow to come to grips with the dynamic nature of change throughout world politics at the level of international organizations, among states, among and within regions, within state-based societies, and among individuals. The personal computer, the fax machine, and now the Internet make world politics penetrable at all levels and they provide individuals and groups with unprecedented access, as James Rosenau insightfully documents in his pioneering work, *Turbulence in World Politics*.[1]

For practitioners, ethnic linkages are yet another complicating factor in an already bewildering world of ever more fractionalized groups. The revolutions in transportation and communications break down the barriers of time and space that for centuries insulated states and helped to centralize the power of political and economic elites. Ethnicity, on the other hand, draws on a sense of peoplehood – real or imagined – based on race, religion, culture, ancestry or language that unite individuals.[2] As Daniel Bell insightfully observed, ethnicity combines material interests with affective ties.[3] Ethnicity, therefore, is hugely relevant to any discussion of international drug trafficking because the production, trafficking, and sale of drugs often take place in ethnic communities within states and across state boundaries. The ethnic group is often the 'venue' for the establishment of new 'territories', be they cities, countries or regions.

Americans have been preoccupied with ethnic-driven crime since the great cities of the Northeast overflowed with immigrants in the late nineteenth century. Nativism and xenophobia often were surface manifestations of anti-immigrant sentiments that were frequently used to justify immigrant restriction laws based on the supposed predisposition toward crime that Irish, Italian, and other Eastern and Southern European immigrant groups displayed.[4] Newer waves of immigrants also used crime as a basis of upward mobility.

The Italian Mafia is but one example. Jewish criminal activities during prohibition in many American cities also constitute another. As outsiders, immigrants and ethnic Americans used ties of culture, kinship, religion, and language as ways of advancing up an often difficult socioeconomic ladder. In a 1996 study, *The New Ethnic Mobs*, William Kleinknecht details the changing face of organized crime in America based on the demographic changes in American cities and the influx of new immigrants. The heightened levels of interdependence among societies allows for greater criminal activities in the United States through the transnational activities of immigrant/ethnic groups members. The involvement of the Chinese and other Asians, Russians, Colombians, Cubans, Nigerians, and Jamaicans in organized crime benefits enormously from a world in which national frontiers are increasingly tattered and permeable.[5]

Ethnic crime is not new to the American and other publics, of course. It has been the focus of the media, featured in novels, films, and on television for almost a generation. But international relations experts appear to have undervalued the role of ethnicity in contemporary world politics.

## Ethnicity and the study of world politics

There is an urgent need to study problems that are global in scope and/ or effect. No one can pick up a newspaper or magazine without being confronted by the ways in which seemingly domestic issues have been globalized in both positive and destructive ways often with simultaneously good and bad effects.[6] Increasingly, levels of interdependence have resulted in the creation of transnational relations – the transfer of tangible or intangible items across state boarders when at least one actor is not a state or international organization.[7]

The proliferation of transnational actors is one of the driving forces of change in contemporary world politics. From transportation and communication channels to the globalized economic and political linkages that now encompass peoples and societies everywhere, transnational relations do matter for governments, policy-makers, groups and individuals.

The study of ethnicity is important because it is one of the fundamental realities of contemporary world politics and it demonstrates the power of transnational relations.[8] The ramifications of ethnic conflict, as with the drug trade, are felt throughout world politics. As an important transnational force, ethnicity will likely exert a major effect on the emerging post-Cold War international system within large and small countries, in dozens of important regions, and on a host of critical transnational issues. The drug trade in the Caribbean has an impact on the national security, foreign policy, and economic relations of states in the Americas, Europe and elsewhere. The impact is real; it is important; and it involves ethnicity.[9]

Ironically, however, the importance of transnational politics in the past 20 years has confounded several of the most important and most prolific scholars. The study of ethnicity and ethnic conflicts was marginalized by the dominant conceptual approaches to the study of world politics – realism and neorealism. Such assumptions reveal much about how world politics is studied and why such an increasingly important transnational force as ethnicity was dismissed as irrelevant.[10] Clearly, how one studies world politics affects the understanding of what is valued as important and useful, notwithstanding the importance of ethnic conflict within and among states as well as a critical factor in regional and perhaps international conflicts in two crucial respects.[11]

First, the dominant theories of international relations failed to understand the importance of ethnic nationalism in the evolving world order of the late twentieth century. The force of ethnicity is discernible in every continent and in the vast majority of states, but most clearly and relentlessly in the transformation of central Europe, the centrifugal forces straining the Russian Federation in the West and in the South, throughout Africa, and in the phenomenal spread of a Muslim identity in Africa and Asia. Increasingly analysts are left pondering the question of how such an inconsequential and disreputable force as ethnicity could pose such a challenge to the international system which developed in the eighteenth and nineteenth centuries and took such distinctive form in the years following World War Two.

Secondly, theorists of international relations whose work focused on that most important element of the world politics – the nation-state –

failed to appreciate the raw power of ethnic nationalism as a touchstone of the very forces that now challenge the Westphalia system.[12] The pioneering work of Daniel Patrick Moynihan demonstrated how liberalism's belief in the power of 'objective' social forces such as class assumed, *a priori*, the fragmentation and disintegration of ethnicity in the United States. American liberalism viewed ethnic identifications as 'recessive, readily explained by immigrant experience, but essentially transitional'.[13] Sociologist Milton Gordon understood, as did Moynihan, that ethnicity simply did not matter to most mainstream social scientists. It was an unfortunate collective group phenomenon that was destined to disappear – to be replaced by supposedly more tangible forms of group differentiation such as social class.[14]

## Why ethnicity matters

Ethnicity, whether as a latent force now made manifest by the inability of the modern state system of 1648 to provide individuals and groups with a meaningful *national identity* or as an unanticipated revival of forces (such as culture, kinship, or religion) that *liberalism* and *Marxism* presumed to be defunct, remains a global force. This is ironic, as noted above, since the literature on international politics and on comparative politics hardly considered it at all.

In the rare instances when students of modernization and development did analyse ethnicity (one of the dominant features of the newly established states of Africa, Asia, and the Middle East following the end of World War Two) it was usually to indicate how ethnicity would wither away as more meaningful associational bonds would help to build integrated states with increasingly robust civic cultures. Such a view belied just how enamored international relations specialists were with the assumption that the nation-state was the building block of the domestic politics and international relations of the latter half of the twentieth century. The presumed limited, parochial, atavistic ties of the ethnic group were, therefore, destined to disappear. The future, it was believed, clearly belonged to the nation acting as a unified state. Ethnicity would simply fade into irrelevance.[15]

The possibility that the inter-state system could be challenged by ethnic nations within states and across many states was not even considered a question worth asking. 'As we look backward on the early postwar years', Crawford Young thoughtfully explained, 'it becomes clear that we witnessed the apotheosis of the nation-state. A confluence of circumstances, whose particularity emerges only in retrospect, yielded a historic moment when this form of polity appeared astonishingly ascendant'.[16] Young clearly recognized the failure of the proliferation of social science models to explain and, as importantly, to predict the transformation of Third World societies into modern secular states. He continued: 'In 1960 Gabriel Almond spoke for a generation: "The political scientist who wishes to study political modernization in the non-western areas will have to master the model of the modern, which in turn can only be derived from the most careful empirical and formal analysis of the functions of the modern Western policies". Many would have added the Soviet Union as an alternative model of modernity in construction, inspirational to large numbers at the time'.[17]

American social scientists brought to the task of studying the developing societies of the newly independent states near evangelical fervor premised on the continued development of secular national states. Notwithstanding a 'compulsive urge to statehood' for the countries emerging from the disintegrating colonial mantel, these scholars overlooked the fragility and novelty of the modern nation-state following the French Revolution.[18]

In assessing the point at which national consciousness emerged in the countries of Western and Eastern Europe or in the Third World, Walker Connor perceptively asked the critical question: 'At what point in its development does a nation come into being?' His answer is as provocative as the question posed: 'There is ample evidence that Europe's presently recognized nations emerged only very recently, in many cases centuries later than the dates customarily assigned for their emergence.'[19] The formation of nationalism is a mass not an élite occurrence, although many scholars have been dependent on the writings of élites about the coalescing of national mass consciousness.

The isolation and the illiteracy of rural populations throughout Europe raises serious doubts about the presumed extent that nationalism captured the loyalty and imagination of the masses in the progressively unidimensional way that it had often been portrayed.[20] Moreover, Connor points out that the establishment of national identity is a process not an isolated event: 'The point in the process at which sufficient portion of a people has internalized the national identity so as to cause nationalism to become an effective force for mobilizing the masses does not lend itself to precise calculation. In any event, claims that a nation existed prior to the late nineteenth century should be treated cautiously'.[21] There is another equally important reason why ethnicity was so disfavored by American scholars. The presumed persistence of

ethnic groups – resistant to the forces of secular assimilation, modernization and development – questioned the state-centered theories in
vogue in the 1950s, 1960s, and much of the 1970s.[22] Theories of
development and modernization had, in fact, become a new type of
social science ideology.[23]

Further, there was the problem of 'culture'. With the horrifying
excesses of European nationalism generally and the Holocaust more
specifically, culture became a concept held in disrepute. Culture became
a code word for buried subjective biases, stereotypes and racist assumptions. Western social scientists worked hard to irradiate culture as a
legitimate explanatory factor even in the world of nation-states increasingly characterized by pervasive conditions of multi-ethnicity. Such
crude cultural stereotypes, as contained in Theodor Adorno's *The Authoritarian Personality*, were shunned. More recently, a firestorm of criticism
greeted the publication of Samuel Huntington's *Foreign Affairs* article
'The Clash of Civilizations', because he used the concept of culture as a
way to explain conflicts among distinctive civilizations in the emerging
new world order.[24] As Huntington stated: 'It is my hypothesis that the
fundamental source of conflict in this new world will not be primarily
ideological or primarily economic. The great divisions among human-
kind and the dominating source of conflict will be cultural'.[25]

Huntington understates the power of ethnic conflict, preferring to
subsume ethnicity under the far more vague rubric of civilization-
based conflicts. More important than whether he is correct or not in
doing so is that his terminology flies in the face of social science methods and the conventional wisdom of the fields of international and
comparative politics. By writing culture out of the literature of international relations theory, American scholars, in particular, failed to consider the persistence of ethnic nationalism as a possible challenge to the
power of the modern secular state. The social–psychological roots of
ethnic passions, once aroused, make ethnic conflicts so much more
intractable because of the powerful sense of group consciousness resulting among the mass members of the ethnic group.[26] Ethnicity, therefore,
comes to resemble a double-edged sword in that it reassures the individual that he or she is not alone 'which is what all but a very few
humans beings most fear to be', yet it may be just as easily used as a
vehicle for mobilizing 'us' against 'them'.[27]

As even the most cursory review of the most intractable ethnic conflicts will reveal, once ethnic nationalism crystallizes it does not easily
abate. As an atavistic force, ethnicity was a premodern holdover that
risked plunging individuals and societies into the non-rational,

anti-intellectual circumstances that eighteenth, nineteenth, and twentieth century international politics sought to move beyond. It is the emotional and psychological power of ethnicity that has been consistently under-estimated by academics, especially political scientists. In assessing the dynamics of ethnic conflict, Connor argues that 'the divergence of basic identity which manifests itself in the "us-them" syndrome... seldom hinges on adherence to overt aspects of culture'.[28] Ethnicity is more basic than that as Connor argues: 'But an individual (or an entire national group) can shed all overt cultural manifestations customarily attributed to his ethnic group and yet maintain his fundamental identity as a member of that nation. Cultural assimilation need not mean psychological assimilation'.[29]

Ethnicity, therefore, has been understudied. This is no where more evident than in the study of international relations. Neither liberal/idealists of the Wilsonian approach, emphasizing international organizations and international law, nor the realists, emphasizing the pursuit of power in the relations among states paid any significant attention to the possible international import of ethnicity. The liberal culture out of which modern international relations emerges conceptualized ethnicity as a premodern hold-over that was fated to disappear as the nation-state evolved into the most powerful geopolitical force since the Peace of Westphalia.

## The failure of realism

Two scholars in particular, E. H. Carr and Hans Morgenthau, reoriented the study of international politics and foreign policy. Realism's emphasis on sovereignty, military power, and the control of foreign policy channels discounted the importance of ethnicity as a factor in international politics. The military capabilities of states ultimately decided global and regional balances of power. If ethnicity played any role in world politics, it was through the foreign policy processes of states. It was the task of foreign policy elites to minimize the effect of the parochial concerns of ethnic groups. The survival of the state was the primary objective of its foreign policy.

The rise of fundamental ethnic conflicts in Northern Ireland, Belgium, Spain, France, Germany and elsewhere was something about which realists were unconcerned, and most of the conflicts certainly were unanticipated.[30] This liberal expectancy envisioned the progressive incorporation of smaller groups into larger groups until fully developed national consciousness emerged. In many ways exactly the reverse process is now unfolding. The sovereignty of states is under siege almost everywhere. The foreign policy-making process must, therefore, contend with the demands of ethnic groups throughout the world. As a response to heightening US–Soviet tensions in the late 1970s and throughout much of the 1980s, realism's emphasis on state power in an anarchical global system gained ascendance.[31] The structure of world politics was its central focus, with a renewed emphasis on the power of states. Neorealism's concern with 'high politics' and a state's political, economic, geopolitical, and military power predictably did not consider ethnicity at all.

The basic questions of how to study international relations and on what level of abstraction had been resolved in favor of the systemic level by a preponderance of the field.[32] Consequently, the study of world politics has been preoccupied with attempts to discern 'the rules of the game' at the highest levels of international politics and international political economy.[33] Such an emphasis deflects attention away from the study of regions and the transnational dimensions of ethnic groups.[34] The emphasis on the structural dynamics of world politics and economy is at such a high level of abstraction that analysts miss the trees in particular forests throughout the world in favor of the outlines of continents and oceans. The trickle down effects of such reified 'rules of the game' have resulted in a dearth of studies of precisely some of the most important contemporary developments of world politics – crime, drugs, ethnicity, the spread of diseases, and environmental concerns.

Ultimately, both realism and neorealism failed to appreciate the increasing attractiveness of ethnicity on a mass basis as the Cold War troded relentlessly onward. As states became more remote from their peoples, the salience of ethnicity increased as the countries of affluent, advanced, post-modern Western Europe attest.[35] Increasingly, ethnic entrepreneurs articulated visions of the ethnic nation which served as an antidote to the alienation that individuals feel when encountering impersonal and seemingly uncaring governmental authorities.[36] In the United States and Western Europe, ethnic affiliations provide groups with an interest and an affective tie, thereby, providing the ethnic group with the ability to place collective demands within the policy-making processes of post industrial societies, while at the same time, providing a means of nurturing isolated individuals.[37] Realism's emphasis on state power and the pursuit of the national interest fails to account for the resurgence of ethnicity in Western Europe, North America, Asia, Africa, or the Middle East.

## Transnational politics

Realism has been challenged by students of transnational relations. As early as the late 1960s the cracks in classical realism's emphasis on unified states and the pursuit of power politics were apparent. States were clearly the most important actors in world politics but they were not the only actors. International organizations both public and private, multinational corporations, and the domestic bureaucracies of states increasingly exerted influence on the global economy and in the domestic and international politics of states. The work of Robert Keohane and Joseph Nye offered a framework that encouraged the study of a plurality of actors affecting world politics.[38]

The power of transnational corporations with global production, marketing, and sales strategies is but one potent example. The technological revolution in information gathering, processing, and dissemination provide non-state actors with the ability to act internationally.[39] As Anthony Smith explained: 'We have been witnessing the crumbling of even the most powerful of political and military blocs in a manner that has been both sudden and decisive'.[40] The ideological thrusts of American liberalism and Soviet communism showed signs of strain, as the demands of feminists, ethnic groups, and environmental movements 'absorbed the spiritual and political energies of many people for whom the slogans of capitalism and communism had become meaningless. Hence the vitality of these blocs had already been sapped from within'.[41]

In underscoring the limitation of realism with its emphasis on state centered international relations, the study of transnational relations encouraged the study of ethnicity as the result of embracing patterns of global interdependence. As emerging transnational actors, ethnic groups seemed destined to play a more significant role in world politics: 'The ethnic nation cannot yet compete with the state in nuclear warheads and warships, but it continues to exercise formidable influence over the primary authority patterns of men. It is from this exercise of power that revolutions are born.'[42]

## Ethnicity and transnational organized crime

Ethnicity is a natural vehicle for the activities of Russians, Chinese, Colombians, Jamaicans, Nigerians, and others in the proliferation of transnational organized crime activities. Finland, Germany, Israel, Italy, and the United States have all called attention to the domestic and international danger of what is now referred to as Russian Organized

Crime.[43] Russian criminal activities in the United States has been linked to extortion, contract murders, prostitution, insurance and Medicaid fraud, money laundering and drug trafficking. The Federal Bureau of Investigation (FBI) has estimated that at least 15 Russian groups are operating in such American cities as New York, Miami, Los Angeles, San Francisco, Seattle, Chicago, Detroit and Baltimore. Parallels have been drawn with the establishment of the Italian crime families, La Cosa Nostra, in the early twentieth century.

Russians like Italians entered the United States during periods of relatively large migration, established residences in small, close knit urban ethnic enclaves, immigrated to the United States during times of economic upheaval and scarcity in their homeland, and began criminal activities by extorting their fellow ethnics.[44] Russian groups have become a powerful criminal force with global influence. In the United States, Russians have contacts with other ethnic-based transnational groups that are major players in international drug trafficking, such as the American-based La Cosa Nostra, the Italian Mafias and the Colombians.[45]

The South Asia heroin trade also relies on transnational ethnic-based Chinese groups in Burma, Laos, and Thailand (the so-called Golden Triangle) in order to more than 70 per cent of the heroin produced in South Asia to the United States. An effective transnational Chinese subculture that facilitates the importation of heroin in the United States, Hong Kong, Australia, Canada, and Europe has developed. It is highly mobile, with few identifiable organizations, and few prior criminal convictions. The oldest organized Chinese crime groups in the United States are the Triads. It is important to note that the Triads also engage in non-criminal activities commercial activities.

The Chiu Chao ethnic group plays a central role in drug trafficking because most ethnic Chinese in Thailand are Chiu Chao. The Chiu Chao triad group based in Hong Kong is well connected with drug traffickers in Bangkok.[46] During the 1980s and 1990s, the old Chinese merchant associations, the Tongs, have also been linked to criminal activities and increasingly money laundering and drug trafficking. Although the Triads and the Tongs first established themselves in San Francisco some 150 years ago, New York City now surpasses any other US city in the number of Chinese gangs. Since 1986, the Chinese have displaced Italians in the wholesale importation of heroin into the United States, especially in New York City, providing the drug to Italians, African-Americans or Hispanics for retail distribution.[47]

The transnational basis of Russian organized crime and the drug trafficking of Chinese Triads and Tongs underscore the profound importance of ethnicity and/or small cohesive families as a means of differentiating members of the group, the 'we' from outsiders, the 'they'. That differentiation is a fundamental element of the ethnic ties that bind individuals to the group. Ethnicity, therefore, serves two masters. It reassures the individual that he/she is not alone – a worldview that is especially important for first-generation immigrants in a foreign land. The ties of ethnicity make non-member infiltration more difficult thus serving, the self-preservation needs of ethnic groups involved in transnational criminal activities. The likelihood of betrayal by a member of the ethnic group is also lessened since, members of the extended family living in the originating country, are vulnerable to reprisal. Ethnicity becomes a truly double-edged sword.

## Conclusion

In 1993, the National Strategy Information Center (NSIC) issued a report written by Roy Godson and W. J. Olson, *International Organized Crime: Emerging Threat to US Security*, that analysed the transnational nature of organized criminal activity, not only in the Americas but also throughout the world. The threat to the national security of the United States, the countries of South America, Central America, the Caribbean, as well as Western Europe is very real. The linkage between ethnic-based transnational criminal organizations and international politics is indisputable, irrespective of whether one is focusing on the Medellín or Cali Cartels, the Sicilian Mafia, Russian Organized Crime or Chiu Chao Chinese in South Asia.

It is ironic, therefore, that the dominant conceptual approaches to the study of world politics relegated the study of transnational relations to an unimportant arena and down-played the role of ethnicity. Part of the explanation lies in the fact that scholars saw ethnicity as peripherally relevant to the hard, difficult task confronting states in the Cold War era. On an epistemological level, ethnicity was conceptualized as an atavistic force destined to disappear once it has run its course as more enduring 'realities' such as socio-economic class take hold. With the irrelevance of ethnicity assured, ethnic attachments were by definition a kind of false consciousness that would become readily apparent as individuals, states, and the global system moved on to more complex developmental stages. Realism certainly shared in this cultural heritage, drawing from such common experiences as the establishment of civil societies and secular political systems within the umbrella of the expanding Westphalia international system.

The problem is that the attractiveness of ethnicity has not abated while ethnic conflicts have increased world-wide. In 1972 Walker Connor described the pervasiveness of multi-ethnic societies and predicted the declining congruence between the nation and the state. He also warned of the likely disruptive consequences of heightened levels of ethnonationalism, seeing a clear trend in the inexorable ethnic conflicts of the twentieth century. Clearly, then, ethnicity does matter; so do transnational relations. The study of international relations in the new millennium will likely be the unfolding struggle of states and international organizations to fend off the penetration by transnational organizations that threaten their national security, political stability, and economic well being. In that context, the story of drugs in the Caribbean, which is a transnational phenomenon where ethnic national and non-state actors feature, may well be the tip of the iceberg of one of the great forthcoming battles of world politics.

## Notes

1  James N. Rosenau, *Turbulence in World Politics: A Theory of Change and Continuity* (Princeton, NJ: Princeton University Press, 1990).
2  R.A. Schermerhorn, *Comparative Ethnic Relations: A Framework for Theory and Research* (New York: Random House, 1970).
3  Daniel Bell, 'Ethnicity and Social Change', in Nathan Glazer and Daniel P. Moynihan (eds), *Ethnicity: Theory and Experience* (Cambridge: Harvard University Press, 1995), p. 159.
4  The classic works remain: John Higham, *Strangers in the Land: Patterns of American Nativism 1860–1825* (New York: Athenaeum, 1974); and Richard Hofstadter, *The Age of Reform* (New York: Random House, 1955).
5  William Kleinknecht, *The New Ethnic Mobs: The Changing Face of Organized Crime in America* (New York: The Free Press, 1996).
6  Rosenau, op. cit., pp. 5–10, 348–415.
7  Robert O. Keohane and Joseph S. Nye, 'Transnational Relations and World Politics: An Introduction', in Joseph S. Nye and Robert O. Keohane (eds), *Transnational Relations and World Politics* (Cambridge: Harvard University Press, 1971).
8  Daniel P. Moynihan, *Pandaemonium: Ethnicity in International Politics* (London: Oxford University Press, 1993), p. 27.
9  See Ivelaw L. Griffith, *Drugs and Security in the Caribbean: Sovereignty Under Siege* (University Park, PA: Pennsylvania State University Press, 1997).
10  Moynihan, op. cit., pp. 145–7.
11  Keohane and Nye, op. cit., pp. ix–xxix.
12  Kenneth N. Waltz, *Theory of International Politics* (McGraw Hill, 1979), pp. 88–9. Robert Gilpin, *War and Change in World Politics* (Cambridge: Cambridge

University Press, 1981), pp. 95–6, 35–6; and Robert O. Keohane, 'Realism, Neorealism and the Study of World Politics', in Robert O. Keohane (ed.), *Neorealism and its Critics* (New York: Columbia University Press, 1986), pp. 24–5.

13 Moynihan, op. cit., p. 27.

14 Ibid., p. 27.

15 Crawford Young, 'The Dialectics of Cultural Pluralism', in Crawford Young (ed.), *The Rising Tide of Cultural Pluralism: The Nation-State at Bay?* (Madison: The University of Wisconsin Press, 1993), p. 7.

16 Ibid., p. 8.

17 Ibid., p. 8.

18 Ibid., p. 8.

19 Walker Connor, *Ethnonationalism: The Ouest for Understanding* (Princeton: Princeton University Press, 1994), p. 223.

20 Ibid., p. 223

21 Ibid., pp. 223–4.

22 Walker Connor, 'Nation-Building or Nation-Destroying?', *World Politics*, 24 (April 1972), pp. 341–2.

23 Young, op. cit., pp. 7–8.

24 Samuel P. Huntington, 'The Clash of Civilizations?', *Foreign Affairs*, 72 (Summer 1993), pp. 22–49.

25 Ibid., p. 22.

26 Connor, op. cit., pp. 204–8.

27 Harold A. Isaacs, *Idols of the Tribe: Group Identity and Political Change* ( New York: Harper and Row, 1975), p. 43; and Clifford Geertz, *The Interpretation of Cultures: Selected Essays.* (New York: Basic Books, 1973), p. 260.

28 Connor, op. cit., pp. 341–2.

29 Chadwick F. Alger, 'Bridging the Micro and the Macro in International Relations Research', *Alternatives* 10 (winter 1984) pp. 319–44.

30 Moynihan, op. cit., pp. 145–6.

31 Waltz, op. cit., pp. 88–9; and Gilpin, op. cit., pp. 35–6, 95–6.

32 Patrick James, 'Structural Realism and the Causes of War', *Mershon International Studies Review* 39 (October 1995), pp. 181–6.

33 Randall L. Schweller and David Priess, 'A Tale of Two Realisms: Expanding The Institutional Debate', *Mershon International Studies Review*, 41 (May 1997), pp 1–32; and Charles S. Taber and Richard J. Timpone, 'Beyond Simplicity: Focused Realism and Computational Modeling in International Relations', *Mershon International Studies Review*, 40 (April 1996), pp. 41–79.

34 David Carment and Patrick James, 'Ethnic Conflict at the International Level: An Appraisal of Theories and Evidence', in David Carment and Patrick James, (eds), *Wars in the Midst of Peace: The International Politics of Ethnic Conflict*, (Pittsburgh: University of Pittsburgh Press, 1997), p. 253; and John F. Stack, Jr, 'The Ethnic Challenge to International Relations Theory', in Carment and James, op. cit., pp. 22–3.

35 Anthony D. Smith, *The Ethnic Revival in the Modern World* (London: Cambridge University Press, 1981), p. 165.

36 Ibid., p. 105

37 Bell, op. cit., pp. 151–2.

38 Nye and Keohane, op. cit., p. xii

39   Rosenau, op. cit., pp. 104–5.
40   Anthony D. Smith, *National Identity* (Reno, Nevada: University of Nevada Press, 1994), pp. 155–6.
41   Ibid., p. 156.
42   Abdul Said and Luis Simmons, *Ethnicity in an International Contest: The Politics of Disassociation* (New Brunswick, NJ: Transaction Books, 1976), p. 14.
43   US Department of Justice, National Drug Intelligence Center (NDIC), *Russian Organized Crime: A Baseline Perspective* (November 1993), p. 1.
44   Ibid., pp. 4–5.
45   Ibid., pp. 8–10.
46   US Department of Justice, National Drug Intelligence Center (NDIC), *Triads, Tongs and Street Gangs: A Baseline Assessment of Asian Organized Crime* (March 1994), p. 1.
47   NDIC op. cit., pp. 14–15.

# Part II
# Connections and Consequences

# 5
# Narco-criminality in the Caribbean

*Gary Brana-Shute*

## Drugs and scholarship: a historiography of sorts

In 1980 Rosemary Brana-Shute and I edited *Crime and Punishment in the Caribbean*. The chapters were written by Caribbean scholars, legal practitioners and criminal justice professionals. We had gathered in Paramaribo, Suriname late in 1978, after meeting in Santo Domingo in 1976, and examined regional cooperation, research, and policy formation among and between the English-, French-, Spanish- and Dutch-speaking Caribbean countries.[1] The 146–page book has ten chapters and the item 'drugs' appears six times in the index, far fewer times than the entry of 'rape', for example. In analysing Jamaica's surge of violence in the late 1970s, Dudley Allen points to Kingston's rapid urbanization and mentions, in passing, 'a connection between gun crimes and drugs', while Rafael Santos del Valle's discussion on Puerto Rico analyses the island's drug problem in terms of medical care and rehabilitation services. Michael Parris concludes his chapter on Guyana noting that 'The use of drugs is not a widespread feature of Guyanese society...'. Crime is examined in country-specific terms and, in several cases, city-specific terms, with no attention paid to regional or international connections.

The situation has changed dramatically since then. Illegal narcotics and related crime have reached significant proportions throughout the Caribbean, constituting a major security threat to the region. The mid-1980s witnessed an explosion of drug-related crime, corruption, production, consumption and, not incidentally, scholarship related to these. In 1988 Rosemary Brana-Shute and I produced 'The Anglophone Eastern Caribbean and British Dependencies' for the fifth volume of *Latin America and Caribbean Contemporary Record*. We had been writing this series of national/sub-regional reports since volume I in 1982.[2] Prior to 1988

97

essays had been decidedly 'Cold War' in profile dealing largely with, for example, the New Jewel Movement in Grenada, the US invasion of the island, and the consequences of the military action for the region.

Our 1988 chapter was the first time that we had included a separate section on drugs; a grand total of one page and two lines, dealing primarily with interdiction operations in the Bahamas, and, in what now seems almost prescient, the remark 'One of the United States' justifications for an increase in military hardware, primarily armed patrol boats, and training for local paramilitary forces in cooperating countries in the Eastern Caribbean – the militarization of the Caribbean – has been to provide for a drug interdiction capability'.[3] Other contributors to the Caribbean section of the volume, including such leading scholars as Anthony Maingot, Carl Stone, and Jonathan Hartlyn, do not mention the issue of drugs, probably because the issue paled in comparison with the other problems. Volumes VI through VIII are laden with rich description and sound analysis of narco-crime, and to read the volumes in order is to see the complexity and import of the conundrum unfold. In effect, a paradigm shift occurred in the scholarship between the 1980s and the 1990s: from preoccupation with a Marxist threat and US countermeasures to it, to a narcotics threat and its consequences.

Ivelaw Griffith, the leading scholar of Caribbean security, put it boldly in a 1997 National Defense University *Strategic Forum*: 'Drugs are the primary threat ... the top security concerns of the region are drug production, consumption and abuse, trafficking, and money laundering'.[4] Three of his books on drugs and security chronicle the dimensions of the 'new wave': *Caribbean Security on the Eve of the 21st Century, The Quest for Security in the Caribbean*, and *Strategy and Security in the Caribbean*.[5] Griffith's solid scholarship, shrewd insights, and scholarly vision are matched by the clear-thinking, no-nonsense leader of Caribbean studies, Anthony Maingot, who devotes two chapters of *The United States and the Caribbean* to drugs, corruption, violence, money laundering and national security in the synergistic context of Caribbean–US relations.[6]

From the obscurity of Jimmy Cliff blowin' weed in the 1970s cult movie classic *The Harder They Come* and scary tales of housewives being accidentally shot in a Dadeland mall drug-gang shoot out, we come to the late 1990s with drug-related problems as the single most serious security issue confronting the internal order of Caribbean nations, their regional policies with other Caribbean states, and their international relations with the US and European powers. Journalism and literature have not been far behind in production. Jamaica Kincaid's *A Small Place* and Robert Coram's *Caribbean Time Bomb*, both of which deal with Antigua–Barbuda, tease out the dynamics of corruption and politics in small scale societies.[7] The money is in cocaine.

Not to be outdone, the US military, through its regional commands – the Atlantic Command (USACOM) based in Norfolk, Virginia and the Southern Command (SOUTHCOM) based in Miami, Florida – over the past several years have sponsored numerous conferences, symposia, and publications which examined the subject of drugs.[8] For example, in May 1997, the conference 'Eye of a Hurricane', sponsored by the National Defense University, SOUTHCOM, and the Woodrow Wilson Center devoted sessions to drugs and a collective, cooperative security system to defend the region against destabilization from drug-related crime syndicates.

Caribbean countries themselves organize annually a Caribbean Island Nations Security Conference (CINSEC). The 13th annual meeting was held in 1997 in Trinidad and Tobago and devoted one afternoon of the two-day conference to drug interdiction.[9] Looming as a sub-text in discussion was the centerpiece of US Caribbean policy: the Maritime Law Enforcement 'Shiprider' Agreement. After rancorous debate, Caribbean concern about the erosion of their long-fought-for sovereignty, and some astute horse trading, particularly by Jamaica and Barbados, Agreements were signed between 1995 and 1997 by the US and all Caribbean countries except Suriname (as of September 1997).[10]

In providing testimony to the Subcommittee on the Western Hemisphere of the US House of Representatives, Georges Fauriol enumerated Cuba, Haiti, bananas,[11] and narcotics trafficking as the major US policy concerns in the region. The Plan of Action signed by President Bill Clinton and 15 Caribbean leaders at the 10 May 1997 US/CARICOM summit held in Barbados identifies 17 topical areas of concern and cooperation between the US and the region; nine of these deal in some fashion with crime and have some connection with narcotics. They include: justice and security, arms trafficking control, illicit drugs and rehabilitation, criminal justice systems, combating corrupt officials, money laundering, witness protection, strengthening regional security systems and intelligence gathering, alien smuggling, and criminal deportation. Thus, drugs, conferences to deal with the subject, and drug-related scholarship seem to constitute a growth industry for the Caribbean.

## Crime in the Caribbean

No country in the Caribbean – independent or European possession, island or mainland Belize, Guyana, Suriname and French Guiana – is spared the impact of illegal drugs and the related violence, crimes against property, money laundering, corruption, addiction, moral decay and international stigma. In places such as Jamaica and Puerto Rico gang violence is visible and a fact of everyday life. This is perhaps not surprising, as both of these countries have strong ties with the US – the Jamaicans through their famed posse gangs and the Puerto Ricans by virtue of their citizenship, freedom of movement and access to US markets.

The Dutch islands of Aruba and St Maarten are penetrated by various organized crime syndicates, notably the Colombian cartels and the Sicilian and American Mafia. And as members of the Kingdom of the Netherlands, they serve as customs free conduits to the European market. There are strong allegations that Suriname's one-time authoritarian leader and now *de facto* strongman, despite democratic elections in 1991 and 1996, is the king pin and mastermind of Suriname's voluminous drug trafficking to the Netherlands through the country's vast and virtually borderless jungle interior. Less dramatic and visible, but of equal danger, like a low-grade cancer, is the pervasive presence of drug money corruption in the Eastern Caribbean and Trinidad. It is, therefore, important to examine narcotics-related crime as it affects daily life, governance, and international relations in the Caribbean, especially in St Vincent and the Grenadines, Jamaica and Suriname.

## St Vincent and the Grenadines

Writing in *The Vincentian*, the daily newspaper of St Vincent and the Grenadines, the witty Canadian/Vincentian anthropologist Hymie Rubenstein tackles the thorny issue of the dimensions of the drug problem and crime in these islands. Marijuana – ganja – and cocaine are still relatively new to St Vincent and the Grenadines, the latter not arriving until the mid-1980s. The plant has been taken up with such vigor that St Vincent now produces more ganja than any of the other small states of the region, a fact reinforced by the US–Vincentian regular sweeps of the Soufriere region on their continuing marijuana eradication deployments. Estimating that about 10 per cent of the crop is destroyed, Rubenstein projects the annual sales of Vincentian ganja at about US$40 million, several millions more than the value of the national banana exports.[12]

Limiting himself to marijuana the author is candid about his reluctance to explore cocaine trafficking, local sale and consumption. Prowling through the alley's of Kingstown's baddest neighborhood, Paul's Lot, might be injurious to the life of any anthropologist or any other scholar. In fact, Ken Pryce, the noted Trinidadian sociologist was drowned under mysterious circumstances while investigating Jamaica's drug scene. Rubenstein's discretion is wise if disappointing; we find that cocaine is sold by pushers in Paul's Lot to young male consumers in the city and through a marketing network in the countryside. But, alas, no more data is provided.

Nevertheless, ganja is the drug of choice; cheap, available, easy to grow and not demonized in the minds of many Vincentians.[13] Grown commercially for the past 15 years, about 1,500 males are involved in its cultivation. Ganja is consumed locally by about 12,000 Vincentians, mostly males – roughly one in every five adults. The country is also a small but active player in the international drug trade, shipping its ganja to Barbados, Grenada, Trinidad and Tobago, St Lucia, Martinique, and to a much lesser extent the US and UK. Selling ganja is not a full-time job and the product is sold in the form of spliffs, US 80 cents each, and bags at US$8 each (prices circa 1994). The profile of ganja smokers would reveal a population of young (under 30), male (three-quarters), and poor (as opposed to middle- or working-class).

Until 1986 young men in the rural areas would openly 'blow weed' in 'high daytime' and purchase their ganja at well-known 'herb gates' or 'ital shacks' where one could also enjoy a noontime spliff on lunch break. Generally, ganja entrepreneurs organized themselves into fluid, informal networks of friends, relatives, and acquaintances rather than formal, tightly knit, durable gangs, something found with Jamaica's infamous posses. Also, there are thousands of Vincentians who regularly use ganja as an infusion but would never dream of 'taking a pull'. Ganja tea or 'herb sip' is used as a 'bush medicine' to treat colds, high blood pressure, constipation, and intestinal parasites.

However, ganja and, of course, cocaine and heroin, are illegal as stipulated by the 1937 'Dangerous Drug Ordinance' and therefore users are criminals. Nevertheless, Rubenstein ends his ruminations on a rather benign note locating ganja in the Eastern Caribbean tradition of smuggling and contraband, and the peasant farmers' search for a new cash crop to supplement their coconuts, bananas and root crops.

Writing in a 1996 series of articles in the Barbados-based *Caribbean Week*, sociologist Klaus de Albuquerque argued that cocaine has made in-roads into St Vincent and the Grenadines, that the number of addicts, particularly in the capital, is unsettling, and that crack users and pushers operate openly.[14] Quoting a police officer, he noted that users and pushers have to be caught 'red handed' in order to be prosecuted, and that on a small island 'there are rumors about everybody'. The penalties remain nevertheless light and 'small island big men' get away with a 'slap on the wrist', reminiscent of the involuted deal-making portrayed in Kincaid's *A Small Place.*

According to a prominent local politician and leader of a small but active opposition party, laundering of drug profits, local consumption, and widespread corruption are the most serious by-products of narcotics transshipping through the tiny archipelago. The US State Department's annual *International Narcotics Control Strategy Report* for 1996 endorsed this view by reporting that for the entire Eastern Caribbean the stability of these traditionally democratic governments is threatened by narcotics trafficking and organized criminal activity.[15]

### Jamaica

'Is three set ah gunman all like me have fi deal wid yu know: gunman, police, and soljah' (People like me live with three forms of violence: the gunmen, police, and soldiers) said Cutty, a young odd-jobber living in Tel Aviv, a 'bad ass' neighborhood in Kingston. Jamaica: ganja, reggae, ragga, dance hall, rastas, garrison communities, political tribalism, uptown and downtown, and the ultimate cocaine warlords – the most violent, ethnic based gangs operating in the United States, the paladins of the streets of West Kingston, the fearsome Jamaican posses. With their usual quick turn of phrase many Jamaicans now say their country is 'Idiaminized' and suffers from tragic danger.

Politics and cocaine have conflated in Kingston. If one asked a Jamaican on the island what he or she associates with the term 'garrison community' the answer most likely would be 'Tivoli' – the pride and joy of Eddie Seaga's opposition Jamaican Labor Party (JLP). However, Tivoli is not the only garrison community based on violence, drugs, crime and political clientilism. Other neighborhoods, such as Jones Town and Jungle associated with the ruling Peoples' National Party (PNP), are mini-states with their own armies which frequently invade each other to capture political and drug-dealing turf.

A combined security force of heavily armed police and soldiers, accompanied by armored personnel carriers and helicopters armed with machine guns, was deployed to the neighborhood. Yet, in spite of a remarkable display of state firepower the Tivoli gunmen managed to keep the force at bay for almost 18 hours. What was the purpose of the military mission? A sweep to clean out drugs, guns, and criminals? A show of political force by the government to crush a JLP fortress? JLPers argue that there were no gunman returning fire and that the whole affair was staged by the government to secure political capital for the ruling PNP.

Neighborhoods such as Tivoli were originally created as bulwarks of political support for political leaders who literally kept the communities going through clientage in exchange for votes. But, over the past 10 years, precisely at the time cocaine made its dramatic entry into the calculus of gangland life, there has been a change in the internal power relations of garrison communities. No longer are politicians the source of economic and military resources; they have been replaced by 'drug dons', known euphemistically as community leaders. Although political influence has weakened there is a tendency for these gangs, known as 'posses', to realign with their former political patrons during election years when political parties need support, votes, and financial contributions, and the gunmen need political protection and insurance for the future. Hence, the drug barons have the leverage.

Consider, for example, one man's infamous story and that of his progeny who would follow in his footsteps; that of Jim Brown, a.k.a Lester Coke, one-time co-leader of the Shower posse (loosely associated with the JLP and has gangland outposts primarily along the east coast of the US). He was responsible for 68 homicides and the shooting of 13 police officers in Jamaica during the first six months of 1990.[16] Brown had been tried 14 times for murder, and had always been acquitted because the witnesses either disappear or are killed. In July, 1990 he and about 60 of his posse were involved in a shootout with police. Armed with two 9-mm pistols and an Uzi machine gun, Brown survived, thanks to the high quality bullet proof vest he was wearing.

While being held for extradition to the US where he was wanted on charges of murder, attempted murder, and conspiracy to commit murder, his son and aspiring 'don', Anthony Mark Coke, known locally as Jah Tee, was gunned down by a rival posse. Violence exploded between the groups. While the mêlée ensued, Brown died mysteriously in a jailhouse fire. He is survived by three sons; one is in jail in Jamaica on charges of murder and narcotics trafficking, another is a prominent don, and the third, at the tender age of 13, is operating his own gang of hitmen and claims allegiance to no one. Although dramatic, this story is not unusual. In fact it fits the general pattern of young male careers in many of Kingston's worst neighborhoods and the pattern of drug crime in Jamaica. Bernard Headley's scholarly *The Jamaican Crime Scene* and Laurie Gunst's under-stated *Born Fi' Dead* convey the dimensions and stress of everyday life 'downtown'.[17]

The posses are home grown, a mix of politics, ganja, poverty, a rotten life of scufflin' and cotchin', the constant 'sufferation' of living in some of the worst urban neighborhoods in the western hemisphere, and of cocaine. But they do not exist just in a Jamaican context. Rather, they project power overseas, particularly in the United States, Canada, and in the United Kingdom (where they are known as 'yardies'). Particularly from the United States, the posses ship back guns, ammunition, drugs, and money to their counterparts back home, with the consequence that turf wars fought in cities in the US are fought out along the same lines as in Jamaica, as are hits ordered in the US for Jamaica and visa versa: Spangler versus Shower posse in Trenton, NJ; Spangler versus Shower in Tivoli, Kingston.

The structure of posses is rather like the idea of a clan or lineage in anthropological literature. Although a group may be named – the Gulleymen, for example – and number in the hundreds, the operational, local posses numbers usually about 20 to 25 members, coordinated by a 25–to–30–year old don. Less structured and hierarchical, and more fluid than Chicago street gangs, and the Bloods and the Crips of Los Angeles, there is even a local apprenticeship program for youth. Teenagers, as young as 11 or 12, called 'fryers' (small chickens) undertake contract work such as robberies and rub-outs, and the conveying of narcotics as innocent looking bagmen. Often they operate with 'loaner' or 'rent-a-guns', which they return after their mission. If they keep the gun or fumble the mission they in turn are rubbed out. There is no overarching gang structure as such and the acephalous nature of authority and leadership probably encourages violent resolution of conflict rather than gangland arbitration.

One Jamaica Defense Force (JDF) Coast guard Commander and one army Major with whom I spoke in May 1997 speculated that with elections then but five months off, 'the heavy guns soon come out', and that 1997 would be a record-breaking year for murders. (Over 900 murders were committed in 1996.) The JDF's strategy, the Commander reported with remarkable frankness, was to contain the violence, or at least limit it to downtown. With the gallows humor of some police and soldiers, he observed that Jamaica's open borders and long coast line act as a magnet for cocaine traffickers, all the more encouraged by the country's lack of blue water patrol craft. 'There was a cigarette boat bound for the Bahamas from Colombia. Crashed on one of our cays and when we got to the carcass we could tell it had been laden with half high octane fuel and half cocaine. The coke had disappeared. Must have been a hellovaparty.'

The US Bureau of Alcohol, Tobacco and Firearms states the following about posses in the US: 'Jamaican posses are bold and aggressive bands of criminals who traffick in large quantities of narcotics and firearms, reaping a billion dollars annually from their drug proceeds. These groups are also involved in money laundering, fraud, kidnapping, robbery, burglary, assault, and murder.'[18] As early as 1982, US law enforcement officials began to arrest hundreds of Jamaican nationals for possession and sale of marijuana and for drug-related murders.

Operating principally out of Miami, New York City, Baltimore, Washington, DC, and Chicago, the posse men seek smaller, lucrative drug markets throughout the country, such as Orangeberg, SC. Mercenary in nature, the groups invade and conquer rival gangs in communities and establish a base of operations. The Shower and Spangler posses maintain the largest number of affiliates. All posses maintain a connection to their 'parent posse' in, primarily, New York or Miami. An estimated 40 posses, with approximately 20,000 members, continue to operate within the United States. The Northeast and Southeast areas are most active, with the Midwest and Farwest being pursued as new drug territories. When captured by authorities in the US they are repatriated – dumped Jamaican authorities say – where they can ply their deadly skills honed in the US.

Jamaican posses are unique because they originally controlled the importation, distribution and sale of marijuana from Jamaica at the retail level in the US as early as the late 1970s. They have enlarged their menu to include cocaine, crack, heroin, carachi, PCP, 'ice' and methamphetamine. For example, the Gulleymen posse, under the leadership of Eric Vassel, has been involved in the sale of heroin, cocaine and crack since the early 1980s. Most of the members were originally from the same neighborhood in Jamaica. In addition to drugs, the Gulleymen were involved in passport fraud, illegal money wire transactions, life insurance fraud, and the usual robberies, rapes, assaults, and murders.[19]

In penetrating new territory, posses have had to deal with indigenous criminal elements. Their most successful alliances have been with Los Angeles-based gangs, the Crips and the Bloods. The kind of alliance varies, but in the Southwest posses and Crips have agreed to share market territories in order to avoid confrontation. In Los Angeles, for example, Crips once were protecting a Jamaican crackhouse. A Crip was arrested in Fayetteville, N.C. while ferrying cocaine from a posse drug depository in New York City to a posse enclave in North Carolina. Close collaboration is also alleged between Jamaicans and Nigerians, although most American witnesses inevitably get the two groups confused, or do not know that often one is trying to 'pass' for the other.

## Suriname

As in real estate so too with drugs; it is location, location, location, and Suriname has it. Moreover, there is a vast, open jungle interior, a well connected, ethnically based (East Indian) commercial community, a bankrupt revolutionary regime in the 1980s that went shopping internationally for financing, a civil war in the 1980s which tore the fabric of life for Maroons and Amerindians in the interior, a government suspected of deep and pervasive corruption, an impoverished population, and the country's *de facto* leader wanted on charges of narcotics transshipping by the former colonial power, the Netherlands. Suriname is in very serious trouble and almost everybody is implicated.[20]

In 1979, in researching juvenile delinquency in Paramaribo, less than imaginatively I used the model of rapid urbanization to explain the city's burgeoning crime rate among poor youth.[21] I regularly visited a poor, rough neighborhood with a section called 'suikertuin' (sugar garden), a drug emporium. Both the cops and I thought it was marijuana; it was not. It was 'poirie' (powder): cocaine. Scammed in from Amsterdam, it was still a little known product on the streets and salons of Paramaribo.[22] There have been several dramatic developments since then, but space limitations permit only examination of some of the high points that have transpired since that time.[23]

Displaying an inability to govern but an immense appetite for graft, the parliamentary government of Suriname was overthrown by a sergeant's coup in 1980. First flirting with, and later falling into the arms of the international left, the young radicals sent emissaries hither and yon; one, the redoubtable and peripatetic Henk Herrenberg, went in early 1982 to Colombia to seal a $50 million drug deal using Suriname as a transshipment point. By 1985, Lt Colonel Boerenveen, close to the military strongman, Desi Bouterse, was arrested by the US Drug Enforcement Administration (DEA) in Biscayne Bay, Miami, while negotiating a several million dollar deal to smuggle cocaine into the US on the state-owned Suriname Airways.

Civil war, with Ronnie Brunswijk and the so-called Jungle Commando, erupted in 1986 and continued as an intermittent insurgency until the early 1990s. The interior of Suriname was wide open with insurgents and government-sponsored gangs of counter-insurgents, and out of control. The Dutch press disclosed stories of landing strips in the interior guarded by elements of the military and their auxiliaries. Even the CIA was involved when they arranged for a light plane to ferry in 1000 lb of cocaine into contested territory between the military and the Jungle Commando to disrupt negotiations just when the two were close to sealing a cooked-up peace accord that excluded civilian government endorsement.[24]

The military-backed political party won the national elections in 1996 and formed a government with several high positions filled by persons allegedly involved in narcotics dealings, including Boerenveen who was promoted to full Colonel after his release from prison in the US and headed military intelligence before his promotion to his current position: Senior Coordinator of military activities. Immense, palatial estates owned primarily by East Indian businessmen have sprung up around Paramaribo, while the amount of gold and BMW ownership has grown at an astonishing rate among young black men. Cocaine can be purchased virtually anywhere in Paramaribo. Dutch customs search every single Surinamer coming into the Netherlands for narcotics. Ivelaw Griffith, with his usual candor, has written of the human body and its orifices used as a narcotics pipeline; this work should be required reading for Dutch customs.[25]

The Director of the Central Bank of Suriname was indicted in absentia in Holland for money laundering. Pyramid, near-banking schemes offered by East Indian businessmen, give 10 per cent *monthly* on your equity; no paperwork, no questions asked, no guarantees. One collapsed in mid-1997; 'no span' (don't get excited), this is not Albania, say Surinamers. Remarkably, the burglary and theft rate in Paramaribo has declined as young men, seeing more money in narco-trafficking and retail sales refer to petty crime as 'shiken fit' (chicken feed). Not surprisingly, cocaine-crime, which still remains dangerously high, has grown excessively violent. Unexplained, gangland murders periodically 'takeout' visiting Brazilians, police, errant soldiers and others.

Desi Bouterse, former Special Adviser to the President of Suriname, and several others have been charged with narcotics transshipping. He was tried and sentenced, in absentia, to 16 years in prison. The sentence was announced in July 1999. Ronnie Brunswijk, Bouterse's alter ego and a former insurgent, lives comfortably in the East Suriname provincial town of Moengo. Several Corvette automobiles are parked in his yard and friends and associates are regularly arrested at Schiphol Airport in possession of cocaine. Remnants of the Tukuyana Amazones pro-military counter-insurgents allegedly control small airstrips in the Saramacca District to which couriers fly from Colombia and from which cocaine is transported to Paramaribo for retailing and transshipment to Holland.[26]

Of all the social consequences this implosion of narcotics, money, and crime has had, the conflation has impacted most on three groups: young coastal black men (called Creoles in Suriname), young black Maroon men (who consider themselves to be a different ethnic group), and East Indian merchants. Young, generally poor Creoles, are the retailers in Paramaribo; flashy and daring, princes of the streets, they know the neighborhoods, the rum shops, the drug dens, and the 'sugar gardens'. They do not operate in gangs. Nor do they operate an organization anywhere compared to the posses. But they affiliate with a patron, who in turn is linked to his patron, and so on. In fact, one of the organizing principles of Suriname social structure is a vertically arranged, overlapping series of patron–client relations articulating economic, political, and criminal spheres of activity. An extension of this Creole population resides in Amsterdam, particularly in a segregated high rise housing project called the Bijlmermeer.[27]

Young Maroons, disrupted by the seven year internal war, have changed life styles as well. First, there was a wholesale evacuation of parts of the interior to the 'big city' of Paramaribo and across the river to French Guiana. The power of the Granman and his council of elders was disrupted, the old gods and oracles lost their grip and control, and young Maroons entered a hitherto unheard life of opportunity and fast lane. Knowing the interior, they became, in the jungle as well as the city, the interlocutors of narco-commerce and, like their Creole counterparts, maintain a mobile population within Suriname. Moreover, because they know the value of a penny, young Maroons invest profits wisely in gold mining technology which they then sub-contract to prospectors.[28]

East Indian businessmen have been prominent in the commercial sector, along with their Lebanese counterparts, since after World War II. International connections, accumulated capital, talent, and a general disinterest in the public sector, conflated to give the two groups prominence in the import–export sector. Although immense amounts of money were made from the parallel financial exchange rates in the 1980s and 1990s – the export of rice, for example, in dollars while local wages were paid in guilders – serious money is earned through money laundering, pyramid near-banking schemes, and facilitating narcotics transport. In a mutually reinforcing, interlocking relationship, East Indian capital supports Creole state control, and vice versa. Who says the races cannot get along in a plural society?

## Conclusion

In the first of his five part series, de Albuquerque chronicles the inflation involved in begging or hustling in order to purchase a spliff throughout the Eastern Caribbean. More dramatically, he points out:

> I argued that there was a clear link between the drug trade and increasing drug use and the escalation in murder, robbery, felonious wounding, burglary, and larceny rates. I specifically linked the majority of these crimes to emerging drug subcultures. These subcultures are to be distinguished from older drug subcultures based on ganja (marijuana), by their drug of choice, crack cocaine, and their proclivity to violence.... Much of the current violence in the region is the result of turf/drug wars between rival posses.... Drugs and crime in the region have become inseparable.[29]

Throughout the region, drug barons, dons, small island 'bigmen', and international entrepreneurs all have connections with government, commercial houses, and political party bosses. Overlapping, vertically integrated chains of patron–client relationships, ripple throughout society connecting top to bottom, eventually to the unemployed, disaffected youth who hustle, scrap, scuffle, retail, and kill each other. In the three cases examined briefly above we see a range of issues in various levels of severity and complexity. Each case shows the complicity of various kinds of élites. St Vincent is still a national emporium with regional traffic undertaken by loose, shifting alliances dealing primarily with marijuana; freebooters as it were. Jamaica displays a remarkable gang organization with posses deeply rooted in the indigenous social–political organization and connected to overseas communities. Suriname comes close to the model some suggest is emerging – narco-democracy and state involvement.

Examination of these cases is not to suggest that narco-criminality is limited to those countries. I did not delve into any of the following: the violence of Puerto Rico and its mainline to the US market; the mafia/organized crime penetration of Aruba, St Maarten, and the US Virgin Islands; corruption in Antigua's 'Birdland'; prison riots and murders in St Kitts-Nevis; piracy on the high seas in Trinidad's Gulf of Paria; the newly opened artery in Guyana from Boa Vista in Brazil, through Lethem, and on to Georgetown and points north; the collapse of post-intervention law and order in Haiti; marijuana cultivation and gangland connections in Belize with their counterparts in Los Angeles; Colombian cartel stations in San Andres and Providencia; and the French connection through the overseas Departments, among others.

There is a solid grasp of the macro-dimensions of the danger and everyone – from the US military and their regional counterparts, the US State Department, DEA and the CIA, to Caribbean national law enforcement agencies – seems to understand that what was once a national level problem has now become a regional security threat. What we do not seem to understand very well is how this narco-activity plays out on the ground, in backyards and on street corners throughout the region; among young men whose life chances are circumscribed, in what Jamaicans call the 'dungle', and who seek alternative fulfillment in narcotics consumption and trafficking for meager highs and financial rewards, and risk death doing it. Youth in the Caribbean are populations dangerously at risk.

Ken Pryce tried to learn. Fieldwork anybody?

## Notes

1  A total of three workshops were sponsored by UNICA, the Association of Caribbean Universities and Research Institutes, which was administered by Sir Philip Sherlock, then resident scholar at the University of Florida. See Gary Brana-Shute and Rosemary Brana-Shute (eds), *Crime and Punishment in the Caribbean* (Gainesville: Center for Latin American Studies, University of Florida, 1980).

2  Volumes I–IV, with same title and publisher, were edited by Jack Hopkins. Volume VI was edited by Abraham Lowenthal Volumes VII and VIII were edited by Jack Hopkins and Eduardo Gamarra.

3  Gary Brana-Shute and Rosemary Brana-Shute, 'The Anglophone Eastern Caribbean and British Dependencies', in Abraham Lowenthal (ed.), *Latin American and Caribbean Contemporary Record, Volume V: 1985–86* (New York: Holmes and Meier, 1988), p. B451.

4  Ivelaw L. Griffith, 'Caribbean Regional Security', *Strategic Forum*, No. 102 (February 1997), p. 1.

5  Ivelaw L. Griffith, *Caribbean Security on the Eve of the 21st Century*, McNair Paper No. 54. (Washington, DC: National Defense University, 1996); Ivelaw Griffith, *The Quest for Security in the Caribbean*. (Armonk: M.E. Sharpe, 1993); Ivelaw Griffith (ed.), *Strategy and Security in the Caribbean*. (Westport: Praeger, 1991).

6  Maingot's work is interesting because it is transitional and links 'cold war' issues with the burgeoning narco-corruption complex of the Caribbean. Young and Phillips, writing in the 1980s use the authoritarian state, Commies, and imperialists model. See Anthony Maingot, *The United States and the Caribbean*. (Boulder: Westview, 1994); and in 'Internationalization of Corruption and

Violence', in Jorge Domínquez, Robert Pastor, and DeLilse Worrell (eds), *Democracy in the Caribbean* (Baltimore: John Hopkins University Press, 1993); Alma Young and Dion Phillips (eds), *Militarization in the Non-Hispanic Caribbean* (Boulder: Lynne Rienner, 1986).

7   Essentially, the rule of thumb in a small society where everyone knows everyone else is to keep one's back to the wall, head down, and mouth shut, thus promoting what Coram calls the 'carnival of corruption in "Birdland"'. Robert Coram, *Caribbean Time Bomb: The United States' Complicity in the Corruption of Antigua*. (New York: William Morrow, 1993), p. 3.

8   For largely Cold War strategic reasons, such as maintaining open 'sea lanes of commerce' to Europe, Caribbean defense issues were under the responsibility of USACOM. As of June 1997 the responsibility was transferred to SOUTH-COM, and the emphasis will be on collective defense, interdiction efforts, and intelligence sharing with Caribbean Basin countries. See *Proceedings of United States Southern Command and National Defense University Western Hemisphere Strategy Symposium*, Miami, Florida, 1997; United States Southern Command and National Defense University, *Cooperative Security in the Caribbean*, Coral Gables, Florida, 1995.

9   At the 1997 CINSEC conference, representatives of the defense and police forces of every independent Caribbean island nation, plus Belize, Guyana, and Suriname attended. Observers included the US, UK, France, the Netherlands, Canada, Puerto Rico, Venezuela, and the US. Virgin Islands.

10  The 'shiprider' protocol includes cooperation on 'shipboarding', 'shiprider', 'pursuit', 'entry-to-investigate', 'overflight', 'order-to-land', and 'maritime alien interdiction'.

11  Bananas too are a security issue, because banana producing countries, particularly in the Eastern Caribbean, fear that the elimination of their banana preference to European Common Market through the Lome Convention would result in the collapse of banana cultivation, a dramatic drop in national revenues, massive unemployment, and a breakdown of internal security and order. See Georges Fauriol, *US Policy on the Caribbean, Testimony before the US House of Representatives Committee on International Relations, Subcommittee on the Western Hemisphere* (Washington, DC: Center for Strategic and International Studies, Americas Program, 1997).

12  See Hymie Rubenstein, 'The Drug Dilemma', *The Vincentian*, 11, 18, 23, 31 December 1992; 8, 15, 21 January 1993; 26 March 1993; 16, 30 April 1993; and 15 April 1994.

13  See Lambros Comitas and Vera Rubin, *Ganja in Jamaica: a Medical Anthropological Study of Chronic Marihuana Use* (The Hague: Mouton, 1975); and Melanie Dreher, *Working Men and Ganja: Marihuana Use In Rural Jamaica* (Philadelphia: Institute for the Study of Human Issues, 1982), for a discussion of routine uses of ganja in Jamaica, especially in folk medicine.

14  Klaus de Albuquerque, 'Drugs in the Caribbean', *Caribbean Weak*, January–February, 1996; February, 1996; February-March, 1996; 2–15 March, 1996; and 16–29 March, 1996.

15  US Department of State, *International Narcotics Control Strategy Report*, March 1996.

16  Gary Brana-Shute, 'Jamaican Posse Gangs in the US', *Suriname Journal of Social Sciences* Vol. 4 (June 1997).

17   Bernard Headley, *The Jamaican Crime Scene* (Washington, DC: Howard University Press, 1996); and Laure Gunst, *Born Fi' Dead: A Journey through the Jamaican Posse Underworld* (New York: Henry Holt, 1995).

18   Brana-Shute, op.cit.

19   See Statistical Institute of Jamaica, *Statistical Yearbook of Jamaica, 1995* (Kingston: Statistical Institute of Jamaica, 1995), pp. 171–84.

20   See Ed Dew's excellent *The Trouble in Suriname, 1975–1993* (Westport: Praeger, 1994); and Gary Brana-Shute, 'Security Issues and Indigenous Groups in the Guianas', *Small Wars and Insurgencies*, Vol. 7(2) (1996), pp. 121–38.

21   As a Fulbright Fellow in Suriname in 1979 I worked with the University of Suriname, the Ministry of Justice, the Police, the Criminal Courts, and the penal system on an ethnography of juvenile delinquency in Paramaribo.

22   See Gary Brana-Shute, 'Mothers in University: The Children's Police of Suriname', *Urban Anthropology*, Vol. 10 (1982); Gary Brana-Shute, 'Juvenile Delinquency in Paramaribo', paper delivered at the Caribbean Studies Association conference, Kingston, Jamaica, 1982.

23   Haakmat offers his 'insider's' assessment in *De Revolutie Uitgegleden* (Amsterdam: Jan Mets, 1987).

24   Frits Hirshland, a Dutch journalist, worked with the Jungle Commando at that time and chronicles the 'scam' and some of the unsavory characters who were passing in and out of Suriname at the time. See his *Dossier Moengo' 290 Uur.'* (The Hague: Cast, 1993).

25   See Ivelaw Griffith, op.cit.

26   De Jong, writing for the Netherlands' newspaper of record, the *NRC Handelsblad,* has over the years produced articles on narco-trafficking in Suriname. The government of Suriname denounces this reportage as overblown. See Sjoerd de Jong, 'Cocaine per legerauto naar Paramaribo', *NRC Handelsblad,* Amsterdam, 25 August 1993.

27   See Livio Sansone, *Hangen Boven de Oceaan.* (Amsterdam: Spinhuis, 1992) on the Paramaribo–Amsterdam connection and his thoughts on international consumerism.

28   The impact of the civil war of the late 1980s and subsequent penetration of the interior by gold mining corporations, illegal gold miners, and timber cutting concessionaires has further disrupted life for both Maroons and Amerindians, especially young males.

29   Alburquerque, 'Drug in the Caribbean', *Caribbean Week* (January–February 1996,), pp. 2, 4.

# 6
# Democracy and Political Economy in the Caribbean

*Clifford E. Griffin*

## Introduction

The Caribbean forms part of Samuel P. Huntington's second and third waves of transition to democracy.[1] The English- speaking subset of the region, with one or two exceptions, has held democratic elections where the contestation for executive and legislative power has taken place since adult suffrage was first granted to Jamaica in 1944.[2] Elections are held approximately every five years, with governments mostly serving their full terms. The 23 years between 1972 and 1994 have witnessed a flourishing of democratic freedoms guaranteed by the rule of law among all of these countries, but especially among those in the English-speaking sub-region. On a scale of one to seven, one being the highest, the countries there averaged political rights and civil liberties scores of 1.9 and 2.3, respectively, during this period.[3] These scores, which rank these countries significantly above the global average, underscore the fact that they represent one of the most developed zones of democracy in the world.

Notwithstanding these democratic credentials, the region also stands out as an important transshipment point for illicit drugs to the US and Europe. The United Nations International Drug Control Program (UNDCP) estimates that 20–40 per cent of the cocaine imported into the US and Europe transits the Caribbean. The Eastern Caribbean countries of Antigua and Barbuda, Barbados, Dominica, Grenada, St Kitts and Nevis, St Lucia and St Vincent and the Grenadines, along with the British, French and Dutch dependencies, represent gateways into the following US ports of entry: Vieques Island, Puerto Rico; and the US Virgin Islands. Antigua and Barbuda, for example, is a transshipment point for more than US$1 billion of cocaine and marijuana smuggled into the US Virgin Islands and US mainland each year.[4] Collectively, these ports are designated as high intensity drug trafficking areas through which, according to the US DEA, an estimated seven tons of cocaine were smuggled successfully each month between 1992 and 1995. Facilitating this transit in illegal narcotics are the international airports and large port facilities in Antigua and Barbuda, Barbados, Jamaica, St Lucia and elsewhere. Other facilitating factors include: easy navigation, rugged and inadequately patrolled coastlines and waters, attractive under-regulated banking practices, well entrenched local drug subcultures, severely limited resources for law enforcement, fragile economies and the susceptibility to corruption of a number of government officials.

Further, the Caribbean is host to the world's greatest concentration of offshore secrecy centers, through which approximately 75 per cent of all sophisticated drug money laundering activities are conducted.[5] Increasing amounts of the proceeds from the illicit drug trade are being invested throughout the region in the form of real estate, shopping centers, and other legitimate enterprises. Proceeds are finding their way into the political process as well. For example, credible allegations of drug money influencing electoral competition in St Kitts and Nevis surfaced in 1993 and 1995. More recently, individuals allegedly closely linked to government leaders, and facing the threat of extradition to the US to answer drug charges, were cleared in the local court to the befuddlement of several people. Further, Jamie Astaphan, a medical doctor from St Kitts and Nevis, who was arrested in New York in 1994 on drug charges, reputedly told US authorities that he had evidence linking top Antigua and Barbuda officials and their associates to drug trafficking and organized crime.

However, Caribbean countries face a dilemma. While the US appears to view drug trafficking and money laundering rather narrowly, Caribbean countries have difficulty separating this problem from broader economic, political and social issues. One reason for this dilemma is the relationship between the structural, political and economic characteristics of a country and its receptivity to drug trafficking and money laundering. Poor countries and countries experiencing economic and political transformation may be highly susceptible to drug trafficking and money laundering activities as they wrestle with problems of adjustment. And drug trafficking and money laundering are likely to produce corruption and other social problems such as increased crime, thereby undermining the social fabric of a given society. According to a British Foreign and Commonwealth Office study: 'the problems associated with drugs and drug trafficking pose the greatest threat to the stability and economic and social development of the Caribbean, and are now undermining democracy there...the corruption from drugs is affecting every level of society, and threatening to destroy the institutions needed to sustain democracy'.[6]

The growing concern over the impact of illicit drugs on the political economy of the Caribbean is related to the larger issue of the dual transformation in the global political economy that became most evident during the 1980s, especially with the collapse of world communism and the disintegration of the USSR. This dual transformation reflects two worldwide reform movements: one toward free market economic systems, and the other toward liberal democratic forms of government. It is this emergence of a more uniformly democratic and free market global political economy that is producing some undesired outcomes for Caribbean countries. Thus, this analysis, which follows the globalization paradigm, examines globalization's impact upon the political economy of the Caribbean by focusing on the following interrelated national interest/security issues: aid, trade and development; offshore financial services; illegal drug trafficking and money laundering; and economic and political stability. I posit that factors such as commodity price deflation, sustained high levels of unemployment and economic recessions make countries susceptible to drug trafficking and money laundering. These developments, in turn, have important implications for social, political and economic security within Caribbean countries.

Accordingly, three interrelated arguments are made. First, the drastic reductions in (mainly US) foreign assistance, the NAFTA erosion of the competitive edge that Caribbean countries had in the textile industry, and efforts by the United States to secure access to EU markets at the expense of CARICOM countries will prove counterproductive to US interests by undermining the economic base and threatening the endurance of democracy in the Caribbean. Secondly, weakened economies may leave Caribbean countries less able and, perhaps less willing, to combat the trafficking in illegal narcotics and the laundering of drug money through the offshore financial sector. Finally, these societies may be incapable of handling the increasing numbers of nationals being repatriated from the US after having been convicted of narcotics-related crimes.

Thus, given the central role that Caribbean countries play in the narcotrafficking and money laundering aspects of international organized crime, the threat posed by these activities to demand countries such as the United States and those in Europe, and the sense that drug operations represent multilateral threats warranting multinational solutions, Caribbean leaders should bargain with those countries for economic concessions to mitigate some of the adverse political, economic and social consequences of globalization. The bargaining outcomes should go beyond the traditional emphasis on aid as food, grants, loans and preferential market access to include aid that promotes human resource development in education and information technology. Such a focus would better serve these countries as they seek to compete with the rest of the world in the new global political economy. Moreover, it would help to cement the economic base necessary for the endurance of democratic governance.

## Globalism

Globalism reflects the movement of information, money, physical objects, people, and other tangible and intangible goods across state boundaries, with at least one of the entities involved in the process being a non-governmental actor, and all operating in a competitive arena according to the rules of free trade.[7] Several interrelated events combine to characterize this increasing uniformity of the international political economy. Included are: the collapse of world communism and the dual transformation to more open political systems and free market economic processes; the successful conclusion of the Uruguay round of negotiations for the General Agreement on Trade and Tariffs (GATT) that resulted in the establishment of the WTO; the passage of NAFTA; the establishment of the European Single Market (ESM); the agreement reached at the 1994 Summit of the Americas to establish the Free Trade Area of the Americas (FTAA) by the year 2005; the increasing porosity of international borders; the transnationalization of financial networks; and the revolution in telecommunications technology that has reduced not only the size of the world but also the ability of states to regulate the transnational flows of money. Hence, an important feature of globalism is the growing interdependence among states and other international actors, which is producing some national interest/security 'levelling' between large and many not- so-small states. This development, however, does not hold true for several states, especially Caribbean countries, whose national interest/security concerns are being undermined by various dimensions of globalism.[8]

For example, not only are these countries experiencing substantial declines in foreign economic assistance but they are being pressured by the United States to assume greater responsibility for managing the problems that confront the hemisphere. At the same time, NAFTA is eroding the competitive edge in textiles production, to the benefit of Mexico. Globalism also threatens to end the Lomé agreements that provide preferential access for a number of Caribbean products to Western European markets. Another outcome of globalism is the elevation of the trafficking of illegal narcotics and money laundering to the status of security agenda items for many countries, including the US and many in Europe. However, for Caribbean countries centrally involved in these illicit activities, drug trafficking and money laundering constitute high-agenda security items, for reasons shown below and elsewhere in this volume.

Several of the region's problems persist because international economic competitiveness among countries, enunciated originally by David Ricardo and others, which is grounded in the doctrine of comparative advantage and specialization, does not work well for these small states. The past decade-and-a-half has witnessed net capital flows into the developing world increase from about US$38 billion in 1981 to more than US$155 billion in 1993, leading to and reflecting the integration and increasing interdependence of national economies.[9] Despite this influx of capital, the developing world boasts only a few successes such as Taiwan, Singapore, and South Korea. The main reason for this unimpressive record is that developing countries have been unable, by and large, to create internationally competitive manufacturing or other types of industries and, consequently, have not achieved the promised and expected levels of development.

Although many Caribbean countries have made impressive gains in living conditions, many face an uncertain future because poverty remains a major social and economic concern. This uncertainty stems from, but is not limited to, the following interrelated, factors: (1) the challenges of increased levels of economic competition driven by global economic and political changes in trade and capital markets; (2) the erosion of preferential access to markets and continued threats to existing preferential arrangements; (3) the susceptibility of the tourist industry to domestic political stability as well as competition from other tourist destinations; and (4) the decline in official capital flows from bilateral and multilateral donors.[10]

For example, net US transfers to the Caribbean doubled to US$353.5 million between 1981 and 1984, following the Grenada intervention. Between 1984 and 1995, US exports to the region grew 160 per cent to some US$15 billion annually, making the Caribbean the only region where the US enjoyed a favorable balance of trade during this period.[11] By 1988, however, US net transfers to the region had nosedived to US$44.5 million.[12] Thus, whereas Direct Foreign Investment (DFI) flows to the Caribbean averaged US$70 per capita during 1980–82, they averaged US$31 per capita between 1990 and 1992. Further, despite increased demand for cooperation on political issues such as narcotrafficking and money laundering, the US ended in August 1996 the 936 Loan Program that provided approximately US$1.1 billion in private investment and low interest loans to Caribbean countries;[13] and US aid to the region is now less than US$25 million.[14]

Further, Caribbean countries are not adjusting well to free trade regimes. For example, from the apparel plants of Jamaica to the sugar cane fields of Trinidad and Tobago, NAFTA already has resulted in job, markets and income losses for these highly vulnerable island states. Capital and investment projects so vitally needed for their future growth are flowing out of the Caribbean and into Mexico. And although many Caribbean countries have petitioned the US government for NAFTA parity, the Clinton Administration remains lukewarm toward it and the Congress appears to be sceptical about it. The implication is that without NAFTA parity, more than one-third of the approximately US$12.5 billion worth of goods currently exported from the Caribbean to the US could be shifted to Mexico. According to the Jamaica-based Caribbean Textile and Apparel Institute, more than 150 apparel plants in the Caribbean closed between 1995 and 1997, at a cost of 123 000 jobs. Further, whereas Jamaica's garment exports grew from approximately US$10 million annually in 1985 to more than US$600 million, at an average annual rate of 28 per cent, Mexican textile exports have grown approximately three times that of Jamaica's rate since NAFTA came on stream in 1994. Meanwhile, Jamaica's apparel exports fell by 7 per cent in 1996, eliminating some 7000 jobs. Similar or even larger decreases were recorded in Guyana, Belize and especially St Lucia, whose economy remains highly dependent on banana exports.[15]

Economically and socially, the banana industry is well-suited to the Windward Islands of Dominica, Grenada, St Lucia and St Vincent. Unlike any alternative crop, bananas can recover to their full productive capacity after a mere nine months if the crops are destroyed by one of region's frequent hurricanes. The industry functions well under the family farm operations especially because production takes place under conditions that guarantee at least minimum standards of living.[16] Further, not only does the industry provide direct employment for one-quarter of the labor force of these islands and accounts for three-quarters of all export earnings but it accounts also for 50 per cent of their total visible exports and 15 per cent of their GDP.[17]

However, while the US has endorsed, repeatedly, the system of tariff preferences for Caribbean bananas and allows a number of Caribbean exports to enter its markets duty free under the 1984 CBI, Caribbean bananas have not been able to penetrate the US market. Furthermore, Caribbean bananas cannot compete with the 'dollar bananas', of the far bigger and more efficient Latin American producers in Guatemala, Honduras, Ecuador, and Mexico on whose behalf the US has complained to the dispute settlement body of the WTO that the Lomé Agreements violate the principles of free trade. Intensive lobbying of the Clinton Administration by Carl Lindner, head of Chiquita Brands, has led to a preliminary ruling by the WTO in favor of the free trade faction. Lindner's companies, which spent approximately US$2 million since 1990 lobbying the US government to pry open the banana markets in Europe, stand to gain millions in revenues from increased access to those markets.[18]

The irony is that very few American jobs are at stake in the banana issue; most of Chiquita's 45, 000 employees are in Honduras and Guatemala. The down side to this is that the final ruling by the WTO in favor of the free trade faction will lead almost inevitably to economic, political, and social instability throughout the Windward Islands that depend heavily upon the banana industry. Possible repercussions of this decision include waves of migrants – legal and illegal, making their exodus from the Windward Islands to North America and elsewhere. But an even more poignant concern was expressed by Grenada's Prime Minister, Dr Keith Mitchell: that US actions not only will hamper the banana industry but also will increase the level of illegal narcotics activity in his country.[19] Thus, one of globalism's paradoxes is huge adjustment costs that create and exacerbate conditions conducive to drug trafficking and money laundering and undermine economic and political stability throughout the region, as the following analysis of the offshore financial services sector suggests.

## Globalism and offshore financial centers

By 1957, the US dollar had replaced the pound sterling as the new key currency for international transactions because balance-of-payment problems in the UK resulted in tight controls on the British pound which, in turn, led to a greater demand for US dollars. Simultaneously, the US government instituted legislation restricting foreign lending by US banks, thereby stimulating the expansion of US bank branches in London, the traditional international financial center. These branches were used to finance the growing number of transnational companies engaged in increasing numbers of international transactions.

A consequent divergence of interests between national governments and transnational companies led to the emergence of offshore financing and offshore banking centers. Moreover, a combination of factors, including relatively low costs of establishing branches, low taxes, more liberal legal provisions for registration and licensing, and the fact that the Caribbean is located in the same time zone as New York, made the Caribbean more attractive than London as offshore financial centers.[20] Offshore banking, therefore, marked the beginning of the offshore financial industry in the Caribbean, providing services including banking and finance companies, captive insurance and reinsurance, holding companies, IBCs, Foreign Sales Corporations (FSCs), licensing and patent holding mutual funds, ship registry and trusts. The main objective of companies and individuals using these services is either to avoid taxes and exchange controls or to protect assets from confiscation or expropriation. These countries, therefore, provide tax paradises and/or tax shelters while generating substantial revenues for themselves.[21] (See Table 6.1.)

From a global perspective, the Caribbean does not play a trivial role in the handling of financial assets and liabilities. The BIS estimates that of the US$12 billion in offshore banks around the world in 1993, offshore banks in the Caribbean held more than US$5 billion, with approximately two-thirds of this amount in other offshore financial instruments.[22] This figure, however, seems to be grossly underestimated. According to a UN report, three of the 20 largest offshore banking centers are located in the Caribbean. Of an estimated US$6992 billion of global foreign liabilities in 1993, approximately US$389 billion, or 5.6 per cent, were administered by the banks in the Cayman Islands, US$168 billion, or 2.4 per cent, by banks in the Bahamas, and US$27 billion, or 0.4 per cent, in the Netherlands Antilles. The aggregate foreign deposits in these three Caribbean countries thus totalled approximately half of the US$1134 billion held in banks in the United Kingdom.[23]

The offshore financial services sector in the Caribbean is a growing industry. According to the 1996 *International Narcotics Control Strategy Report* and anonymous sources, the number of offshore banks in Antigua and Barbuda jumped from 25 in 1994 to 42 in 1995, a 75 per cent

Table 6.1  Estimated Number of Registered Companies in the Caribbean

| Country | IBCs/ECs | FSCs | OBs | TCs | CICs | SRs | MFs | Date |
|---|---|---|---|---|---|---|---|---|
| Anguilla | 2,669 | 0 | 2 | 0 | 17 | 0 | 0 | 09/94 |
| Bahamas | 38,000 | 0 | 413[a] | 413[a] | 30 | 1500 | 300 | 1995 |
| Barbados | 1,486 | 1,173 | 25 | 39 | 232[b] | 33 | – | 12/94 |
| Belize | 1,750 | 0 | – | – | – | 770 | – | Q4/94 |
| Bermuda | 5,947 | 118 | 0 | 28 | 1,326 | 93 | 318 | Q4/94 |
| BVI | 100,000 | 0 | <10 | – | 200–300 | – | – | Q4/94 |
| Cayman Islands | 26,000 | 0 | 507[c] | 277 | 361 | 784 | 891 | 12/94 |
| NA | 22,000[d] | 0 | 56 | 39[e] | 29 | 20 | 450 | 12/93 |
| Nevis | 5,000 | 0 | 0 | 0[f] | 0 | 0 | 0 | 10/96 |
| Turks & Caicos | 9,376 | 0 | 7[g] | 13 | 1,600 | 150 | 0 | 09/94 |

*Notes*:
[a] Refers to both Offshore Banks and Trust Companies;
[b] Refers to both Exempt Insurance Companies and Exempt Insurance Management Companies;
[c] 224 institutions have both banking and trust licenses;
[d] Offshore Naamloze Vennootschappen (NV);
[e] Corporate Management Companies;
[f] Trust ordinance effective May 1994;
[g] Offshore and domestic banks.
IBCs/ECs – International Business Companies/Exempted Companies
FSCs – Foreign Sales Companies
OBs – Offshore Banks; TCs – Trust Companies
CICs – Captive Insurance Companies
SRs – Ships Registered; MFs – Mutual Funds
*Source*: Adapted from national data, ECLAC estimates, and *International Narcotics Control Strategy Report 1996*.

increase. Approximately 38 000 IBCs are registered in the Commonwealth of the Bahamas, employing more than 3000 people and generating approximately US$16 million annually from licensing fees and work permits. An estimated 26 000 companies plus several hundred banks are registered in the Cayman Islands, employing about 1500 persons and generating approximately US$26 million annually from licensing fees. In the British Virgin Islands, the registrar of companies database indicates that the number of IBCs jumped from 253 in 1984 to 15 328 in 1990 and skyrocketed to 32 523 in 1995, producing revenues approximating US$9.2 million. However, a UN report puts that figure at 100 000, creating about 400 jobs and generating approximately US$38 million annually in direct government revenues. And newcomer Nevis currently has some 7000 IBCs, netting the government US$1 143 718 in 1994 and US$1 868 677 in 1995.[24] (See Table 6.2.)

*Table 6.2*  Estimated Annual Employment and Direct Government Revenues
from the Offshore Sector

| Country | Year | No. of employees | Year | Revenue ($m) | % of Current govt revenue |
|---|---|---|---|---|---|
| Bahamas | 1985 | 3,035 | 1994 | 16.0 | 3 |
| Barbados | 1994 | 2,000 | 1993 | 9.7 | 2 |
| Bermuda | 1992 | 2,006 | 1992 | 23.6 | 7 |
| British Virgin Islands | 1994 | 400 | 1994 | 38.0 | 63 |
| Cayman Islands | 1994 | 1,500 | 1994 | 26.0 | 16 |
| Montserrat | 1994 | 4 | 1993 | 0.3 | 2 |
| Netherlands Antilles | 1994 | 3,000 | 1993 | 111.7 | 28 |
| Nevis | 1994 | 30 | 1996 | 0.4 | 1 |
| Turks & Caicos Islands | – | – | 1994 | 2.6 | 10 |

*Source*: Adapted from national data and ECLAC estimates.

The benefits of the offshore financial sector are mixed: on the one hand, it generates much needed revenues; on the other hand, it makes these countries vulnerable to the lure of illicit drug money as well as monies from unknown sources. For example, several banks in Antigua and Barbuda are known to have links to Russia, generating concern about investors and that depositors may be connected to the Russian *Mafiya*. And although the financial services sector pre-dates the narco-trafficking boom, its growth accelerated with the expansion of drug trafficking. Globalism, therefore, not only conduces to the growth of these financial services but also to the continued rise in the market for international narcotics.

## Globalism, illegal narcotics and money laundering

Globalism reflects the increased interdependence among states and other international actors, the ease of international travel and communications, the porosity of international borders and the transnationalization of financial networks that combine to create global markets for both licit and illicit goods. In fact, globalism has altered fundamentally the context in which licit and illicit businesses operate and has opened up unprecedented opportunities for transnational organized crime. Essentially, transnational organized crime such as drug trafficking and money laundering represents an extension of a legitimate market function into areas normally proscribed. Moreover, international criminal operators are driven by the same operational considerations that govern entrepreneurship in the legitimate market place: the need to maintain and increase market share.

As occurs in the licit arena, entrepreneurs locate and/or relocate their operations to lower cost areas, thereby enabling them to maximize global profits. Thus, by acting transnationally, criminal organizations are able to gain access to lucrative markets and identify and penetrate areas of vulnerability while remaining relatively immune to law enforcement. These organizations also channel proceeds from illicit activities through the global financial system, often using tax havens and relatively unregulated banking centers as major points of access. And one of the most worrisome examples of a global market for illicit transactions is the market for illegal narcotics and the offshore financial centers that are used regularly to launder the profits generated by this market. While the choice of illegal narcotic varies from one region to the next, the global trade in these illegal substances was estimated at US$500 billion in 1988, exceeding the global trade in oil.[25] More recent UN figures indicate that approximately US$750 billion in illegal narcotics proceeds are laundered annually, suggesting a significant increase in the revenues generated by this illicit activity.[26]

Illicit narcotics activities can best be viewed as an industry with distinct stages of production and distribution at the wholesale and retail levels. These activities also can be understood as globally tradable commodities that function under the same laws of supply and demand and the same rules of international competitiveness as licit commerce. Three factors make this illicit area highly lucrative: (1) limited competition among the cartels and entities involved; (2) little threat from substitute products; and (3) the limited power of both the suppliers of the raw materials and the consumers of the final product.[27] And several factors account for the growth of global markets for these illicit activities: (1) a rise in the number of cosmopolitan cities that function as the central nervous system of the global economy, the sources of capital and wealth, and as major facilitators of international transactions in both legal and illegal activities; (2) the surplus wealth in these cities that creates increased opportunities for recreation and leisure as well as a demand for illicit goods and services; and (3) the revolution in communication technology that illuminates the inequalities among countries, stimulates the desire among the economically underdeveloped to emulate the consumption patterns of the economically developed, and facilitates the movement of people and goods between developing and developed countries. Consequently, a global market is constantly developing in which consumers have immediate access to information about consumer tastes and desires, and in which entrepreneurs readily capitalize on the marketing opportunities that globalization presents.[28] The Caribbean, which plays a central role in these activities, continues to experience uncomfortable political and economic repercussions.

## Some political realities

Illicit drug trafficking and money laundering continue to take a huge toll on Caribbean societies. Whereas the Latin American drug producer viewed the Caribbean simply as a transit zone through which his product must pass in order to reach the lucrative markets in the US, Europe and elsewhere, most Caribbean states, until recently, viewed drug trafficking as a problem for the Latin American producer countries and North American and European consumer countries. However, by exploiting the territorial integrity of these countries, the Latin American producer made drug trafficking a Caribbean problem. This was achieved largely by paying their trafficking associates in the Caribbean in cash as well as in kind. As a result, a local demand has been created, drug related crime has increased, and governments now acknowledge that drug trafficking is indeed a Caribbean problem.

According to Barry McCaffrey, the Clinton Administration's drug 'Czar', about 154 tonne of cocaine pass through the Eastern Caribbean into the US annually during the late 1990s while another 180 metric tonne finds its way into Europe. Contributing to this volume of illicit drugs transiting the region is the significant reduction of resources dedicated to interdicting activities, falling from US$1.03 billion in 1992 to US$569 million in 1995.[29] (See Table 6.3.) As a result, drug traffickers, who spend about US$2000 per kilo of cocaine in corruption and shipping costs in the Eastern Caribbean, leave behind US$400 million to US$600 million a year, much more than the national budgets of most of these countries. Not only are illicit drug trafficking and drug money leaving behind a pattern of violence, drug addiction, scandals and political corruption but drug traffickers have also penetrated the highest levels of society and government institutions in Antigua and Barbuda, Aruba, the Dominican Republic, Jamaica, St Kitts and Nevis, and Trinidad and Tobago, according to one US Department of State official.[30]

Drug trafficking through the Caribbean is not new. Much of the cocaine and marijuana entering the US during the late 1970s and early 1980s passed through the Caribbean, especially Jamaica and the Bahamas. However, intense surveillance by US and Colombian authorities in

*Table 6.3* US Counternarcotics Funding for the Caribbean for Fiscal Years 1991–95 ($m)

| Agency | 1991 | 1992 | 1993 | 1994 | 1995 |
|---|---|---|---|---|---|
| Defense | 407.1 | 504.5 | 426.0 | 220.4 | 214.7 |
| Coast Guard | 565.2 | 443.9 | 310.5 | 314.4 | 301.2 |
| Customs | NA | NA | 16.2 | 12.5 | 12.8 |
| DEA | 26.2 | 28.8 | 29.1 | 28.7 | 29.6 |
| State | 35.9 | 36.2 | 14.0 | 7.9 | 10.6 |
| Total | 1034.4 | 1013.4 | 795.8 | 583.9 | 568.9 |

*Note*: NA – not applicable.
*Source*: General Accounting Office, adapted from the *Washington Post* (23 September 1996).

the mid-1980s forced traffickers to shift their operations to Mexico. When US law enforcement authorities responded by focusing their interdiction on Mexico, traffickers shifted back to the traditional Caribbean routes while developing new ones through the Eastern Caribbean. One of these new places narcotics traffickers looked at and liked was Antigua and Barbuda, a country alleged to be so plagued by rampant corruption that drug lords and their Antiguan surrogates find it easy to infiltrate the poorly paid police force and customs officers and, in some cases, the highest levels of government. As a result, the Antigua and Barbuda transshipment route has proved lucrative for Colombian cartels.

United States federal agents estimate the street value of cocaine and marijuana smuggled into the US Virgin Islands and the US mainland via Antigua during 1993 at more than US$1 billion – eight times Antigua and Barbuda's 1993 budget. What concerns US federal officers is the development of what appears to be a strong, corporate type structure among traffickers in the Eastern Caribbean where specialization has led to fewer slip-ups. The situation is especially acute in Antigua and Barbuda, where respected businessmen, offshore bankers and international confidence men have made millions of dollars in drug money virtually untraceable due to clever accounting and money laundering.[31]

Antigua and Barbuda is not the only country in the Eastern Caribbean implicated in the drug trade. However, it is the country whose government officials and prominent businessmen are most often accused of at least tangential links to the trade. Facing drug charges in two states, Jamie Astaphan claims to have had close contact with several members of Antigua's government, including chairman of the ruling Labor Party,

Vere Bird Jr. And according to reports, Astaphan gave US federal agents copies of canceled checks and other financial documents as proof of the Bird regime's involvement in drug trafficking and other illegal activities.[32]

Reports of Antiguan government officials involvement in the shadowy world of drug-related crime are not new. In 1990, Vere Bird Jr was removed from his cabinet position of public works minister after being identified as a key player in a plot to arm Colombian drug lords. The Blom-Cooper Commission of Inquiry that probed the scandal recommended that Vere Jr be debarred from holding public office. The Commission also implicated Lt Colonel Clyde Walker, then Commander of the Antigua and Barbuda Defense Force because, among other things, investigators discovered that a call had been made from Walker's office to a clandestine Medellín drug cartel telephone number in Colombia. But the Antigua and Barbuda government official most often linked to drug trafficking by political opponents as well as those in the drug trade is the new leader of the ruling party and Prime Minister, Lester Bird. Back in 1989, immediately following his election as Prime Minister and even more recently, Bird announced 'new' initiatives in Antigua and Barbuda's anti-drug war, promising to release the names of drug pushers operating in the country. There have been no new initiatives, sources say, and Bird has yet to release any names. Sources contend that because so many citizens supplement their income directly or indirectly from the lucrative underground economy created by the drug trade, there is little public pressure on police or politicians to do more.

Like Antigua and Barbuda, St Kitts and Nevis became targeted as a new transshipment point partly because its coastal area is littered with coves that facilitate drug transfer and partly because, with only one coast guard boat to patrol the entire area, the coast guard is both out-gunned and out-manned by the traffickers. To demonstrate its resolve to combat drugs, the government has conducted several raids on the homes of suspected traffickers, including a major operation in conjunction with the Regional Security System (RSS) during the early hours of Father's Day 1993. In the process, Noel 'Zambo' Heath, reputed to be a business partner of high ranking members of the Labor Party, was arrested and charged with illegal possession of drugs and ammunition. US federal drug agents identify Heath as one of the major figures in drug trafficking in the Eastern Caribbean, and they believe that he, along with Antiguan Ickford 'Ocean' Karr, are key players in a drug ring that ran a multi-million-dollar smuggling operation between the US Virgin Islands and New York. According to investigators, a wiretap of Heath's home telephone in St Kitts linked him to co-conspirators in Tortola, St Croix, St Thomas and New York. This information, later confirmed by co-operating defendants, led investigators to 'people, planes and drugs'[33]. Heath, who is wanted in the US to answer drug trafficking charges, successfully fought extradition to the US despite overwhelming evidence against him.

During the 1993 election campaign, incumbent Prime Minister Kennedy Simmonds intimated that it was perhaps the most crucial election in the country's history because 'for the first time, drug money was being used in an attempt to influence the outcome of the election'[34]. Ironically, Simmonds' minority government was forced to face the electorate on 8 July 1995, less than half way through his term, and lost largely because of three major scandals surrounding his government. The first was the June 1994 disappearance at sea of Dr William Herbert, former leader of the People's Action Movement (PAM), then the country's Ambassador to the UN. Herbert was accompanied by family members and friends, who also disappeared. US officials allege that Herbert had been involved in money laundering activities, supposedly for drug dealers.

The second event was the forced resignation of Sidney Morris, Deputy Prime Minister and Minister of Education. During September 1994, Morris' three sons found themselves at the center of a drugs and weapons controversy. One son was charged with importing about 50 kg of cocaine while another was arrested on weapons charges; and the third son and his female companion, Joan Walsh, disappeared and later were found dead in the middle of a sugar cane field in a burnt-out automobile. They were presumed to have been executed by drug hit men. The real crisis erupted, however, after both brothers were released on bail. Resentment over the perception of preferential treatment led to violent protest by inmates at the central prison in the capital city, Basseterre. Prisoners rioted and burned the prison and the government was forced to request a RSS contingent to support the police in restoring order and securing the temporary prison facilities. The third event was the assassination of Superintendent Jude Matthew, head of the Special Branch of the St. Kitts and Nevis police force. Matthew, who headed a team investigating the disappearance of Morris and his female companion, was allegedly close to unmasking highly placed individuals involved in the drug trade.[35]

Basdeo Panday was elected as Prime Minister of Trinidad and Tobago in 1995, largely by campaigning on an anti-drug platform. His Attorney General, Ramesh Lawrence Maraj, is being watched closely to see how he helps the prime minister fulfill his campaign promise. Maraj, who acknowledged that more than 2000 kg of cocaine transit the country monthly during the late 1990s,[36] already has been successful in convicting the Dole Chadee group. This group, which was prosecuted for murdering the families of drug associates, is believed to be the most important drug trafficking organization in the Eastern Caribbean. Many citizens of Trinidad and Tobago were sceptical that the case against the Chadee group would succeed as witnesses against the group or their families have been murdered. One significant such murder occurred during the 1996 carnival celebrations, when Clint Huggins, who was under protective custody and feared for his life, was reputed to have been given permission by the security forces to attend some of the festivities. Huggins was murdered on carnival Tuesday.

The situation in Trinidad and Tobago is even more alarming because the country is a mere seven miles from Venezuela – well within easy access from Colombia. In addition, the Trinidad and Tobago coast guard, like that of the other Anglophone Caribbean countries, is little match for the traffickers who control enormous resources. Even more disconcerting is the practice of the Colombian cartels to compensate local traffickers with cocaine – approximately 40 per cent of shipments – and not with cash. Consequently, as the number of local traffickers increases, competition becomes more keen, violence and bloodshed and upwardly spiralling criminal activity become the norm, individual safety is compromised, and democracy's foundations begin to founder.

## Some social and economic consequences

As discussed above and in Chapters 1 and 3, poverty remains a major social and economic concern among Caribbean countries despite the impressive gains in living conditions made by a number of them. And poverty, according to a 1996 World Bank report, is closely associated with the level of crime and violence in the region, which has been increasing steadily since the early 1980s. Stories of shootings, gang killings, minor disputes that turn violent, sexual attacks, personal robberies, aggravated assaults, and domestic violence abound in cities such as Belize City, Belize, Kingston, Jamaica, and Port of Spain, Trinidad and Tobago. Moreover, the use of illegal drugs and crime go hand in hand because, in many cases, drug users will do just about anything to obtain enough drugs to satisfy a habit. The crimes committed most frequently by drug abusers are theft, prostitution and drug peddling. This list, however, does not exhaust the types of crimes committed, as exemplified by stories of business executives who have embezzled company funds and of workers who have intentionally damaged goods in order to purchase them at a reduced rate and sell them for additional money to support their drug habit. Further, while all crimes are not necessarily connected with the acquisition of drugs, many are committed by individuals while under their influence.

These problems have created and continue to create huge social costs for these various countries by undermining their populations' sense of trust, eroding social capital, elevating the level of fear and anxiety and, in some cases, destroying the sense of community and social cohesion. An increasing proportion of limited public resources is required to strengthen the level of police enforcement, support the growing prison population, finance the demands placed on the judicial system, and provide health care for the victims of crime and violence. In Antigua and Barbuda, for example, the cost of crime, including maintaining the police, courts and prisons, increased from US$4 128 756 to US$7 312 183 in 1985 to US$13 147 571 in 1988. During this same period, the number of cases reported to and accepted by the police ranged from 7095 in 1980 to 6469 in 1985 to 6561 in 1988.[37]

In Trinidad and Tobago, the conservatively estimated cost of spending six months in prison was US$42 217: US$9205 for the cost of imprisonment, US$11 197 for cost of arrest by the police, US$11 015 for five court appearances, and US$10 800 for loss of income.[38] Other costs include the installation of expensive security systems, including armed guards by homeowners and businesses. Even more serious is the loss of potential revenues from investors and tourists, who choose other destinations as a result of the threat of crime. Further, estimates indicate that drug trafficking and related criminal activity cost Barbados approximately $200 million annually; that Trinidad and Tobago spends more than 30 per cent of its health budget on drug rehabilitation programs; and that Jamaica's costs of increased policing and national security operations to counter trafficking and violent drug related crime have doubled.[39]

## Responses

At the 1994 Summit of the Americas, Caribbean countries agreed with other countries in the hemisphere that drug trafficking and money laundering constitute serious challenges to the maintenance of law and order throughout the region and may threaten the integrity and stability of governments, financial systems, and commerce. As a result, governments began to further coordinate strategies to counteract this threat. At their 1995 summit in Guyana, for example, CARICOM heads of government agreed to coordinate regional security efforts and assistance requests, including technical advice and equipment and, to develop, to the extent possible, common legislation against money laundering. Bankers are encouraged to be diligent when dealing with clients, to keep good records, and to look out for suspicious transactions.

The global dimensions of this twin problem led to a three day meeting of the UNDCP in Barbados from 15–17 May 1996 to develop an action plan to counter this threat. More than 250 delegates from every Caribbean country participated alongside delegations from North America and Europe, including from Britain, France, the Netherlands and Spain – the countries with the closest traditional links with the Caribbean region. Participating as well were representatives from Australia, Greece, Italy, the Commonwealth Secretariat, Interpol, the WTO and various UN organizations, and from several non-governmental organizations, including the American Bar Association (ABA), the Addiction Research Foundation and Drug Abuse Resistance Education (DARE). This diverse group of participants agreed on two interrelated aspects of the drug problem: (1) the Caribbean countries form a geostrategic zone of democracy that is central to peace and security in the Western Hemisphere; and (2) one of the most crucial problems facing the Caribbean is the trafficking of illicit drugs from South America to Europe and North America. And it is this transit traffic that poses one of the greatest threats to their democratic endurance and, by extension, their peace and security.[40] The group agreed on collaborative initiatives to address the various dimensions of the drug problem, from police and customs interdiction, to prosecution and money laundering, demand reduction and rehabilitation.

The meeting acknowledged a number of structural problems that prevent Caribbean countries from being more effective in their anti-drug efforts. For example, the different legal jurisdictions and legal systems – English, French, Dutch, and Spanish – undermine the ability of the region to harmonize and implement anti-drug legislation. Further, drug offenders fail to get convicted in the courts in the region partly because of weaknesses in the prosecutorial systems. For example, when a drug trafficker is caught in the Caribbean, invariably he or she immediately retains the services of a highly paid, experienced lawyer. Typically, these lawyers can move from one jurisdiction to another with little difficulty. Moreover, they have acquired a level of expertise in drug cases that far surpasses that of the underpaid and overworked prosecuting attorneys of area governments. As a partial solution, the group agreed to develop a regional cadre of experienced drug prosecutors, who would be readily available to assist any of these countries in prosecuting traffickers.[41]

Among their efforts to combat the trafficking in illicit narcotics, Caribbean countries have signed a number of bilateral treaties and agreements with the US, including Mutual Legal Assistance Treaties (MLATs), extradition treaties, overflight and maritime agreements. MLATs are negotiated between Caribbean governments and the US Department of State in cooperation with the US Department of Justice to facilitate cooperation in criminal matters, including money laundering and asset forfeiture. Some MLATs, know as shiprider agreements, were very controversial. They require US and individual Caribbean countries to allow armed law enforcement officials on each other's coast guard vessel and Caribbean countries to approve hot pursuit of suspected drug traffickers by US vessels in their territorial waters. Moreover, they sanction 'counter drug' patrols and give US law enforcers the right to enforce the laws of the country that is party to the agreement. Further, US officials assigned to the coast guard vessels of Caribbean countries would authorize Caribbean ships to enforce US laws outside the country's territorial waters while helping Caribbean coast guard officials board vessels suspected of ferrying drugs. However, Barbados was very concerned that the agreements did not grant any reciprocal rights of hot pursuit that would allow Caribbean countries to pursue suspected drug traffickers into US territory such as the US Virgin Islands and Puerto Rico.

While Antigua and Barbuda, Dominica, Grenada, St Kitts and Nevis, St Vincent and the Grenadines, and Trinidad and Tobago, quickly signed shiprider agreements, Barbados, and Jamaica initially refused to do so. There were several concerns. First, proposed agreements did not guarantee compensation for any of these countries should any US official act improperly in during a drug operation within that country's jurisdiction. Secondly, all US officials involved in anti-narcotics activities would be granted diplomatic immunity, which means that none of these officials may be arrested or sued for actions undertaken in the performance of their duties. Thirdly, Caribbean countries would have the right to dispose of assets seized in their respective territorial waters while the US would have the right to control and dispose of any assets seized outside of the individual country's territory. Fourthly, US officials would be permitted to use force in the process of stopping and boarding any commercial or private vessel, including fishing boats, flying the flags of the various countries, in and out of their waters, if those officials suspect the vessel to be transporting drugs.

Another major concern was that the proposals did not address the issue of gun running; neither did the United States offer technical nor other types of assistance. A complicating factor was the US policy of repatriating individuals convicted of narcotics related crimes in the US to their respective countries, all of which lack the law enforcement and economic infrastructure to receive and resettle them. The influx of repatriates, especially under current economic and social conditions, will only produce further hardships for these countries. Approximately 9000 criminals were repatriated to the Caribbean between 1986 and 1994. Of these, 208 were returned to Guyana, 401 to Trinidad and Tobago, 3396 to Jamaica, and 3684 to the Dominican Republic (see Table 6. 4). It is highly unlikely that many of these deportees, many of whom are hard core criminals, will resettle in their native lands as model citizens. What is more likely is that they will remain active in various aspects of the international illicit drug trade as well as other criminal activities, including gun running and crimes against property and person.

*Table 6.4*   US Deportees for Narcotics Violations by Nationality

| Year | Bah | Bar | Bel | Dom | DR | Guy | Hai | Jam | TnT | Other | Totals |
|---|---|---|---|---|---|---|---|---|---|---|---|
| 1980 | – | – | – | – | 3 | 1 | – | 4 | 2 | 2 | 12 |
| 1981 | – | – | – | – | 2 | 1 | 1 | 4 | 2 | 2 | 12 |
| 1982 | – | – | – | – | 3 | – | 1 | 7 | 3 | 3 | 17 |
| 1983 | 1 | – | 3 | – | 2 | – | – | 7 | 2 | 1 | 16 |
| 1984 | 1 | 2 | – | – | 9 | 1 | – | 21 | 4 | 6 | 44 |
| 1985 | 1 | 1 | 5 | – | 19 | 2 | 1 | 31 | 6 | 3 | 69 |
| 1986 | 4 | – | 8 | – | 18 | 4 | 4 | 40 | 4 | 4 | 86 |
| 1987 | 7 | – | 9 | – | 54 | – | 33 | 82 | 1 | 2 | 188 |
| 1988 | 16 | – | 20 | – | 164 | 9 | 53 | 134 | 23 | 16 | 435 |
| 1989 | 7 | – | 16 | 16 | 195 | 20 | 61 | 264 | 31 | 19 | 629 |
| 1990 | 17 | – | 38 | 28 | 378 | 26 | 97 | 416 | 39 | 21 | 1060 |
| 1991 | 18 | – | 36 | 11 | 348 | 33 | 93 | 381 | 49 | 37 | 1006 |
| 1992 | 33 | – | 55 | 17 | 742 | 73 | 118 | 688 | 63 | 48 | 1837 |
| 1993 | 38 | 24 | 64 | 20 | 847 | 53 | 127 | 686 | 99 | 45 | 2003 |
| 1994 | 45 | 27 | 65 | 23 | 919 | 68 | 98 | 705 | 92 | 43 | 2085 |
| Totals | 188 | 54 | 319 | 115 | 3703 | 291 | 687 | 3470 | 420 | 252 | 9499 |

*Notes*: Bah=Bahamas; Bar=Barbados; Bel=Belize; Dom=Dominica; DR=Dominican Republic; Guy=Guyana; Hai=Haiti; Jam=Jamaica; TnT=Trinidad and Tobago; Other includes Antigua and Barbuda; Bermuda; the British Virgin Islands; the Cayman Islands, Cuba; the Netherlands Antilles and Eastern Caribbean islands.
*Source: Annual Statistical Report of the Immigration and Naturalization Service* (various years).

The situation in Guyana seems typical. Some 1053 persons were deported to Guyana in 1996 from 23 countries, including countries in the Caribbean, North and South America and Europe, for offences ranging from overstaying their time to attempted murder. Of these, 402 were deported from French Guiana, 219 from the US, and 182 from Suriname. Police in Guyana have become increasingly concerned for public safety due to increasing incidents of violent crime involving deportees. Such crimes have included drug-related Mafia-style executions, kidnapping, police murders with high-powered weapons and illegal migration.[42] Similar accounts reflect the situation in Jamaica where 61 per cent of the 1434 deportees in 1994 were repatriated from the US, and where a total of 872 or 61 per cent of the returnees were deported for illicit drugs and/or weapons charges. Many of the deportees have been linked to criminal activity in Jamaica, especially the importation and use of firearms, the illicit drug trade and money laundering.[43]

## Conclusion

Despite a few success stories in controlling the supply, production and trafficking of illegal drugs, the scope of the narcotics problem today transcends law enforcement and public health questions, posing what is arguably the greatest single threat to the security and integrity and economic and social development of the Caribbean. The narcotics trade stands to undermine governments and officials through corruption, intimidation, and economic destabilization; drug money also can – and in some cases do – buy governments, finance political parties and purchase votes. The ebb and flow and sheer volume of drug money have a destabilizing effect on the supply of money and exchange markets.

For the Caribbean, the problem stems partly from the consequences of US policy toward the Caribbean, including its drastic reductions in foreign assistance, NAFTA's erosion of the competitive edge that Caribbean countries enjoyed in the textile industry, US attempts to secure access to the banana markets of the EU at the expense of Caribbean producers, and US criminal repatriation policy. These factors combine to engender economic dislocations in many Caribbean states, and threaten to undermine the democratic foundations of these countries, producing collateral problems, including political instability, increased levels of illicit drug trafficking, use, abuse and money laundering, and increased levels of legal and illegal migration to the US.

According to former Barbados Minister of International Trade and Business, Philip Goddard, 'there is a direct correlation between the efforts to contain drug trafficking and the maintenance of strong economies in the region'.[44] This means that success at reduction depends on the overall economic situation in the Caribbean. But, there must be other initiatives. The economies of the region must become reoriented to the dynamics of globalism. This entails a vision and derivative policy geared toward, at a minimum, a major investment in human capital, as is being attempted in Barbados. The information age demands skills in data processing, data transcription, and software development and manufacturing. With the Lomé Agreements due to expire in the year 2000 and with pressure coming from the US, Caribbean countries should not count on a renewal of that program. They should begin to negotiate support for human resource development to avoid further marginalization in this global, technology-driven economy.

## Notes

1   Huntington defines a 'wave of democratization' as a group of countries that undergoes the transition from nondemocratic to democratic systems of government during a specific period and that significantly outnumbers a group of transitions in the opposite direction during the same period. See his *The Third Wave: Democratization in the Late Twentieth Century*, (Norman, Oklahoma, University of Oklahoma Press, 1991); and, 'How Countries Democratize,' *Political Science Quarterly*, Vol. 108, No. 4, (1991), pp. 579–616.

2   The democratic system did not function in Guyana from 1974 to 1992, notably during the rule of Forbes Burnham and the People's National Congress (PNC); it did not function in Grenada between 1979 and 1983, when the New Jewel Movement (NJM) suspended the constitution; and it has been malfunctioning in Antigua and Barbuda, where there have been claims of electoral fraud and corruption related to the empowerment of the Antigua Labour Party (ALP), since 1976.

3   See Raymond Gastil, *Freedom in the World: Political Rights and Civil Liberties*, (New York: Freedom House, 1972–95).

4   See Melvin Claxton, 'Antigua Hotbed of Corruption: Top Officials Linked to Guns, Drugs, and Murder', *Virgin Islands Daily News* (3 March 1994).

5   See Anthony P. Maingot, 'Offshore Secrecy Centers and the Necessary Role of States: Bucking the Trend', *Journal of Interamerican Studies and World Affairs*, Vol. 37, No. 4 (1995), p. 3.

6   See British Information Services, New York, 'The Problem of Drugs in the Caribbean: A European Union Initiative' (September 1996). Also, see Baytoram Ramharack, 'Drug Trafficking and Money Laundering in the Caribbean 'Mini'-States and Dependent Territories: The US Response', *Round Table*, Vol. 335 (1995), pp. 319–41; Ivelaw L. Griffith, 'Drugs and Security in the Commonwealth Caribbean', *Journal of Commonwealth and Comparative Politics*, Vol. 21,

No. 2 (1993), pp. 70–102; Rensselaer W. Lee, III, 'Global Reach: The Threat of International Drug Trafficking', *Current History* (May 1995), pp. 207–12; and Clifford E. Griffin, *Democracy and Neoliberalism in the Developing World: Lessons From the Anglophone Caribbean* (Aldershot: Avebury Publishers, 1997), esp. ch 7–10.

7 See Robert Keohane and Joseph Nye, *Transnational Relations and World Politics* (Cambridge, Massachusetts: Harvard University Press, 1971), p. xii.

8 I am indebted to Ivelaw L. Griffith of Florida International University for this insight.

9 See 'A Dynamic New World', *Business Week* (18 November 1994), p. 22.

10 See *Economic Commission for Latin America and the Caribbean /CDCC Newsletter,* (January-March 1995) pp. 1–4; and *Poverty Reduction and Human Resource Development in the Caribbean,* World Bank Report No. 15342 LAC (May 1996), p. vii.

11 Larry Rohter, 'Impact of NAFTA Pounds Economies of the Caribbean', *New York Times* (30 January 1997), pp. A1, A4.

12 See Charles Skeete, 'Performance and Prospects of the Caribbean Group for Cooperation in Economic Development', paper prepared for the World Peace Foundation, October 1990.

13 Under the US Federal Government's 936 Loan Program, US private investors were provided with tax rebates for investing in Puerto Rico. The program was expanded subsequently to include other Caribbean countries. However, the Dominican Republic and Jamaica became the main secondary beneficiaries while the Eastern Caribbean did not secure any benefits from this program. (Interview with officer at in the US Embassy's economic and political division, Bridgetown, Barbados, 5 May 1997)

14 Rohter, op. cit.

15 Rohter, op. cit.

16 See 'EU Banana Rules Fair', *Newsletter of the Delegations of the European Commission in Trinidad and Tobago, Barbados and the Eastern Caribbean,* Vols 4 and 5, 1995.

17 See 'Will West Indies Bananas Survive?', *Express* (26 May 1996), p. 8.

18 Not only does power asymmetry reflect the lack of success among Caribbean banana producers to penetrate US markets and underscore their difficulties in maintaining preferential access to European markets, but it also explains the success of companies such as Chiquita at playing the influence peddling game. For example, Lindner and his top executives reputedly began to funnel more than $US500 000 into the Democratic National Committee on 12 April 1996, the day after US Trade Representative Mickey Kantor agreed to plead Chiquita's case at the WTO. See Michael Weisskopf and Viveca Novak, 'The Busy Back-Door Men', *Time* (31 March 1997), p. 40; also William Safire, 'Bananagate', *New York Times* (26 March 1997), p. A19.

19 See 'Straight Case – Bananas or Drugs', *Caribbean Week* (22 June–5 July 1996), pp. 17–18.

20 See UN Economic Commission for Latin America and the Caribbean, *Offshore Financial Centers in the Caribbean,* LC/CAR/G.441 (31 March 1995).

21 Countries that do not levy taxes on foreign companies are considered tax paradises; countries where taxes are levied only on internal taxable events, or

not at all, or at very low rates, on profits from foreign sources are considered tax shelters.

22  See Financial Crimes and Money Laundering Report', in UN Economic Commission for Latin America and the Caribbean/Caribbean Development and Cooperation Committee, *Offshore Financial Centers in the Caribbean*, LC/CAR/g.441, 31 March 1995.

23  See *Offshore Financial Centers in the Caribbean*, op. cit.

24  See US Department of State, *International Narcotics Control Strategy Report 1996;* interview conducted at the US Information Agency, Bridgetown, Barbados (August 1996); Government of Nevis, Ministry of Tourism, Trade, Industry, Planning and Development *Memorandum*, (10 October 1996); also Government of the British Virgin Islands, *Memorandum* (22 January 1997).

25  See Louis Kraar, 'The Drug Trade', *Fortune*, (20 June 1988), pp. 27–38.

26  See Maingot, 'Offshore Secrecy Centers...'pp. 1–24.

27  See Phil Williams and Ernesto U. Savona, (eds), *The United Nations and Transnational Organized Crime*, (London: Frank Cass, 1996), p. 21.

28  Ibid., p. 21.

29  See Douglas Farah, 'Caribbean Key to US Drug Trade', *Washington Post* (23 September 1996), pp. A1, A9.

30  Ibid.

31  Quoted in Melvin Claxton, 'V.I. Drugs Linked to Antigua: Cops Pin Crime Rise on Smuggled Dope', *Virgin Islands Daily News* (3 March 1994).

32  Astaphan gained international notoriety in the wake of the Seoul Olympics after admitting that he supplied disgraced Canadian sprinter Ben Johnson anabolic steroids.

33  See Melvin Claxton, 'Drug Sealers Prosper in Antigua: Tentacles Stretch From Colombia to V.I.', *Virgin Islands Daily News* (4 March 1994).

34  See 'St Kitts and Nevis Prime Minister Says Drug Money is Major Election Issue', *Democrat* (20 November 1993).

35  See 'Simmonds Says Forces of Law Will Not Be Intimidated', and 'Policeman Killed', *New York Carib News* (25 October 1994), p. 14; 'Dr. Douglas Responds to US State Department's Report on St Kitts-Nevis', *New York Carib News* (28 March 1995), p. 4; also, Farah, op. cit.

36  See *New York Carib News* (4 March 1997), p. 8.

37  See Government of Antigua and Barbuda, *Statistical Yearbook of Antigua 1988* (St Johns, 1988), pp. 46–54.

38  The majority of prisoners, 65 per cent, spend up to six months in prison. The cost of lost earnings is averaged at US$1800 per month. Although the cost of legal representation is not included in the overall estimate, five court appearances is not unusual due to a variety of institutional and resource factors such as the heavy workload of the magistrates to the lack of transport to take prisoners to court on the designated day. See *Poverty Reduction and Human Resource Development in the Caribbean*, op. cit., pp. 58–9.

39  See Richard Cox, 'EC Official: Drugs Infesting Region', *New York Carib News*, 28 May 1996, p. 3. Given the huge increase in the volume of trafficking and enormous sums of money involved, one could assume that the costs of drug interdiction have doubled since the early 1990s.

40  See *Proceedings of the UNDCP Regional Meeting on Drug Control Cooperation in the Caribbean*, UNDCP/CAR/1996/INF.4/Rev.1 (23 May 1996).

41  See P.A. Penfold, 'Fighting Drugs in the Caribbean: A Regional Approach', *Courier*, No. 161, (January–February 1997), pp. 10–12.

42  See 'Deported Criminals Pose Problems', *Caribbean Week*, Vol. 8. No. 10 (15–28 February 1997).

43  See *Economic and Social Survey Jamaica 1994*, op. cit.

44  See Farah, op. cit.

# 7
# Drugs and Post-Intervention Political Economy in Haiti and Panama

*Orlando J. Pérez*

This chapter examines the political economy dynamics of Haiti and Panama after the 1994 and 1989 interventions, and the role of drug trafficking and money laundering in those dynamics. No other countries in the Caribbean Basin – with the exception of Mexico – have been more closely linked to the United States and have had more impact on US hemispheric policy than Panama and Haiti. The United States has intervened militarily in both countries several times during the twentieth century.[1] Moreover, issues such as immigration, drug production and trafficking, and money laundering, so important to US domestic politics, have been at the forefront of US relations with both countries.

The latest US interventions in Haiti and Panama – in 1994 and 1989 respectively – sought to 'restore' democracy and wrest control of the government from the hands of corrupt military dictatorships. The military regimes in Panama and Haiti had been able to maintain themselves in power through repression, manipulation of elections, and general corruption including heavy involvement in drug trafficking and other illicit enterprises. In Panama and Haiti the military had each established a 'mafiacracy'. Among the issues this chapter seeks to explore is the extent to which the new civilian governments in these countries have been able to curb drug trafficking and money laundering. First, I outline a theoretical framework for analysing a country's involvement in the drug trade. Secondly, I will examine the political economy of each country before and after the interventions.

## Theoretical framework

Five criteria may be used to explain a nation's involvement in drug trafficking and other illicit activities:

1. the institutional weakness of the state;
2. the geographical location and size of the country;
3. the nature of the political culture; primarily, the culture of the nation's elites;
4. the presence of large numbers of legal and illegal immigrants living outside the territorial limits of the nation-state; and
5. the nature of a country's entrepreneurial class.

Some criteria may not apply to all countries involved in illicit activities. However, the more characteristics a nation exhibits the more susceptible it will be to penetration by drug traffickers and other illicit enterprises.

Institutional weakness is a necessary, but not sufficient condition for a country to be a haven for drug traffickers. Weak states[2] are unable to exercise control over many social and economic relationships within their territory. This factor makes them ideal places for the growth of illicit enterprises. Officials of such weak states often use the apparatus of government to enrich themselves. Thus the state is no longer an independent arbiter of social relations, but is actively involved in illicit activities. In addition to their regular salaries, state officials receive perquisites of office either as bribes or by siphoning public moneys from the various government agencies or state enterprises for private ends. Moreover, state officials use their positions to assist those involved in illicit enterprises in exchange for money or other benefits.[3]

Weak states are consistent with global post-cold war moves toward liberalization and economic integration, which have led to increased cross-border flows of goods and services and provide a golden opportunity to illicit entrepreneurs to hide their profits among the licit flows. All nations, but particularly those of the Third World, are under increasing pressures to remove trade barriers and loosen banking and other commercial restrictions.[4] Ironically, states have relinquished control of licit markets while attempting to exercise greater control over illicit flows.

These controls come primarily from 'policing' of borders and from industry specific regulations.[5] Policing efforts extend to Transnational Criminal Organizations (TCO). However, TCOs are extremely problematic for weak states because they will seek to change state policy – on extradition, banking regulation, and taxes, for example – to suit their needs. Weak states are largely unable to withstand such pressures. Through violence or the threat of violence, TCOs seek to intimidate and coerce state officials, for example, judges.[6] Furthermore, TCOs entice lawyers and coopt the business sector with money and power,[7] becoming an extreme example of a special interest group, with ability to influence and sometimes control state policy. Special interest groups, however, further reduce the efficiency of the state in reallocating resources and generally 'stultify' national economies.[8] The interaction involving weak states, the market and non-state actors ultimately calls into question state sovereignty. A state which struggles to physically control its borders as well as capital flows through its economic system, suffers from 'ailing sovereignty'.

Geography and size constitute another factor. Both tend to affect the nature and direction of the flow of goods and services. Countries, such as Haiti and Panama, located in strategically important international trade routes, or in close proximity to large consumers of licit and illicit goods, will inevitably attract the attention of those involved in commercial enterprises. Geography and size also shape the pattern of integration into the world economy. Some nations are assigned the role of cheap labor providers for extraterritorial manufacturing interests and/or transshipment points for goods and services flowing to the First World. Geography and size contribute to the level of economic dependence a country suffers, and thus can contribute to a state's weakness.

Political culture is another important factor why countries are susceptible to illicit enterprises. A nation's political culture – understood as the pattern of beliefs and attitudes about politics – influences greatly the atmosphere in which illicit activities are permitted. Furthermore, the nature of élite political culture is particularly important in shaping the behavior of business and government élites. An élite political culture that permits, and indeed encourages, corruption serves as a breeding ground for illicit activities. In countries were the political culture sees the state as a means of personal enrichment, illicit activities are common. In an atmosphere where élites are openly engaged in illegal and corrupt practices, the poor are readily enticed into illicit activities. For the latter, illicit enterprises become the sole means of surviving in a generalized climate of corruption. Under these circumstances the ability of the state to fight illegal activities is extremely reduced.

Migration is another factor that influences a nation's involvement in illicit activities. A large immigrant group with relatively weak loyalties to the host country provides an excellent distribution network for illegal imports. Moreover, the remittances from immigrants can also be linked to illicit activities.[9] Finally, the nature of entrepreneurship affects a nation's involvement in drug trafficking and other illegal activities. The sector engaged in drug trafficking is a component of business that operates with the expectation of high short-term profits. The process of globalization has created an 'entrepreneurial free-for-all' in which transnational organized crime operates with potential high payoffs and little risk from law enforcement or regulation.[10]

All five of the factors noted above are neither necessary nor sufficient for a country to be implicated in illicit activities. However, to the extent that a nation meets all five criteria they will be far more susceptible to drug trafficking, money laundering and other illegal enterprises. As the discussion below shows, Haiti and Panama are two cases where the five factors have featured in variable ways, making those countries deeply vulnerable to various drug and drug-related activities.

## Corruption and the development of Haiti's prebendary state

The small and poverty-stricken nation of Haiti, occupying the western third of the island of Hispañola, is among the few nations in the hemisphere that meet all five criteria mentioned above. Since its birth, after a bloody revolution in 1804, the Haitian state has been extremely weak *vis-à-vis* elements of the economic and political élite and has been used by the élites as a means of acquiring personal wealth. For all these reasons the Haitian state has been classified as a 'prebendary state', one in which a political regime where those who hold office or political power live off politics.[11] Haitian politics is characterized by cults of personality and a reliance on spoils and revenge. In such an environment the state fails to act as an independent arbiter of social relations.

Throughout most of Haitian history an educated urban and largely mulatto élite used the state to enrich itself by any means possible. Its members paid little taxes or customs duties, or even their utility bills. With these gains they manipulated the ambitious military leaders they placed in office. The military leaders, in turn, made sure they enriched themselves as quickly as possible. This entailed extensive involvement in illicit activities.

Geographically the country is strategically located halfway between the major drug producers in South America and the United States, the world's single largest drug-consuming country. The country sits on the eastern side of the windward passage, one of the most important maritime routes in the hemisphere. Moreover, Haiti and its neighbor to the east, the Dominican Republic, maintain an extremely porous frontier. All these factors make Haiti an ideal transshipment point for drugs into the United States. Moreover, in Haiti, a deeply embedded culture of predation has fostered autocracy and corruption, extreme social injustice, and economic stagnation, all of which are conducive to illicit activities. This political culture has developed as a result of historically defined factors such as traditional African culture, slavery, a bloody war of liberation, the reimposition of relations of élite dominance and mass submission, chronic cycles of tyranny and chaos, and the effects of a prolonged US occupation.

As regards the fourth criteria, migration, an estimated 1.5 million Haitians – about one-fourth of all Haitians – live outside of Haiti. They live in such cities as New York, Boston, Miami, Chicago, Montreal, and Paris as well as in Africa, the Dominican Republic, and other parts of the Caribbean. These immigrants have had a tremendous impact on Haitian politics and economics. Haitians living abroad remit over $100 million back home to families and relatives. During 1993, the US State Department publicly denounced such transfers for spoiling the already porous OAS embargo against the military regime.[12] However, along with hundreds of thousands of ordinary Haitians, most of them law-abiding citizens, the Haitian diaspora in New York and other cities included members of FRAPH (Front for the Advancement and Progress of Haiti), the civilian arm of the military regime. By the spring of 1994, FRAPH had begun importing terror into the US. FRAPH members engaged in intimidation of opponents of the military government, and FRAPH leaders were accused of engaging in a wide variety of corrupt practices, including drug trafficking. FRAPH members in the US serve as a convenient network for the importation of drugs into the country.[13]

While many diaspora Haitians returned to Haiti after the US military intervention of September 1994, many more have remained in their host countries. Some have stayed because of the continued economic problems facing the country. Others remain as integral parts of networks of illicit activities. After the intervention, custom checks and import duties have all been relaxed to encourage the rapid replenishment of goods from abroad. This makes Haiti even more porous than in the past. Between 1791 and 1804, a seesaw revolutionary war destroyed much of the plantation economy and countryside and, in substantial measure, uprooted the European planter class. The French were driven out; nearly all Europeans went with them. But not all the free people of color (mostly mulattoes) left; many fought on the side of the revolution. On 1 January 1804, General Jean Jacques Dessalines proclaimed victory. The revolution was triumphant.[14]

It was during the early years of Haitian independence that the bourgeoisie learned to siphon off every productive effort of the agrarian masses to enhance their personal consumption; and its has always been a consumption that results in zero expansion of domestic production. Without a strong political and economic infrastructure, the essentially adequate peasant production could not be harnessed efficaciously for the general good. Haiti was to become a permanent case study of the debilitating limitations of a peasant economy. Nearly two centuries of political independence have not altered the slide to isolation, poverty, and abandonment of the tropical state that was once the richest colony in the world. By the end of the nineteenth century, Haiti had become the poorest state in the Americas; and it remains so to this day.

Haiti eventually found itself occupied by the United States military in 1915, an occupation that lasted 19 years. The US dissolved the political institutions, which were not reformed until 1930, and controlled the customs receipts until 1947. Despite their promise to reform the political system, the Americans did little to stabilize local politics, and on their departure very little had really changed in Haitian life.

In 1957, François 'Papa Doc' Duvalier, a physician and folklorist, handily won an army-supervised presidential election by appealing to nationalism, racism, and an impenetrable mysticism masquerading as voodoo. Within two years, he had consolidated his position by eliminating his opponents, real and imagined. Duvalier went on to challenge the authority of the army by creating a private army of thugs known as the Tontons Macoutes (named euphemistically as the National Security Volunteers (VSN)). The macoutes were recruited overwhelmingly from the poor, Black and illiterate in a calculated exploitation of poverty.

Duvalier revolutionized Haitian politics and in the process widened and deepened the structure of corruption. The end result of this was parallel systems of private and public corruption. In the private sector the old mulatto élite, displaced from state politics, continued its habits of avoiding taxes, corrupting public officials and expatriating capital. Eventually, especially under Jean-Claude 'Baby Doc' Duvalier, this private sector corruption began to function symbiotically with corruption in the public sector. Corruption became the essential link between the public and private sectors.

Duvalier gave the nation a new constitution in 1964 which declared him president for life. In 1971, shortly before his death, another constitutional change gave the president the power to name his successor (subject to ratification by the electorate), and he named his only son, Jean-Claude as successor. Under Jean-Claude individual senior military officers were encouraged to take private initiatives outside the institution. The military went into business. Beginning in the mid-1980s, a steady stream of evidence emerged linking the Haitian military leaders to the drug trade.

Although less dictatorial and sadistic than his father, Jean-Claude 'Baby Doc' Duvalier was overthrown in February 1986 amid rising economic, political, and social discontent. Political power quickly reverted to the army, with Armed Forces chief General Henri Namphy taking control of a National Government Council (CNG). The drug business became the 'engine' that drove the military and overwhelmed the island's commerce, providing the basis for generalized smuggling and a brisk money laundering operation. The drug business is estimated to be worth about $250 million a year and has involved government agencies devoted to 'public service', and government corporations such as the Port Authority (which controls imports and exports as well as access to both military and international airports) and a state-owned flour mill.[15]

In 1988, Massachusetts Senator John Kerry who chaired the Senate Subcommittee on Terrorism, Narcotics and International Operations, held hearings on the drug trade in Haiti and Central America. One of the witnesses, George Morales, a convicted drug trafficker, stated 'I used the Isle of Haiti mainly as a parking lot, as a place that I would place my aircraft so they could be repaired and also so that I could leave the city of Port-au-Prince without having to do the paperwork necessary to get permission to fly an aircraft over the island...'. Senator Kerry pressed Morales regarding the transshipment of drugs through Haiti, and Morales responded 'Yes! it is something which is done fairly commonly...'. Morales assured Senator Kerry that Haiti was used as a bridge to move drugs from Colombia to the United States, and he claimed to have spoken to Michel François, head of the Port-au-Prince police, in the offices of Pablo Escobar (then head of the Medellín cartel). He also stated that François 'protected the drugs in Haiti...'. Moreover, he implicated General Prosper Avril, leader of the military junta from 1987 to 1990, of being actively involved in dealings with the Medellín cartel. In late 1993, Senator Kerry concluded that 'there is a partnership made in hell, in cocaine, and in dollars between the Colombian cartels and the Haitian military'.[16]

In November 1993, the *New York Times* revealed that the Haitian Intelligence Service, an élite unit created and trained by the CIA in the mid-1980s to combat the drug business and to monitor internal Haitian politics, had actually become involved in trading drugs, machinating against the Aristide government, and committing acts of terror against Aristide supporters. The report indicated that three former chiefs of the

Haitian Intelligence Service – Col. Ernst Prudhomme, Col. Diderot Sylvain and Col. Leopold Derjeune – were named by the United States Treasury Department in a November 1992 order for seizure of their assets in the US.

Col. Jean-Claude Paul, commander of the country's main military unit, the Dessalines Battalion, is reputed to have run Haiti's cocaine-transshipment business. He allegedly used an airstrip on his ranch for deliveries and worked closely with the Medellín cartel, incorporating the members of his battalion and Tontons Macoutes into his operation. Paul's drug business expanded after Duvalier left Haiti. Ernest Bennett, Michèle Duvalier's father, had also been involved with cocaine, and Jean-Claude Duvalier had a useful airstrip on his ranch as well. When Jean-Claude Duvalier left the country, a portion of the drug business was open to the next taker. The United States decided in 1987 to target Col. Paul as a major international drug trader. Col. Paul was eventually indicted by a Miami grand jury on charges of conspiring to ship narcotics to the United States. In September 1988, after a coup staged by Gen. Prosper Avril, Jean-Claude Paul was sacked. He conveniently died a few weeks later from an apparent poisoning.[17]

For the first time since the departure of Duvalier, elections were scheduled for November 1987. The elections were annulled in the midst of state-sponsored violence and repression. Fraudulent elections were held in January 1988 and political scientist Leslie Manigat was named president, but this government lasted only five months. The military continued its repressive rule until February 1991. Under internal and external pressures the regime scheduled another round of elections for December 1990. They were won by Father Jean-Bertrand Aristide, a priest of the Salesian Order, ardent proponent of liberation theology, and one of the most outspoken leaders of the radicalized ecclesiastical base community movement *Ti Légliz* (Little Church). The fusion of mysticism, martyrdom, and antimacoutism added a messianic character to Aristide's leadership and won him the devotion of a population that was ready to accept a savior.

Aristide ruled for seven months before being overthrown by the military with the support of ex-Duvalierist and members of the Haitian bourgeoisie. During those seven months, Aristide made significant efforts at restructuring the Haitian military. He and his prime minister were well aware that any reforms in the public administration and economy would not stand a chance unless Aristide first neutralized the traditional power bases of the prebendary state system. This meant reforming the military institution and dismantling its paramilitary organization. Aristide began by requesting the retirement (or reassignment to obscure posts) of several top-ranking officers who had controlled the armed forces under past regimes, and promoting or commissioning new officers thought to be more supportive of democratization. Among the presumed reform-minded officers was Col. Raoul Cédras (the leader of the coup that eventually ousted Aristide in September 1991). Cédras was promoted in July 1991 to the rank of brigadier general and named interim commander in chief of the army.[18] In 1994, Patrick Elie, Aristide's coordinator for Haiti's anti-drug program, accused Gen. Cédras of being involved in the drug business.

In addition to the reshuffling, the reforms contemplated for the army included three essential measures: separating the army from the police, disarming the paramilitary organization, and dismantling the system of section chiefs in the rural sector. While the Aristide government did not succeed in fully implementing the military reforms, it made significant strides in combating corruption, contraband activities, drug trafficking, and human right abuses. The government established an interministerial commission in February and a second independent commission in August 1991 to investigate and bring to justice those accused of crimes and massacres between 1986 and 1990. Aristide also replaced several 'compromised' Supreme Court justices along with many other judges in the countryside.[19]

The military hierarchy was angered by Aristide's attacks against corruption and drug trafficking and worried that the warming relations between the Aristide government and the US Embassy in Haiti would lead to greater drug enforcement activities in the country. They were also restive about the formation of a presidential security force that would be loyal to Aristide. Moreover, Aristide's inflammatory rhetoric angered the bourgeoisie (which had been against him from the start), without the real ability to carry out his threats against them. Under these circumstances the military launched the 30 September 1991 coup that ousted Aristide.

On 5 November 1992, President Bush ordered US compliance with a UN and OAS sponsored economic embargo of Haiti. The embargo, however, was tough only on paper. There were many reports of drugs slipping out of Haiti despite the embargo. On 15 April 1993, for instance, the US Coast Guard discovered 100 pounds of cocaine on board a Haitian freighter on the Miami River. That same month a United States Congressional delegation visited Haiti and reported that major Colombian cocaine trafficker Fernando Burgos 'continues to live and flourish' in Haiti, untouched by Haitian narcotics services. In 1993 the US ranked

Haiti eighth on a list of 10 nations shipping drugs to the southeast United States. Nonetheless, there were few charges brought against the military. Despite the Haitian military's brutal history of repression, its known corruption and involvement in drug trafficking, and its aversion to democracy, US officials still believed that they could 'professionalize' that institution and convert the high command into ardent democrats.

Tightening economic sanctions and diplomatic pressure failed to remove the Haitian military from power. By September 1994 President Clinton was under increasing domestic and international pressure to act militarily to remove the Haitian military leaders and restore Aristide to power. The president went on national television to announce and justify the impending military intervention. Former President Jimmy Carter, retired Gen. Colin Powell, and Sen. Sam Nunn of Georgia were dispatched to negotiate the terms of the junta's departure and the mode of entry of the 20 000–strong US-led multinational force. On 15 October 1994, jubilant crowds welcomed President Aristide back to Haiti.

The military has been abolished, but the oligarchy remains. The prospects for economic development and a substantive improvement in living conditions are problematic. Even if one takes the optimistic view that the primary obstacle to economic development – the predatory state – is no more, the challenges are enormous. There are few functioning institutions and a long history of waste and corruption. Moreover, the Haitian private sector has been no less predatory that the state. The economic élites have never been that interested in investing in Haiti under competitive conditions, and they are reluctant to face more efficient foreign competitors. The outlook for foreign private investment has not been promising.[20] Lacking investment, Haiti will need foreign aid. International donors have pledged $1.8 billion over five years (1994–99) for the Haiti Economic Recovery Program.[21] Much more will be needed and over a longer period of time if 200 years of misdevelopment are to be reversed.

Another problem lies in the neoliberal economic policies that the US, IMF, and the WB have tried to force on the Haitian government. The restructuring program calls for a dramatic reduction in state bureaucracy and spending. To the extent that the government bureaucracy is streamlined and state enterprises privatized, this will contribute to greater unemployment. In the short-term there is likely to be increase inequality as well. All this is likely to produce more social and political conflict, undermine the legitimacy of both the government and the democratic experiment, and make an economic take-off even more problematic.

Haiti was rocked early 1997 by protesters burning tires and throwing stones in hopes of forcing the resignation of the prime minister and ending the internationally mandated austerity measures. In Port-au-Prince shops were shut down, parents kept children from school and no buses were running during a general strike called for 16 January 1997. The strike was called by the Anti-International Monetary Fund Committee after a man lost his right hand to an exploding tear-gas canister fired by police during peaceful demonstrations.[22] The strikes and protests point to the incredible weakness of the Haitian state. The government continues to rely on UN peacekeeping forces to maintain control. On 30 November 1996 President Preval asked for another extension of the UN mandate in Haiti.

A second important issue at the heart of current problems in Haiti is that of security. The Aristide and later the Preval governments have made significant progress in dismantling the military apparatus which served as the center of the predatory state. All that is left are several hundred former military personnel who were part of the recently dissolved Interim Public Security Force and who are now being absorbed into the Haitian National Police (HNP). But there are major unresolved problems. The new police are sorely lacking in experience at all levels, but particularly at middle and upper-level management. Many leaders lack understanding of police work or are otherwise incompetent. There have been instances of corruption and human rights abuse.[23] Allan Nairn reported in the 8 January 1996 edition of *The Nation* that teams of CIA agents roamed the country and recruited intelligence operatives, mainly from the ranks of the now-disbanded FRAPH. US special forces also secured the release of FRAPH torturers who had been arrested by the upstart Haitian Police.

There is continued uneasiness about the former members of the Army who are being brought into the HNP, especially those in the second-echelon ranks of the command structure. This is a recipe for renewed corruption if these soldiers are not retrained and if the new government is not vigilant. Finally, highly disturbing signs indicate that all is not well within the HNP. There have been growing reports of police violence, incompetence and graft, and a corresponding sharp decline in public support for the institution.[24] In early November 1996, the *Miami Herald* reported how a mob of hundreds of people 'enraged' after police had killed a man, burned down a courthouse and police station. The paper also reported that about 60 officers had been suspended for misconduct. On 23 January 1997, a coalition of human rights groups said that in the 18 months since its deployment, 'members of this US-trained force [the HNP] have committed serious abuses, including torture and summary executions'.[25] The report was prepared by Human Rights Watch/Americas, the National Coalition for Haitian Rights and the Washington Office on Latin America. The group warned that continued violations raised serious doubts about the training and leadership of the police force. Lack of adequate pay and training are conducive to the involvement of the police in illicit activities, such as drug trafficking in order to supplement their income.

In late December 1996, gunmen forced customs inspectors in the northern city of Cap-Haitien to hand over a shipload of contraband. The incident reflects the difficulties the government has had in trying to reform customs procedures and the port authority – one of the principal agencies involved in drug trafficking in the past. Jean-Jacques Valentin, national customs director, was quoted as saying: 'The customs bureau cannot assure its own security. We have to rely on people who often don't have the same interest as we do', alluding to the chronic complicity of government officials and smugglers.[26]

Smuggling continues to undermine Haiti's struggle to rebuild its economy. The *Miami Herald* reported on 28 February 1997 that '70 percent of all the sea cargo manifested for Port-au-Prince from the United States...is diverted to provincial Haitian ports as contraband'. The newspaper reported that port infrastructure is nonexistent and inefficient, and that local authorities often are in league with smugglers. The contraband has three important effects: The state loses substantial revenues; Haitians are being put out of business by dishonest competition; and it undermines the restoration of state authority.[27]

On a positive note, after years of trying to build a case against former military and political figures in Haiti, on 7 March 1997 federal prosecutors unsealed an indictment against exiled police chief of Port-au-Prince Joseph Michel Francois. Francois is widely regarded as the leading drug trafficker among the former military regime. The *Miami Herald* reported that he is expected to be defended by Frank Rubino, a Miami lawyer who defended deposed Panamanian dictator Manuel Noriega.[28] Yet, while the new Haitian governments have made some progress in reducing the power of the military and in establishing the foundations for a democratic government, Haiti is unable to break the cycle of violence, corruption, and poverty that have made it the poorest nation in the Western Hemisphere.

## At the service of the world: Panama's political economy

Four factors have shaped the nature of politics and society in Panama since the colonial period. First, the extent to which the predominance of the transit route shaped the nature of the Panamanian economy. Since the colonial period Panama's economy has been tied to the transfer of goods across the narrow stretch of the Panamanian Isthmus. This phenomenon has affected the behavior and values of élites, as well as the institutional structures of the state. Commercial opportunities, both legal and illegal, presented by its location have attracted a deeply fractionated society. Secondly, the influence and intervention of the United States. The Panamanian constitution of 1904 gave the US the right to intervene militarily to 'secure the public peace' whenever the US deemed necessary. The treaty for the construction of the Panama Canal also gave extraordinary powers to the United States. Thirdly, the level of ideological consensus among Panamanian élites. Liberal ideas have dominated the political dialogue of élites since before the establishment of the republic. Fourthly, a commercial élite that has held tight control over the apparatus of government. While the ruling class has been open to – and indeed has encouraged – the incorporation of wealthy European and US immigrants, they have traditionally excluded popular sectors from participating in the nation's politics.

These factors have led to the development of a weak state, manipulated by US interests and national élites tied to those interests. The state, like the one in Haiti, has been used as a means of obtaining and enlarging large personal fortunes. During the 1970s and 1980s, the state was used by the military to protect and enhance their involvement in illicit activities. The increasing ability of the police/military institution to extract resources from illicit service sector activities partially accounts for its growing power and relative autonomy.

The military was by no means the first sector to build its political power base around the control of illicit service sector activities. In fact, it can be argued that Panama as a nation is largely the product of such activities as practiced since the colonial times. Colonial merchants engaged in contraband trade in African slaves and used the resulting profits to capitalize real estate and other business ventures in Panama City. Historian Omar Jaén Suárez argues that 'contrabanding and smuggling have in Panama such power we cannot consider it to be a marginal activity practiced by a small group of marginal persons in a clandestine fashion. . . . Smuggling is a way in which the Creole natives were able to confront the monopoly of the metropole during the 17th and 18th centuries'.[29]

Since the discovery of Mar del Sur (as Spaniards called the Pacific Ocean), the Isthmus of Panama has been used as a zone of transit. Anthropologist Julian Steward argues that the physical environment influences the formation and development of the social institutions of a nation.[30] Panama demonstrates the veracity of this argument. The use that world commerce has assigned to the geographic position of Panama has had profound effects over its history and culture. According to Panamanian historian, Alfredo Castillero Calvo, the Spanish crown assigned a transit role to the isthmus. In other words, to serve as a land bridge for the transportation of gold, silver, and other merchandise between the Pacific and Atlantic Oceans.[31] As a result, and different from other regions of Latin America, the dominant class came to be composed primarily of merchants.

Ricardo Arias Calderón, former Vice president of Panama, has stated that 'Panama is a transactional, rather than a confrontational society'.[32] Panama therefore can be characterized as the nation of the 'deal'; everything is for sale including politicians and ideologies. The climate that prevailed during the early period of colonization, as described by Castillero Calvo, was one of 'to be there to get rich'.[33] This phenomenon is reflected in the nature of Panamanian entrepreneurs: they seek quick short-term profits in businesses which require little initial capital or investment.

In the 1950s and 1960s individual military leaders such as National Guard Commanders José Antonio Remón and Bolívar Vallarino were involved in numerous illicit activities, including drug trafficking and prostitution. The practice enriched them personally but had little effect on the military as a whole.[34] After the 1968 coup that brought General Omar Torrijos to power, the National Guard's involvement in illicit activities became less personalized, more systematic, and broader in scope. By the 1970s leaders of Latin American states were more capable of engaging in a variety of illicit activities. Domestically, the growth of a public sector encompassing many new autonomous agencies with unclear lines of authority provided expanded opportunity. Moreover, access to vast amounts of foreign capital combined with the confusing organizational environment facilitated corrupt practices.[35]

By the mid-1980s, however, the comfortable relationship between the commercial élite and the National Guard that had secured the stability of the regime came to an end as General Manuel Antonio Noriega began to expand the reach of the military. In testimony before the Kerry

Subcommittee, Francis J. McNeil, former US ambassador to Costa Rica and State Department intelligence officer, stated that in 1977 Noriega was widely known as 'the rent-a-colonel'. By 1982, Noriega was working with the Medellín Cartel – smuggling drugs, protecting traffickers, guarding cocaine-processing plants in Panama, and laundering money.[36] Of all the money-laundering centers in the world, Panama's international banking center has been widely regarded as the most efficient: the US dollar circulates as legal tender, and foreign exchange regulations are completely absent.

The growth in revenue generated by involvement of the Defense Forces in the drug trade also led to growing divisions within the ranks of the officer corps itself.[37] General Noriega surrounded himself with a trusted group of friends that had been with him since he was chief of intelligence. Those outside the inner circle were excluded from participating in lucrative illicit activities. This generated division within the top echelons of the armed institution, leading to General Roberto Díaz Herrera's break with Noriega in June 1987.[38] Around the same time the cozy relationship between the US and Noriega also ended. With increasing accusations of Noriega's involvement in drug trafficking and his opposition to helping the US carry out its policy in the rest of Central America, the usefulness of Noriega began to wane. By July 1987, the US had suspended economic aid to Panama. Between 1987 and 1989, the US along with Panamanian opponents of the regime mobilized in an effort to oust Noriega from power. Elections were held in May 1989, but Noriega refused to accept the defeat of his hand-picked candidate, Carlos Duque, and annulled the elections.

On 20 December 1989, the US military did what Panama's opposition and economic sanctions had failed to do. Using overwhelming firepower against limited and largely ineffective opposition, it destroyed the Panamanian Defense Forces and took control of Panama. Noriega sought refuge in the Vatican embassy, but eventually surrendered to US authorities and was flown to Miami to stand trial on charges of narcotics trafficking.

At the heart of the indictments against Noriega was the charge that he had accepted US$4 million payoff to allow the Colombian cartel to conduct operations in Panama. The indictment also detailed five other payments totaling US$850,000 for protection of individual shipments of cocaine and chemicals. These allegations were the basis for the US government's most serious charge, that Noriega and cartel bosses Pablo Escobar and Gustavo Gaviria and other defendants had been engaged in a criminal enterprise as defined by the Racketeer Influenced and Corrupt

Organizations Act, known as RICO. In exchange for US$4 million, Noriega had allowed the cartel to transport chemical supplies through Panama to cocaine factories in Colombia and to build a large cocaine factory in Panama's Darién province, and when Escobar and Gaviria were fleeing Colombia, Noriega gave them refuge and allowed them to run their business in Panama City. Moreover, seven shipments of cocaine also allegedly moved through Panama, using pilots working for Noriega. Most events in the indictments occurred between October 1982 and June 1984. Noriega was eventually found guilty on most charges and sentenced to 40 years in prison. He is currently appealing the convictions.

The post-invasion government made significant strides in building a democratic regime. It decided to replace the Defense Forces with a Public Force composed of three services: the National Police, the National Air Service, and the National Maritime Service. The new security forces were subordinated to civilian authorities through direct control by the Ministry of Government and Justice and budgetary oversight by the Office of the Comptroller General as well as by the Legislative Assembly. Institutional reforms led to an independent and credible Electoral Tribunal and true separation of powers between the executive, legislative, and judicial branches of government. These were significant steps forward in Panama's struggle to build a democracy, but they did not, however, end all problems. Charges of corruption in the Public Force and in the entire justice system, allegations of increased narcotics trafficking and money laundering, and continued rising crime rates combined to keep public confidence in the force at extremely low levels. Divisions between the Public Force and the smaller, technically separate Technical Judicial Police (PTJ), charged with carrying out the actual investigation of criminal activities, has led to further inefficiency.

A 1991 US GAO report stated that drug activities in Panama were on the increase.[39] The lack of security has contributed to a steady increase in narcotics trafficking and drug use in Panama. Domestic narcotics consumption, formerly limited by the Noriega regime, has now reached near epidemic proportions. By some estimates, Panama now has the worst narcotics usage problem in Latin America.[40] In December, 1992, US Ambassador to Panama Deane R. Hinton used an address to the American Chamber of Commerce to express his concern over the 'formidable menace' created by drug trafficking and usage and by money laundering through banks and through the Colon Free Trade Zone.[41] The following year the Panamanian Catholic Church issued a communiqué in which they condemned the increase levels of corruption and the potential for instability in the country. The statement from the Bishop's Conference of Panama stated in part, 'We are aware of the allegations of corruption, past and current: smuggling, drug trafficking, money laundering, graft and mismanagement of public funds...' They went on to accuse 'white glove criminals' for these and other crimes.[42]

A major scandal erupted in the autumn of 1992 when the Attorney General of Panama, Rogelio Cruz, was accused of illegally unfreezing bank accounts linked to drug traffickers. The scandal engulfed members of the Legislative Assembly, the National Director of Customs, the Director of the Technical Judicial Police, and others in the administration of President Guillermo Endara. The scandal was symptomatic of a general atmosphere of instability, corruption, and political infighting that rocked the civilian government. In the end, Cruz was removed from office by the Supreme Court and placed under house arrest. However, no indictments were ever handed down and Cruz was eventually released. In fact, by 1996 Rogelio Cruz was defending a prominent Colombian citizen linked to the Calí cartel, José Castrillón Henao, arrested in Panama and accused of drug trafficking and money laundering.

The Revolutionary Democratic Party (PRD) won the 1994 elections. Ernesto Pérez Balladares, the party's general secretary and presidential candidate, took office in September 1994. The PRD, founded in 1979 as the political arm of the military regime, had reformed itself after the US invasion and benefited from the unpopularity and corrupt image of the Endara government. The Pérez Balladares administration has made significant strides to arrest a sense of drift about the economy. It has come to terms with Panama's international creditors, moved ahead with privatization and granted concessions to private investors to develop infrastructure and to take advantage of the country's underexploited location, particularly the areas being handed over to Panama by the US as a result of the 1977 Torrijos–Carter Treaty.[43] Moreover, the Pérez Balladares administration has proposed that Howard Air Force Base – one of the US military installations slated to be turned over to Panama – be transformed into a multinational counter-drug center. The center would coordinate antidrug activities between the United States, Panama, and other Latin American nations. According to the Panamanian proposal the main functions would be the gathering and dissemination of information among the participating nations.

Despite the progress, the government faces major problems. An opinion poll published in September 1996 showed a majority of Panamanians believed the current government to be more corrupt than the Endara administration and, incredibly, more corrupt than the Torrijos led military government.[44] In June 1996, in the middle of a growing scandal over drug money going to his 1994 presidential campaign, President Pérez Balladares was forced to admit that his campaign received contributions totaling US$51,000 from José Castrillón Henao a prominent member of the Calí drug cartel.

Reports surfaced in 1996 linking a prominent presidential friend and adviser, Mayor Alfredo Alemán, to drug trafficking and money laundering. The *Miami Herald* reported that Alemán was forced to resign his position as head of the National Bank of Panama under pressure from the US state department, which accused him of involvement with narcotics traffickers. The newspaper gave as evidence the fact that an airline, Trans Latin Air, partly owned by Alemán, was indicted by a federal grand jury in Chicago in 1994. The now-defunct company helped buy a plane for a gang of Colombian drug traffickers who moved tons of cocaine and marijuana into the US. Moreover, a bank that listed Alemán as its vice president collapsed in 1996, and investigators subsequently discovered more than US$50 million missing from its accounts. Banco Agro Industrial y Comercial de Panama (BANAICO), had long been a favorite place for drug traffickers to stash their cash.[45]

On 12 June 1996 the *New York Times* reported that Trans Latin Air's legal counsel, Gabriel Castro, was also a friend and legal adviser to Alemán. Castro is now director of the Panamanian Government's National Defense and Public Security Council, and therefore in charge of the nation's efforts to combat drug trafficking.[46] In its 1996 report on drug trafficking, the US Department of State described Panama as 'a financial and commercial center with a location that is ideal for narcotics smuggling and illicit financial transactions'.[47]

Panama's financial sector, which accounts for about 15 per cent of national income, is struggling to regain the position it enjoyed until the early 1980s. To understand Panama's banking system one must consider its history. Based on an agreement with the United States in 1904 and Law No. 84 of the same year, Panama has no paper money of its own. Rather, the US dollar circulates as legal tender, along with US and Panamanian coins. The purpose of this agreement was to facilitate payment to workers engaged in building the Panama Canal. When the Canal was completed, however, the agreement remained. Panama calls its currency the 'balboa', but it has, according to the 1904 agreement, always run at parity with the US dollar.[48] Lacking both a central bank and its own currency, the monetary authorities have little control over the supply of money in Panama. US dollars enter the Panamanian economy from Panama's exports as well as from loans and transfers.

When an excess of cash develops in the economy, private banks unload their excess dollars into their accounts at the National Bank of Panama (NBP), which serves as a clearinghouse for checks and dollars. The NBP then credits their accounts and sends the excess cash by plane to either a private bank in the US or the New York Federal Reserve Bank. When a cash shortage develops, the BNP draws on its accounts in the US and the money is flown back to Panama.

The biggest impulse to the development of Panama's international banking center was Cabinet Decree No. 238 on 2 July 1970. The decree reorganized Panama's banking system along more systematic lines, allowing both greater stability and efficiency. Several measures provided greater stability: abolishing paper banks, requiring a minimum paid-in capital of US$250,000, establishing new regulations for reserves and capital structures in domestic banking, and creating the National Banking Commission with regulatory authority. The decree enhanced the secrecy provisions governing the banking system: the Banking Commission is prohibited from conducting or ordering investigations concerning the private affairs of any bank's clients; it prohibited the publication of any information without the consent in writing of the bank or client concerned; it stipulates sanctions to bank or Commission employees who release any information in violation of the decree. These secrecy provisions are in addition to those that permit numbered bank accounts, which conceal the depositor's identity to all but one or two bank employees.[49]

The banking sector's contributions to Panama's economy were significant: By 1986 it employed over 9000 people, earning on average over 50 per cent above those in the rest of the nonagricultural sectors. The center also stimulated substantial indirect employment in construction of bank headquarters, housing for employees, hotels, and infrastructure and auxiliary activities. At its peak in the in the early 1980s, Luis Moreno estimated that for every person directly employed in the center at least four outside the center owed their jobs to it; thus, the center's direct and indirect contribution to GDP was between 3 and 4 per cent.[50]

For years Panama's banking center thrived on its competitive advantage as a result of numbered accounts, secrecy laws, dollar economy, and relative political stability. However, political instability in the late 1980s, a sleazy reputation that is proving hard to erase, and changes to the global banking business that successive governments appear not to have understood, have combined to damage the sector. The government of President Guillermo Endara signed a Mutual Legal Assistance Treaty with the US in April 1991. The treaty makes bank records more available to investigators looking for money laundering activities. It also established the extradition of criminals wanted by one of the signatory countries. In 1996, legislation to tighten controls on drug money laundering went into effect, including US-style regulations that call for cash deposits of more than $10,000 to be reported. The government is also pledged to reform the 1970 banking law to create an autonomous regulating entity. The need for reform was underlined by the collapse in January 1996 of BANAICO; of the bank's $88 million loan portfolio, $59 million was in 'bad' loans.

Panama's reputation as a money laundering haven also affects legitimate business. Some US banks, for example, have withdrawn from the trade finance for the Colón Free Trade Zone because of suspicions that it is used for money laundering, and the Hongkong & Shanghai Bank is still fighting a case that has been pending in the US since 1992 over alleged money laundering. To some extent, massive corruption may be becoming riskier, despite the widespread feeling that it is still endemic, as Panama now gets more national and international media scrutiny than before. The US also retains a role as public arbiter, particularly when it believes US interests have been damaged by corruption.[51] Moreover, the increased independence of the legislative and judicial branch, and a rebirth of civic and other organizations, have made wholesale corruption more difficult and costly.

## Conclusion

Haiti and Panama have traditionally been havens for illicit enterprises. Their geographic location, weak states, political culture, and the nature of their business élites are factors that make the two countries ideal places from which to run drug trafficking and/or money laundering activities. This chapter has shown the historical roots of those phenomena, and how they have developed over time. Moreover, both Haiti and Panama have been subject to intense US scrutiny, and both were victims of US military interventions recently. In both countries the US wanted to end brutal military dictatorships and restore civilian-led democratic governments. Throughout the 1980s the US was also concerned about the level of drug trafficking and other illicit activities emanating from the two countries. While there is clear evidence that the US was aware of the presence of those activities decades before the military interventions, by the 1980s domestic and international pressures made it very difficult for the US to continue to ignore the pervasiveness of illicit activities in Haiti and Panama and in the rest of the hemisphere.

This analysis, however, demonstrates that despite the US interventions and the establishment of civilian democratic governments in Panama and Haiti those countries continue to be havens for drug trafficking and money laundering. In fact, there is evidence that in both countries these activities have pick-up steam since the interventions. The problem lies partly in the historical structures that characterize each society. Illicit activities have been an important part of the economies of Haiti and Panama since the colonial period. These activities are ingrained in the culture and socioeconomic structures, and thus are exceedingly difficult to eliminate. Short term military occupations cannot possibly end long-standing political and economic practices; neither can they change the political culture in a few months or years.

Both Haiti and Panama have made significant strides in establishing the foundations for democratic governance, and one can argue that this would not have been possible without US intervention. However, if they are to be weaned away from reliance on illicit enterprises, both nations must be encouraged to diversify their economies and construct the necessary infrastructure that will provide adequate employment for the poor, and the necessary business atmosphere for legitimate entrepreneurs. In the short term, however, these changes are not likely given the pressure on both countries from international financial institutions to implement neoliberal restructuring plans. The policies required under these plans are likely to lead to more poverty, and to more illicit activity as the state is weakened even further.

## Notes

1   Apart from 1994 the US intervened in Haiti in 1915–34. In Panama, the US interventions prior to 1989 were in 1906, 1908, 1912, 1918, 1921, 1925, and 1964, not to mention a permanent US military presence in the Panama Canal Zone until 1999.

2   Following the work of Max Weber, I define the state as follows: an organization, composed of various agencies led and coordinated by the state's leadership (executive authority) that has the ability or authority to make and implement the binding rules for all the people as well as the parameters of rule making for other social organizations in a given territory, using force if necessary. A weak state is thus one that is unable to make and/or implement the binding rules for a society. See Max Weber, *The Theory of Social and Economic Organization*, edited by Talcott Parson (New York: The Free Press, 1964), p. 156.

3  For an examination of the nature and impact of weak states, see Joel Migdal, *Strong Societies and Weak States: State–Society Relations and State Capabilities in the Third World* (Princeton: Princeton University Press, 1988).

4  Eduardo A. Gamarra, 'Market-oriented Reforms and Democratization in Latin America: Challenges in the 1990s', in William C. Smith, Carlos H. Acuña, and Eduardo A. Gamarra (eds), *Latin American Political Economy in the Age of Neoliberal Reform* (Boulder, CO: Lynne Rienner Press, 1994); and Aldo Vacs, 'Convergence and Dissension: Democracy, Markets and Structural Reform in World Perspective', in *Latin American Political Economy in the Age of Neoliberal Reform*, op. cit.

5  See Ethan A. Nadelman, *Cops Across Borders: The Internalization of US Criminal Law Enforcement.* (University Park: Penn State University Press, 1993).

6  See Peter Andreas, 'The Retreat and Resurgence of the State: Liberalizing and Criminalizing Cross-Border Flows in an Integrated World', paper presented at the 1995 meeting of the American Political Science Association; P. Williams, 'Transnational Criminal Organizations: Strategic Alliances', *Washington Quarterly*, winter 1995, pp. 57–72.

7  D. Von Drehle, 'Ohhhhh Miami', *American Bar Association Journal*, 1 April 1988, pp. 62–66.

8  Mancur Olson, *The Rise and Decline of Nations* (New Haven, CT: Yale University Press, 1982).

9  Francisco F. Thoumi, *Political Economy and Illegal Drugs in Colombia* (Boulder, CO: Lynne Rienner Press, 1995) p. 175.

10  Ibid., p. 174.

11  For a discussion of the meaning and effect of this prebendary state, see Alex Dupuy, *Haiti in the New World Order: The Limits of the Democratic Revolution* (Boulder, CO: Westview Press, 1997).

12  Jean Jean-Pierre, 'The Tenth Department', *NACLA Report on the Americas*, v. XXVII, no. 4 (January/February 1994).

13  James Ridgeway, 'Haiti is Here', *The Village Voice*, 3 May 1994.

14  For a detailed discussion of the Haitian revolution see, C.L.R. James, *The Black Jacobins: Toussaint L'Ouverture and the San Domingo Revolution* (New York: New Vintage Books, 1963).

15  Patrick Elie, 'Press Briefing on the Haitian Drug Trade', *The Haiti Files: Decoding the Crisis* (Washington, DC: Essential Books/Azul Editions, 1994), pp. 163–4.

16  Ibid., pp. 165–70.

17  See Amy Wilentz, *The Rainy Season: Haiti since Duvalier* (New York: Simon and Schuster, 1989), pp. 172–3; Creg Chamberlain, 'An Interregnum: Haitian History from 1987 to 1990', in Deidre McFadyen *et al.* (eds), *Haiti: Dangerous Crossroads* (Boston, MA: South End Press, 1995).

18  Dupuy, op. cit., pp. 131–2.

19  Ibid., p. 118.

20  Don Bohning, 'Intervention in Haiti Slowly Restoring Peace', *Miami Herald*, 16 September 1995.

21  Testimony of Norma Parker, deputy assistant administrator for Latin America and the Caribbean, US Agency for International Development, before the US House of Representatives Sub-Committee on Western Hemisphere Affairs, 12 October 1995, p. 22.

22   *Miami Herald*, 17 January 1997, via Internet.
23   Human Rights Watch/Americas National Coalition for Haitian Refugees, 'Haiti: Human Rights After President Aristide's Return', Vol. 7, No. 11, October 1995.
24   See Tammerlin Drummond, 'A Constabulary of Thugs', *Time Magazine*, 17 February 1997. pp. 62–3.
25   *Miami Herald*, 23 January 1997, via Internet.
26   Ibid., 28 December 1996, via Internet.
27   Ibid., 28 February 1997, via Internet.
28   Ibid., 8 March 1997, via Internet.
29   Omar Jaén Suárez, *La población del Istmo de Panamá del siglo XVI al siglo XX* (Panama City: Impresora de la Nación, 1978), pp. 305–7.
30   Julian Steward, 'Basin-Plateau Aboriginal Sociopolitical Groups', Smithsonian Institution, *Bureau of American Ethnology Bulletin*, Vol 120, 1979, p. 2.
31   Alfredo Castillero Calvo, 'Transitismo y dependencia: El caso del Istmo de Panama', *Loteria*, no. 210, July, 1973; pp. 17–40; Alfredo Castillero Calvo, *Economia Terciaria y Sociedad: Panamá Siglos XVI y XVII*. (Panamá: Impresora de la Nación, 1980); Alfredo Castillero Calvo, *America Hispana: Aproximaciones a la historia economica* (Panamá: Impresora de la Nación/INAC, 1983).
32   Ricardo Arias Calderón, 'Panama: Disaster or Democracy?', *Foreign Affairs*, Vol. 66, Winter 1987/88, p.329.
33   Castillero Calvo, 1980, op. cit., p. 46.
34   Larry LaRae Pippin, *The Remon Era* (Stanford, CA: Institute of Hispanic American and Luso-Brazilian Studies, Stanford University, 1964).
35   Robin Theobald, *Corruption, Development and Underdevelopment*. (Durharm, NC: Duke University Press, 1990), pp. 86, 98, and 101.
36   US Congress. Senate. Committee on Foreign Relations, *Hearings Before the Subcommittee on Terrorism, Narcotics and International Operations*, 100th Cong. 2nd sess., 1988, pts 2 and 3.
37   From the various testimonies, it appears that total money laundering resulting from drug trade exceeded $10 billion a year after 1984. See US Congress, Committee on Foreign Relations, Subcommittee on Terrorism, Narcotics and International Operations, *Drugs, Law Enforcement and Foreign Policy: Report*, 100th Cong., 2nd sess. (Washington, DC: USGPO, 1989).
38   Frederick Kempe, *Divorcing the Dictator* (New York: Putnam, 1990). For other accounts of the Noriega years, see John, Dinges, *Our Man in Panama*. (New York: Random House); Margaret Scranton, *The Noriega Years: US–Panamanian Relations, 1981–1990* (Boulder, CO: Lynne Rienner Press, 1991); and see Kevin Buckley, *Panama: The Whole Story* (New York: Simon and Schuster, 1991).
39   See Mark Sullivan, 'Panama–US Relations: Continuing Policy Concerns', *CRS Issue Brief*, 15 January 1993, p. 10.
40   *Miami Herald*, 20 November 1992, pp. A1 and A6; *Central America Report*, 5 June 1992, pp. 153–4; *New York Times*, 13 August 1991, pp. A1 and A9.
41   Speech by Ambassador Deane R. Hinton to the American Chamber of Commerce of Panama, 15 December 1992.
42   'Comunicado de la Conferencia Episcopal Panameña', *Panorama Católico*, 10 January 1993, p. 3.
43   The treaty established a process by which Panama would gradually gain control of the old Panama Canal Zone. By the end of 1999, Panama was to

have full control over all the areas previously held by the US, including military installations and the Panama Canal.

44   Poll conducted by Diechter & Neira for *La Prensa*, via Internet.
45   *Miami Herald*, International Satellite Edition, 10 June 1996, pp. 1A, 3A.
46   *New York Times*, 12 June 1996, pp. A1 and A8.
47   Quoted in *New York Times*, 12 June 1996, p. A8.
48   See Jorge Conte-Porras, *El crédito, la banca y la moneda panameña* (Panama City: Banco Nacional de Panamá, 1983).
49   See Luis Moreno, *Panamá: centro bancario internacional*. (Panama City: Asociación Bancaria de Panamá, 1988); Comisión Bancaria Nacional, *Banking Law of Panama*. (Panama City: Republic of Panama, 1986).
50   Moreno, op. cit., p. 196.
51   It is worth noting that in late February 1997 the United States Department of State officially 'certified' Panama's anti-drug efforts, thus indicating its satisfaction with the policies undertaken by the Panamanian government.

# 8

# 'Narcodemocracy' or Anti-drug Leviathan: Political Consequences of the Drug War in the Puerto Rican High-intensity Drug-trafficking Area

*Jorge Rodríguez Beruff*

This chapter explores some propositions regarding the political consequences of drugs-driven state restructuring, particularly in relation to
security policies and forces.[1] This process of change has been conditioned by the new post-Cold War security agenda that emphasizes
'non-traditional' threats – mainly drugs and illegal migration in the
case of the Caribbean – as well as by broader economic and social
transformations that have elicited new forms of state control. The case
of Puerto Rico is analysed from this perspective, with the caveat that
present trends in Puerto Rico are by no means unique, though perhaps
more pronounced than in other Caribbean societies. However, it should
also be stressed that Puerto Rico is set apart from the rest of the Caribbean due to the character of its political relationship with the United
States and the geostrategic position it has occupied and continues to
occupy within the region.

The discourse associated with the 'war on drugs' has witnessed coinage
of the terms 'narcodemocracy' and 'narcostate' to refer to the political
threats that production, consumption and drug trafficking pose for
democratic institutions.[2] However diffuse in meaning, it serves to convey the notion that drug interests govern behind a façade of democracy
or have, at least, penetrated strategic political institutions. Initially
applied to Colombia[3] and other producing countries of the Andean
region, the concept is used exclusively with regard to producing and
transit countries. The considerable capacity of a multi-billion dollar
illegal business to bribe functionaries, use financial institutions for

money-laundering and manipulate the electoral system, and the desta-bilizing effects of rising violence and criminal activities associated with drugs are among factors mentioned as challenges to governability and even to the viability of democratic practices.

Authors such as Ivelaw Griffith, Anthony Maingot, and Michel Laguerre, among others, have stressed that the political challenge of the drug trade is magnified in the Caribbean due to the vulnerability of the microstates and territories to its impact on political institutions.[4] These approaches seem to suggest that a form of 'Colombianization' threatens the region. Griffith, in particular, has suggested that the drug business undermines the sovereignty of Caribbean states.[5] The conclu-sions of a symposium held in Miami in 1995 state that '. . . [t]he trade has in many instances sought to compromise the national integrity, political will and subvert traditional democratic institutions in the region'.[6]

The magnitude of the political challenge posed by illegal drugs should not be underestimated. Evidence abounds on high-level corruption scandals in governments and the private sector in the Caribbean, includ-ing Puerto Rico, and in circum-Caribbean states. The 1996 and 1997 episodes in Panama (the 'narco-checks scandal') and Mexico (the desti-tution of the Mexican anti-drugs 'czar' and the disclosure of widespread corruption in the Army) must be added to the numerous cases in the insular Caribbean, such as in Antigua and Bahamas. In Puerto Rico, a political scandal related to the alleged corruption of legislators, includ-ing the Vice-President of the Senate, attracted public attention during 1995. During the last two years there have been numerous instances of corruption of policemen, National Guard personnel and employees of the international airport. The vulnerability of the airport was under-scored by the arrest, in August 1997, of about a dozen Delta Airlines employees, followed by an official statement that more arrests would follow. In addition, the banking system of Puerto Rico has been used in the past for money-laundering operations. The burgeoning drug busi-ness has also been a factor in the steeply increasing incidence of violence.

Despite all this, the 'narcodemocracy' hypothesis does not seem to apply to the Puerto Rican case, as the drug interests do not seem to have the capability to politically destabilize the state or to become major political actors. On the contrary, anti-drug strategies may have had the effect of strengthening state power and its instruments of force. Seen from this perspective, the political impact of the drug business is mainly indirect, through the 'accumulated results' of the state's responses to the problem, and may pose more an issue of the compatibility between the 'anti-drug war' policies and democratic institutions, than of governability.

Therefore, the problem of the political consequences of the illegal drug business and dominant anti-drug measures is approached from a different angle, namely, whether the main danger of subversion to democratic institutions emanates from the 'accumulated results' of the present 'anti-drug war' strategy that may tend to constitute what could be called the 'anti-drug security state'. This raises questions such as the following: To what extent are drug trafficking and consumption functional to the type of society and state that are emerging? Could it be that the apparent impotence of the state to respond effectively to the constantly worsening problem of drugs may be partly the result of the policies that it has adopted, or of deeper processes of social and economic transformation that underlie those policies? Are the anti-drugs policies conditioned by systemic considerations that go beyond the issue of drugs and may point to new forms of authoritarianism?

## Drugs, the crime scare and politics in Puerto Rico

Puerto Rico was a society with very low level of criminality and violence during the 1950s despite episodes of political violence such as the Nationalist uprising of 1950. The economy had been steadily growing since the 1940s and large-scale migration served to remove a large part of the surplus labor that could not be absorbed by the expanding manufacturing sector or by government employment. The most common violent crimes involved acquaintances, using knives or *machetes*, and for passional reasons. The first bank robbery did not occur until the 1960s. (In March 1997 three banks were held up in a single day.[7]) Clandestine rum production (*pitorro*) was a much greater problem for the police than illegal drugs. However, drug consumption was beginning to become a concern and the Narcotics Law was approved in 1959.

A fundamental change took place between 1968 and 1973. Those were years of momentous global transformation. In Puerto Rico the prevailing economic model began to falter, the political arrangement constructed during World War II began to break down, and the impact of the Vietnam War was at its peak. The first year marks the foundation of Hogares CREA, a private initiative for the rehabilitation of addicts, and the latter the establishment by the government of the *Departamento de Servicios Contra la Adicción*. This responded to a rapid rise in drug consumption, particularly of heroin, and a parallel increase in the incidence of robberies and other 'crimes against property'.[8] Drug related deaths

and arrests also rapidly rose. The official estimates of the addict population during the early seventies ranged between a few thousand to as
many as 70,000.

Public opinion perceived this as a 'crime wave' and attributed it to
drugs. An opinion poll conducted in 1975 found that 87 per cent of
respondents thought that violence was more serious than previously,
and 29.5 per cent attributed it to 'drugs and vice', although 18.9 per cent
also mentioned unemployment and inflation as causes.[9] By 1996, 43 per
cent of respondents of another poll placed crime in the first place among
the problems of Puerto Rico and an additional 18 per cent mentioned
drugs. Only 5 per cent mentioned in the first place an economic issue
such as the permanence of Section 936 companies.[10] Thus, crime and
drugs, and the perceived connection between the two, became a major
political issue in political campaigns in Puerto Rico much before the 'war
on drugs' was launched in the US in the mid-1980s. The issues of drugs
and crime was already important politically in the 1972 and 1976 elections. Henceforth crime and drugs became crucial issues in all elections,
used with particular effectiveness by the New Progressive Party whenever it was in the opposition.

The late 1960s and early 1970s period was important for several reasons. First, a large addict population – calculated in the tens of thousands – crystallized, thus ensuring a broad market for drugs, and the
consequent consolidation of international drug trafficking organizations and routes. By 1976 there were 7,262 addicts in private and public
treatment programs, with an additional number in the penal population
(2000 in 1973, over 50 per cent of the total). Most of the addicts in
treatment were under 24 years of age.[11] Secondly, a study entitled *Socio-
ecology of Criminality in Puerto Rico* confirmed that public housing projects in major urban centers had become locations for many violent
crimes.[12] In addition, crime rates, although following an uncertain
path, tended to continue increasing over the next decades.[13] Thirdly, a
long-term 'state of opinion' formed that consistently placed crime and
drugs first and second among the major problems of Puerto Rico, and
increasingly established a causal connection between the two.

During the late 1980s and early 1990s a dramatic increase in violent
crime occurred. Murders, for example, nearly doubled between 1987
(509) and 1994 (995) as Table 8.1 indicates. Serious crimes, known as
Type I crimes, also rose steeply. In addition, a series of incidents seemed
to underscore that some public housing projects (*residenciales*), mainly in
San Juan, had become safe havens for criminals and for drug traffickers, a
kind of no man's land, beyond police control. Often the police would be

received with rocks or gunshot when they ventured into a residencial and on more than one occasion a police station in Puerta de Tierra was attacked with rifle fire from a nearby high-rise building. Battles among criminal groups were fought with sophisticated automatic weapons. Television news projected an endless stream of killings, mainly poor youngsters from residenciales and *barriadas* (traditional urban neighborhoods). The penal system could no longer hold the prisoners and was subjected to hefty fines by the Federal Court, due to overcrowding.

Crime became a lucrative business for the media, capable of ensuring the success of the daily (*El Vocero*) with the highest circulation. Rising crime statistics, together with the daily visual evidence provided by the media, enhanced the public perception that a bloodbath was enveloping the island. Upper- and middle-class neighborhoods pressed for legal means to close access to their *urbanizaciones*, neighborhood security committees sprang up with official support in urban centers, and the private security business (from alarms to private guards) burgeoned. The population also increasingly armed itself. As Table 8.2 shows, by 1997,

**Table 8.1**   Murders in Puerto Rico, 1985–96

| Year | Murders | Year | Murders |
| --- | --- | --- | --- |
| 1985 | 573 | 1991 | 817 |
| 1986 | 719 | 1992 | 864 |
| 1987 | 509 | 1993 | 954 |
| 1988 | 596 | 1994 | 995 |
| 1989 | 667 | 1995 | 864 |
| 1990 | 600 | 1996 | 865 |

*Source*: Amelia Estades Santaliz, 'Redobla el paso la criminalidad', *El Nuevo Dia*, 18 December 1996, p. 4.

**Table 8.2**   Legal Weapons in Puerto Rico, 1997

| | |
| --- | --- |
| Possession license | 53,750 |
| Target practise | 95,407 |
| Hunting | 3,800 (estimate) |
| Police (central and municipal) | 18,890 |
| Govt. functionaries | 5,391 |
| Federal functionaries | 900 |
| **Total** | 180,138 |

*Source*: Gerardo Montero, 'Piden limitar aún más la ley local', *El Nuevo Día* 9 February 1997, p. 5.

there were 180,138 legal weapons, of which over 150,000 were in private hands. This does not include many thousands of illegal weapons and those held by military bodies such as the National Guard and the regular Armed Forces. About 25,000 additional weapons have been reported stolen and 10,017 illegal weapons were confiscated by the police between 1993 to 1996.

The concern with public security has also gradually produced many legal changes. The legislation to allow the closing of neighborhoods is a case in point. Harsher mandatory sentences were also introduced. Moreover, the treatment of juveniles was revised, permitting their prosecution as adults. More recently, a law has been approved establishing mandatory drug tests for private and public employees. Further, curfews for youths have been enforced in several municipalities, and are being considered for San Juan. The federal government established a precedent by asking for the death penalty in several cases in the Puerto Rican jurisdiction, where capital punishment is banned by the local Constitution. Stronger federal anti-crime legislation, applicable to Puerto Rico, has also redefined the legal structure. The trend is clearly in the direction of enhancing the repressive power of the state, sometimes at the cost of an erosion of civil liberties.

The crime wave perceived as unstoppable was clearly a factor in the 1992 defeat of the Popular Democratic Party. The Rafael Hernández Colón administration (1988–92) tried to respond by creating the *Fuerzas Unidas de Rápida Acción* (FURA) to combat drug trafficking, and began planning to intervene in the residenciales. However, these measures did not offset the political cost of the crime wave. During the 1992 electoral campaign the New Progressive Party and its candidate, the present governor Pedro Rosselló, made anti-drug and anti-crime proposals a central feature of their program under the slogan 'a strong hand against crime and drugs'. This message, plus the promise to establish a health card for the poor, occupied a strategic place in the campaign.

A frontal campaign against drugs and criminality was promised. Its main elements consisted of a harsher treatment for criminals, the strengthening of security agencies – particularly the police – with a larger budget, and more equipment and personnel, the expansion of the penal system, a greater degree of collaboration with federal agencies and the use of the National Guard to occupy, together with the police, the residenciales. Such a hard line approach to crime and drugs enjoyed broad popular support. It was also in line with the stronger anti-crime and anti-drug policies in the US, and with mounting federal concern regarding the role of the island (and the neighboring US Virgin Islands and the Dominican Republic) in drug-trafficking.

## The 'strong hand' policies

The 'strong hand' was put in execution as soon as Rosselló assumed the governorship. He named an FBI agent, Pedro Toledo, to head the police and later another FBI agent was appointed as the second-in-command in that agency. Eventually, even the *Negociado de Investigaciones Especiales* (NIE), under the Puerto Rican Justice Department, was placed under the direction of an FBI agent. But the most spectacular measure was the occupation of many housing projects by the National Guard and the police in quasi-military operations.

The National Guard was assigned to keep watch in the occupied projects. About 5,000 officers and soldiers were involved in the anti-crime measures. For the first time, Puerto Rico, in peacetime, experienced a visible and prolonged military presence in the urban centers, as the National Guard had previously only been used during disturbances and natural disasters. After the occupations, a conglomerate of civilian agencies, known euphemistically as the *Congreso de Calidad de Vida* (Quality of Life Congress), intervened in the residenciales in support of the police action. The subordination of these civilian agencies to the police is indicated by the fact that the funding for the Congreso is included in the police budget. After the occupations, the buildings were spruced up, a wall was constructed, and a single entrance with guards established. By 1997, a total of 77 out of 338 residenciales had been intervened by police and the Congreso. The Education Department began a parallel program known as *Escuelas Libres de Drogas y de Armas* (partly funded by the federal government under the 'Drugs Free Schools and Communities' program), accompanied with much publicity.

The 'strong hand' policy was reflected in a rapid increase in the budgets of all civilian local security agencies between 1992 and 1997, particularly of the police as Table 8.3 shows. The personnel of public security-related agencies also rose steeply during this period as Table 8.4 reveals. A significant increase in the number of municipal police, a force of relatively recent creation which now has several thousand members, has also occurred. The statistics for this force, organized in 77 municipalities, are not readily available.

The government also organized a referendum in 1993 with the purpose of abolishing the constitutional right to bail. A host of political and civic groups, including the Catholic Church and the Evangelical

Table 8.3  Consolidated Budgets (Local plus Federal Funds) of the Main Civilian Public Security Agencies of Puerto Rico, 1992–96 ($m)

|             | 92–93 | 93–94 | 94–95 | 95–96 | 96–97 | 97–98 |
|-------------|-------|-------|-------|-------|-------|-------|
| Police      | 298.7 | 373.5 | 377.2 | 406.2 | 483.9 | 494.2 |
| Corrections | 162.4 | 229.2 | 267.4 | 365.7 | 455.5 | 577.9 |
| Justice     | 58.8  | 72.2  | 73.7  | 82.0  | 95.1  | 101.8 |

Note: The figures for Corrections include the seven agencies under the 'Corrections and Rehabilitation' umbrella Department and the Justice figures include three agencies under the Justice 'umbrella' Department. The police figures refer only to all Police programs, but not all agencies under the 'Law and Order' umbrella (which also includes the National Guard and other agencies). The amounts for 1997–98 are those recommended.
Source: Government of Puerto Rico Bugdet Proposal 1997–1998, San Juan, 1997. Also, Budgets in Leyes de Puerto Rico, 1993–94, 1994–96.

Table 8.4  Total Personnel of Puerto Rico's Police and Corrections Departments, 1992–98

|      | Police               | Corrections           |
|------|----------------------|-----------------------|
| 1992 | 12,000 (estimate)    | NA                    |
| 1993 | 14,475               | 7,666                 |
| 1994 | 16,125               | 7,924                 |
| 1995 | 16,692 (16,269)      | 9,875 (10,524)        |
| 1996 | 18,615 (17,605)      | 10,707 (12,330)       |
| 1997 | (20,008)             | (12,511)              |
| 1998 | (20,500) (requested) | (13,179) (requested)  |

Note: NA – not available.
Source: Budget Proposal 1997–1998, San Juan, 1997. There is a discrepancy in the figures provided in the 1995–96 and in the 1997–98 budgets. The latter are enclosed in parenthesis.

Council, formed a coalition in opposition to the plan.[14] The proposal was defeated by 53 per cent 'No' vote. The governor spoke of 'obstacles and resistance' to explain the results contrary to his 'compromise with change', and a leading politician implied that there existed a connection of the Catholic Church to drug trafficking.

In 1994, the anti-drug policies provoked yet another political controversy, this time related to the Navy's plan to establish a Relocatable Over-the-Horizon Radar (ROTHR) in the Lajas Valley and Vieques. The stated purpose of this radar is to monitor aerial traffic in South America for drug interdiction operations. The announcement also provoked widespread and militant opposition culminating in a large demonstration on 29 October 1995. The project had to be postponed until after the 1996 elections and a new location for the receiver was chosen outside the Lajas Valley (now it is planned for Fort Allen in Juana Díaz).[15] Government spokesmen again linked the opposition to drug traffickers.

Amidst this controversy, a scandal erupted in the legislature regarding allegations against the Vice-President of the Senate and several other legislators of having connections with drug-traffickers. The Vice-President of the Senate was removed from his post and seat and some other law makers chose not to run in the 1996 elections. None of the drugs-related allegations reached the courts, but the former Vice-President of the Senate has been charged with tax evasion.

Despite these political complications, the 'strong hand' remained on course. As evidence of its success, numerous arrests, drug, arms and money seizures were constantly shown on television, together with the display of military force in the *residenciales*. Two visual clichés were constantly repeated – murdered youths lying in a pool of blood in a street corner or inside a car, along with the apparently positive results of police action. The message conveyed by the images were reinforced by a costly public relations campaign that claimed that the police 'did what had to be done'.

In addition to the increase in police personnel (from about 12,000 in 1992 to over 20,000 in 1997), equipment purchases included 3,153 vehicles, 10 000 bullet-proof vests, several helicopters and 34 speed-boats.[16] In May 1996 it was announced that three new privatized prisons in Guayama, Ponce and Bayamón would add 25 per cent capacity to the correctional system. During the 1996 electoral campaign, the ruling party promised to add 2,000 more policemen and to cut by half the number of murders.

Since murders continued climbing to the unprecedented high level of 995 in 1994 and have remained at well over 800 in subsequent years, it was argued that the drug-traffickers were 'killing each other' and that at least the upward trend of violent deaths had been contained. An Interpol study published recently with 1994 figures indicates the magnitude of the violent crime problem in Puerto Rico. While in the United States the murder rate was 9 for every 100,000 inhabitants, in the island it was 26.89. This rate was higher than that of Nicaragua and Venezuela, known for their high levels of violence. And only 38 per cent of the assassinations were resolved, the lowest rate of any of the countries mentioned. Despite this, the government claimed an overall reduction of Type I crimes (106,088 in 1995, 99,788 in 1996, and 94,799 in 1997), but refused to release the figures on Type II crimes. The opposition disputed the reliability of the official statistics.

Despite the government's claims of positive results, by 1996 it was becoming increasingly clear that the 'strong hand' policies were failing to produce the expected results. During the first two months of 1997, assassinations and spectacular robberies took place. In one of these, against the jewelry store 'A Touch of Gold', the thieves stole US$2 million in jewelry and US$300,000 in checks and cash. Another robbery against an armored vehicle in Ponce, though promptly solved, involved a booty of several million dollars. Spectacular shootouts occurred in busy streets of San Juan. Not only did violence seem unstoppable but the problem also appeared to be escalating. Drug trafficking through Puerto Rico to the US also intensified during 1995 and 1996.

Soon after the November 1996 elections, the local director of the DEA, Félix Jiménez, refuted the police's claim that the increasing violence was a result of the scarcity of drugs provoked by the 'strong hand' measures. According to Jiménez, the *guerra por los puntos* (the struggle for control over distribution points) was the result of the heightened competition caused by the oversupply of drugs.[17] In addition, the closing of the urbanizaciones had not shielded the middle class neighborhoods from robberies and drug related executions, while the occupation of the residenciales had resulted in the relocation of criminal activity to barriadas and rural areas.[18] Not even the display of force ensured a secure control over the occupied housing projects, nor could all residenciales be simultaneously occupied.

Bringing the National Guard into police functions and in contact with the lucrative drug business also had negative consequences, as in 1996 a major corruption scandal within that force was unveiled and it became known that more than 380 members of the Guard had been expelled due to their connection with drugs and other crimes. It is thus not surprising that while 74 occupations of residenciales took place in 1995, only three were undertaken in 1996. Further occupation of the housing projects has been de-emphasized in official statements, though funds for 30 additional operations were included in the 1997–98 budget.

On the other hand, the scale of drug trafficking to the US reached alarming proportions. A mid-1996 General Accounting Office study, claimed that 30 per cent of the cocaine that enters the US transits through the Puerto Rico–Virgin Islands area. It also pointed out that 'most of the drugs shipped through the islands are destined for further transit through Puerto Rico to the United States'.[19] Another study notes the use of the Puerto Rican route also by Dominican traffickers.[20]

Guillermo Gil, the chief federal prosecutor in Puerto Rico, claimed that more drugs had been supplied during the last two months of 1996 than during the entire previous year.[21] The shift in 1993 of US anti-drug resources to producing countries and successful interdiction efforts elsewhere in the Caribbean, such as OPBAT – Operation Bahamas and Turks and Caicos – may have worsened the problem.

According to the DEA, Puerto Rico receives annually 84 tons of drugs valued in $20 billion. Of this total, 20 per cent remains in the island to supply the local market, valued in about US$4 billion, and the rest is re-exported to the US. Interdiction operations only affect a fraction of that flow (calculated optimistically in about a third by the US and the UN). If DEA figures are accurate, this implies that the value of drugs exported to the US is roughly equivalent to the value of industrial exports of Section 936 companies. That would make drugs one of the most important economic activities in the island and certainly the one with the highest rate of return (calculated, in the case of cocaine, at 300 per cent at the retail level). This does not include the traffic with heroin and marijuana. The estimated street value of marijuana confiscated in 1996 (18 355 lb) was US$183 million.[22] The DEA also calculates in the hundreds the criminal organizations involved in the drug business, which implies that the dismantling of only a few of these may have the effect of strengthening those remaining. It raises a dilemma not dissimilar, and perhaps more complicated, than that of guerrilla warfare, once several fronts have been opened. The DEA notes that in the past five years 5,000 luxury homes were constructed but only 1 879 taxpayers report income higher that US$150,000.[23]

After five years of the 'strong hand' and many public relations efforts, public perceptions about the gravity of the crime and drug problem have not changed. Indeed, public opinion perceives a serious worsening of the situation. An opinion poll published on 13 August 1997 by *Nuevo Día*, the main daily, showed that 68 per cent of respondents opined that crime was 'much worse' than five years ago, and an additional 19 per cent considered it was 'somewhat worse'. With regards to drugs, 71 per cent thought it was 'much worse', and 14 per cent 'somewhat worse'.[24]

## The High-intensity Drug-trafficking Area, SOUTHCOM and the role of the federal government

From the outset the 'strong hand' policy implied the support of the federal government to the government of Puerto Rico through anti-crime and anti-drugs funds, a greater activism of the federal agencies and a greater degree of collaboration among all security agencies. The nomination of FBI agents to the highest posts in the local security agencies was symbolic of the higher profile of the federal government.

In this regard, it should be mentioned that the increase in local funds to security agencies was supplemented by federal grants. In 1995, for example, FURA received US$2.5 million, local and federal initiatives received $5.5 million, local initiatives US$5 million and the NIE received $500,000. This police program financed 354 additional policemen and 151 municipal guards in 21 municipalities.[25] Funding for the corrections and rehabilitation agencies increased from US$1.2 million in 1995 to US$7.5 million in 1997. In 1995, the National Guard received US$3 million for operations in the residenciales (in addition to the normal US$7.1 million grant). The largest injection of special federal funds went to the police which received US$2.3 million in 1995, US$6.7 million in 1996, and US$21.5 million in 1997.[26]

An important step in increasing federal activism in Puerto Rico was the establishment, in late 1994, of a High Intensity Drug Trafficking Area (HIDTA) for Puerto Rico and the US Virgin Islands. Lee Brown, then drugs 'czar', visited Puerto Rico to announce this measure. It should be noted, however, that the establishment of the HIDTA was preceded by other steps that had been taken to strengthen the federal law enforcement and security structure to confront illegal migration, rising violent crime and increasing drug trafficking through the Puerto Rico–Virgin Islands region. Among these measures were the building of a modern federal jail, strengthening the Border Patrol and Coast Guard, and the plan to build a ROTHR.

The importance attached to the island in the anti-drugs strategy was further underscored when it was subsequently chosen as the venue for the 'anti-drugs' summit attended by Janet Reno, Attorney General, Tom Constantine, head of the DEA, and Gen. Barry McCaffrey, the then recently named anti-drugs 'czar'. The summit was used, among other things, to counter proposals to 'medicalize' drugs. A congressional committee held hearings in San Juan on anti-drugs efforts. The governor emphasized, and held up as a model, the local crime control measures during the US Governor's Conference held in Puerto Rico in 1996, an event also attended by Gen. McCaffrey. Important anti-drugs operations were launched by the federal agencies since mid-1996, such as 'Operation Gateway' to stem the flow of drugs to the US through Puerto Rico, and 'Operation Jetway' to clean the international airport of elements linked to drug trafficking.[27] The airport was an important center for drugs, money and arms trafficking.

The HIDTA, according to the federal anti-drugs strategy document, has the mission of protecting the air, land and sea frontiers of the US from the drug threat. They were assigned $103 million for their operation during 1997. There are six 'Gateway' HIDTAs: (1) southwestern frontier, (2) Houston, (3) Los Angeles, (4) Miami, (5) New York, and (6) Puerto Rico-Virgin Islands. A 'Distribution' HIDTA was created in the Washington DC–Baltimore area and three 'Empowerment' HIDTAs in Atlanta, Chicago and Philadelphia. The HIDTA is fundamentally a collaboration structure encompassing local and federal agencies for 'joint action', funneling anti-drugs funds to the area and sharing intelligence. Each HIDTA is directed by an Executive Committee composed of a federal and state officials (in this case of the government of Puerto Rico) in more or less equivalent numbers.[28] The fact that the Virgin Islands has been included, indicates that its jurisdiction is regional, and it remains to be seen if it is to play a role with regard to the neighboring Dominican Republic.[29] Among the federal agencies that participate in the Puerto Rican HIDTA, alongside the local agencies, are the DEA, FBI, Internal Revenue Service (IRS), Immigration and Naturalization Service (INS), Bureau of Alcohol, Tobacco and Firearms (ATF) and the federal marshalls.[30] It can be assumed that other agencies that perform roles in the 'war against drugs', such as the Coast Guard and the Navy, also form part of this structure. The establishment of the HIDTA has been accompanied by the doubling of the resources of the FBI and the DEA in the island. The FBI, for example, recently opened three regional offices.

The recent decision to locate the SOUTHCOM army garrison in Puerto Rico, once it is removed from Fort Clayton in Panama, adds yet another dimension to the process. The government of Puerto Rico lobbied hard to have SOUTHCOM's headquarters transferred to the island, but lost out to Miami. Though economic and law-enforcement considerations were mentioned, the status of the island was also a factor since the ruling party has consistently sought to court the Pentagon in support of statehood.[31] On 1 June 1997, all military bases and installations in Puerto Rico, formerly controlled by the USACOM, passed to the jurisdiction of SOUTHCOM. The latter now has responsibility for all of the insular Caribbean, in addition to its former missions in Central and South America. SOUTHCOM has been extremely active in the region since its relocation to Miami. Given the Department of Defense's assigned role as 'lead agency' in the monitoring and surveillance of drug trafficking, the Caribbean and anti-drugs measures will occupy a prominent position in SOUTHCOM's agenda, as the move to Puerto Rico of one component indicates.

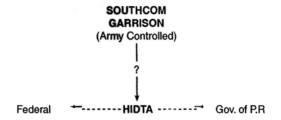

Figure 8.1 The Emerging Military–Police Complex in Puerto Rico Military and Police Security Agencies

The decision to locate SOUTHCOM's garrison – US Army South – in the island was announced in late July 1997. The detachment consists of 3,000 military and 2,000 civilian employees. Of these, about 800 civil and military personnel, along with 2,000 family members, will be deployed by October 1998, mainly in Fort Buchanan. The garrison will have an air component in Isla Grande, San Juan, and a naval component in the Roosevelt Roads Naval Station. Other installations, such as Camp Santiago and Fort Allen, will also be used.[32] This move reinserts the Army in Puerto Rico, hitherto the Navy's turf. It signifies a more visible, and perhaps more intense, presence of the regular armed forces, and will require enhanced security measures.

The military's role in the 'war on drugs' will also imply a close liaison with the HIDTA structure. Plans have also been announced for close collaboration of the garrison with the Army Reserve and National Guard.[33] On a regional level, SOUTHCOM's garrison in Puerto Rico is envisoned as forming part of a strategic triangle together with the Multinational Counter Narcotics Center (MCC) in Howard Air Force Base, Panama, and SOUTHCOM's headquarters and military facilities in Florida. The MCC plan, that has already generated militant opposition in that country, envisages retaining 2,500 US military personnel in Panama and also using Rodman Naval Station and the Fort Sherman Jungle Training Center.[34] Figure 8.1 attempts to depict the emerging security complex.

## The perverse political consequences of the 'drug war'

The new security complex that is crystallizing in Puerto Rico, legitimated by an anti-crime and anti-drug agenda, is characterized by a growing fusion between federal and local agencies, and between military and civil security structures. This process has been justified by the need to achieve 'full integration' of law-enforcement efforts to counter the threat posed by drug trafficking and abuse and violent crime. Thus, what has happened at a local level between the police, the National Guard and the host of civilian agencies known as the Congreso de Calidad de Vida, now is being institutionalized with regard to the constellation of federal and local, civil and military, security agencies. This process is not without contradictions, as exemplified by the recent frictions between the DEA and the Puerto Rican police, but may further enhance the power of the security agencies within the state. Already local civilian agencies such as the Treasury and the Housing Department, not previously seen as performing security functions, are being increasingly drawn into this new security structure.

Additionally, the tendency towards integration of security agencies runs parallel to a considerable build-up of all the security agencies at the local and federal levels. This occurs while drug rehabilitation efforts are not seriously pursued, as the drop from US$21 million in 1992 to US$15.8 million in 1996 in the budget of the government department entrusted with this task indicates.[35] It could be argued that this also signifies a gradual transfer of authority in the realm of internal security from the local to the federal structure, and the blurring of traditional liberal distinction between civil and military spheres (as the military is increasingly drawn into civilian police functions).[36] The new security formation operates within a significantly redefined legal context represented by the 'accumulated results' of both federal and local 'anti-crime' legislation. Politically the process finds support in a state of opinion that expresses great concern with drugs and crime, and this is interpreted by the dominant political forces as prescribing tough measures in the sphere of law-enforcement.

The problem may be magnified as Puerto Rico increasingly becomes a focal point for drug trafficking, and is assigned the role of 'frontier outpost' in the 'war on drugs'. It poses political challenges that are not new to democratic theory: How will the new structure be democratically controlled? What is the proper place and role of military institutions in a democratic polity? How can a different policy approach to the challenge of drugs and violent crime be implemented once the new security structure becomes consolidated? What share of public resources should be devoted to law enforcement *vis-à-vis* other social needs? What is the cost to civil liberties of present trends?

One of the sharpest critiques of the implications of the ever escalating 'drug war' in Puerto Rico came from Juan F. Torruellas, a federal judge who had seen thousands of drug cases and was formerly an advocate of tough measures. He suggested that it was necessary to explore other policy alternatives and proposed the naming of a high-level US federal commission to evaluate the results of the present approach and explore other alternatives:

> First, prohibition's enforcement has had a devastating impact on the rights of the individual citizen. The control costs are seriously threatening the preservation of the values that are central to our form of government...
>
> In leaving this point, let me add what may sound like an exaggeration, but for which I invite your considered ponderation. There are many cases in the history of humankind, some of recent vintage, in which citizens have been willing to give up their collective civil rights in the name of, and in exchange for, an illusory achievement of so-called law and order. Seen from one viewpoint, there undoubtedly was a large measure of law and order in Hitler's Germany or Trujillo's Dominican Republic. But in the long-run, the surrendering of fundamental principles for temporary peace has proven to be short-sighted. I do not say we have yet reached such a crossroads, but I do say to you that I detect considerable public apathy regarding the upholding of rights which have been cherished since this land became a constitutional Republic, when it comes to those accused of drug violations.[37]

## A democratic and structural approach to the drugs–crime problem

The changes that have occurred in the security policies and structures of the state may be seen as conditioned by transnational and regional processes that are not unique to Puerto Rico, namely: (1) the revision by the United States of its security agenda and the convergence with this new agenda of regional political elites and security actors and (2) the social and political consequences of the erosion of previous forms of incorporation of popular sectors to the state as a result of the implementation of new macroeconomic policies, in some cases through the adoption of neoliberal formulas and in others as a response to the need to find new forms of articulation to the world economy. But the latter entails not only the abandonment of redistributive or paternalist policies associated with the concept of the 'welfare state', but a deeper social reorganization. It is in this broad context that present trends in Puerto Rico and the Caribbean should be viewed.

The post-Cold War national security agenda of the US focuses on 'non-traditional' threats that were formerly not considered security challenges. Terrorism, environmental security, peace operations and the promotion of democracy were raised to the status of major security themes in the absence of a bi-polar confrontation and its regional manifestations. However, in the Caribbean the major security concerns became drug trafficking and illegal migration. Both threats were linked in the security discourse and elicited analogous policy measures: strengthening control over frontiers, increasing the effectiveness of law-enforcement agencies, enhancing international collaboration, expanding intelligence capabilities, and so forth.

As the impact of both problems was felt throughout the region, the agenda was not imposed unilaterally by the US, although its actions were sometimes high-handed and controversial, but there was rather a convergence with the security agendas of Caribbean states and other powers represented in the region (mainly France and the UK).[38] This also occurred in Puerto Rico, with the particularity that there US security agencies act without the mediation of a national state. Secondly, in the social and economic spheres, neoliberal and privatization policies have tended to become dominant in the Caribbean and internationally. The ruling party in Puerto Rico has enthusiastically endorsed this ideological orientation, while US policies also impinge directly on social and economic changes. These policies do not necessarily entail a weaker or smaller state, but rather a reorganization of the state apparatus and a redefinition of its relationship with the economy and civil society. While the state retreats from some economic functions and de-emphasizes some aspects of social policy – consequently dismantling specific components of the state structure – new forms of paternalism are put in place and certain parts of the state bureaucracy significantly expand.

In particular, neoliberalism in Puerto Rico has been accompanied by a building up of the security agencies of the state to ensure social control. The need to enhance the repressive power of the state is structurally conditioned by its diminished capacity of incorporating the population through 'populist' measures and the social polarization that results from the thrust of its economic policies. This is accompanied by a style of governance that is increasingly authoritarian.

Although the economic and social changes that underlay the transformation of the state cannot be examined here, one can propose the hypothesis that they have resulted in a deepening of social polarization and in new forms of marginality. Marginalization affects, particularly, certain social groups, such as youths and social sectors that are not incorporated in the formal economy or are expelled from it.[39] This implies that the increase in drug consumption, the drug business and violent crime are not necessarily an unexplainable aberration, but a result of macrosocial and macroeconomic changes of an exclusionary character, and that the 'war on drugs' is the other side of that coin. It is interesting to note that the current US anti-drug strategy does not tackle structural factors, and consequently places almost exclusive emphasis on 'law enforcement' measures. The latter, applied with increasing determination in recent years in Puerto Rico, have failed to show decisive results.

## Conclusion

The drug business and the rise in violent crime should be seen as complex and long-term problems, conditioned by multiple factors, that our societies confront and for which there are no simple solutions. Policies that place undue, or even almost exclusive emphasis on 'law-enforcement' or military solutions, are bound to fail, while posing new challenges to democratic institutions. More than a decade of a steadily escalating 'war on drugs' has not significantly reduced the availability of drugs, drug consumption, or the very high level of violence.

Dora Nevárez, a Puerto Rican criminologist, has called for a 'structural' approach to the problem of crime in the island, that would take into account broader socio-economic factors.[40] This would require heeding the words of Judge Torruellas, while opening up public debate to a consideration of diverse policy alternatives. Such a debate will necessarily have to look beyond police measures and take into account the interconnectedness between the dominant thrust of state policies and the drugs–crime crisis. It may also provide us with a better understanding of the links between criminality and processes of cultural and social change. Otherwise, we will have to live with the (televised) illusion that mounting arrests and drug confiscations, a contemporary form of the Vietnam War 'body count', will eventually make our environment safer and better.

## Notes

1  I use the term 'security forces' to include both the civilian police and the armed forces. Present tendencies point to what can be called the 'military–police complex' due to a symbiosis between civilian and military structures and the blurring of the distinctions between these.
2  In the Caribbean the concept 'narcodemocracy' has been used by Ivelaw L. Griffith and Trevor Munroe in, 'Drugs and Democracy in the Caribbean', *Journal of Commonwealth and Comparative Politics*, Vol. 33, No. 3 (November 1995), pp. 357–76.
3  See, for example, James L. Zackrison and Eileen Bradley, 'Colombian Sovereignty Under Siege', *Strategic Forum*, No. 112 (May 1997).
4  See, for example, Ivelaw L. Griffith, 'Caribbean Manifestations of the Narcotics Phenomenon', in Jorge Rodríguez Beruff and Humberto García Muñiz (eds), *Security Problems and Policies in the Post-Cold War Caribbean* (London: Macmillan, 1996), pp. 181–200; Anthony P. Maingot, *The United States and the Caribbean* (Boulder, CO: Westview Press, 1994), chs 8 and 9; Michel S. Laguerre, 'National Security, Narcotics Control and the Haitian Military', in Rodríquez Beruff and García Muñiz, *Security Problems and Policies in the Post-Cold War Caribbean*, pp. 99–120.
5  Ivelaw L. Griffith, 'Caribbean Regional Security', *Strategic Forum*, No. 102 (February 1997).
6  'The Impact of Crime on Regional Security and Democratic Stability', Executive Summary prepared by O'Neill Hamilton for the Symposium 'Cooperative Security in the Caribbean: Preparing for a Shared Future', North–South Center, University of Miami, 18–19 April 1995.
7  The first robbery, which caused great commotion, was against the Nova Scotia bank in Santurce. On 26 February 1997, PonceBank, Banco Roig, Banco Popular branches in Río Piedras, Puerto Nuevo y Ponce were robbed. Amelia Estades Santaliz, 'Asaltan en dia tres bancos', *El Nuevo Día*, 27 February 1997.
8  Official concern with rising crime resulted in a comprehensive 16-volume study entitled *Etiología de la violencia en Puerto Rico* (San Juan: Technical Services, 1975).

9   Technical Services of Puerto Rico, *La Opinión púlica ante la violencia*, Vol. II of *Etiología*, pp. 16, 51.
10   'Reafirman ser americanos y puertorriqueños', *El Nuevo Día*, 12 June 1996, pp. 4–5.
11   Technical Services of Puerto Rico, *La adicción y la criminalidad*, Vol. XV of *Etiología* ..., op. cit., p. 29.
12   Technical Services Of Puerto Rico, *Socioecología de la criminalidad en Puerto Rico*, Vol. IV of *Etiología* ..., op. cit.
13   In the early 1970s, however, the upsurge of drug consumption was not immediately accompanied by a parallel rise in violent crimes but of 'crimes against property'.
14   For the position of a Catholic Bishop, see, S.E.R. Monseñor Enrique Hernández, *Sobre las propuestas enmiendas a la Constitución de Puerto Rico* (Caguas: Oficina de Medios de Comunicación Social, 1993), cited in Pedro Rosario Barbosa, 'Consideraciones preliminares en torno al discurso de la marina y el gobierno sobre el sistema de radar relocalizable más allá del horizonte', manuscript, December 1995, p. 4.
15   Gloribel Delgado, 'En pie las audiencias del radar', *El Nuevo Día*, 31 October 1995, p. 12.
16   Ismael Fernández, 'Con el crimen no se juega', *El Nuevo Día*, 13 May 1996, p. 50.
17   Pepo García, 'Chocan de frente los argumentos', *El Nuevo Día*, 18 December 1996, p. 5.
18   Andrea Martínez, 'Tierra dentro el azote', *El Nuevo Día*, 30 December 1996, p. 7.
19   Government Accounting Office, *Drug Control, U.S. Interdiction Efforts in the Caribbean Decline* (Washington DC: GAO, April 1996), pp. 4–5.
20   Joseph Rogers, 'Unwanted Fame', *Hemisphere*, Vol. 7, No. 3 (1997), pp. 38–41.
21   Andrea Martínez, 'Tierra adentro el azote', *El Nuevo Día*, 30 December 1996, p. 7.
22   See the table 'Marihuana confiscada en Puerto Rico' and Gerardo Montero, 'Confiscadas 25 libras de marihuana en el aereopuerto', *El Nuevo Día*, 5 August 1997, p. 26.
23   Daisy Sánchez, 'Crece la economía criminal, en todas partes el dinero del narcotráfico', *Diálogo*, November 1996, p. 11.
24   'Peor la criminalidad en la percepción pública', *El Nuevo Día*, 13 August 1997, pp. 4–5.
25   Leonor Mulero, 'Sella el pacto el zar antidrogas', *El Nuevo Día*, 19 January 1995, p. 6; and, 'Refuerzo federal para la mano dura', *El Nuevo Día*, 1 May 1996, p. 8.
26   Government of Puerto Rico, *Budget Proposal 1997–1998*, Vol. II (San Juan, 1997).
27   Andrea Martínez, 'Destacan los logros de la "Operación Gateway"', *El Nuevo Dia*, 19 June 1996, p. 16; 'Rudo golpe al narcotráfico', *El Nuevo Día*, 2 October 1996, p. 20.
28   About the HIDTA, see, White House, *National Drug Control Strategy: 1996* (GPO: Washington, DC, 1996), p. 15, and section IV.
29   On some existing links with the Dominican Republic, see Andrea Martínez, 'Rompen una poderosa pandilla internacional', *El Nuevo Dia*, 6 March 1997, p. 20; also, US Department of State, *International Narcotics Control Strategy Report*, March 1995, pp. 171–2.

30   Mulero, 'Sella el pacto...', op. cit.
31   See, Jorge Rodríguez Beruff, 'Strategic military interests and Puerto Rican self-determination', in Rodríguez Beruff and García Muñiz, *Security Problems and Policies in the Post-Cold War Caribbean*, pp. 155–178.
32   Juanita Colombani, 'Amplia la presencia de las unidades militares', *El Nuevo Día*, 16 August 1997, p. 26.
33   Leonor Mulero, 'Puerto Rico la base escogida', *El Nuevo Día*, 1 August 1997, p. 4; and, 'Desembarco millonario de beneficios', p. 5
34   Hans Binnendjik and Erik Kjonnerod, 'Panana 2000', *Strategic Forum*, No. 117, June 1997, pp. 3–4.
35   Government of Puerto Rico, *Budget Proposal for 1995–1996*, San Juan, 1996.
36   A General Accounting Office (GAO) study notes that: 'At the outset, the lead agency mission was a radical departure from DoD's traditional military role and was accompanied by social and legal questions regarding the proper role of the armed forces in a democratic society' (GAO, *Drug Control, Impact of DoD's Detection and Monitoring on Cocaine Flow*, September 1991, p. 21).
37   Juan R. Torruellas, 'One Judge's Attempt at a Rational Discussion of the So-Called War on Drugs', *Revista Jurídica*, Vol. 66, No. 1 (1996), pp. 34–5.
38   See, Beruff and Muñiz, 'Security Problems...', op. cit.
39   According to a recent study, the profile of the young offender was: 96 per cent drug user (37 per cent combines more than one drug, normally marijuana with cocaine), 95 per cent from a high risk zone, 82 per cent divorced parents, 60 per cent school drop-out, 55 per cent family depends on public assistance, 46 per cent mother as head of the household, 18 per cent father as head of family, 32 per cent victim of family violence, and 23 per cent abused. Homicide is the first cause of death among youths from 15 to 19 years of age, and 1 out 10 youths born in 1970 have criminal records. Ingrid Ortega Nevárez, 'Hijos del caos social', *El Nuevo Día*, 3 June 1996, p. 5., and 'A merced de la violencia'.
40   José Fernández Colón, 'Promotora política pública', *El Nuevo Día*, 8 March 1997, p. 4.

# 9
# Cooperation and Conflict in the US–Caribbean Drug Connection

*Trevor Munroe*

The connection between the United States and CARICOM states in relation to drugs has been characterized by both conflict and cooperation. By and large, cooperation has been the dominant element. This cooperation has derived from both recognition among Caricom élites of coincidence of interests with the United States in the 'war against drugs' as well as pressure on Caribbean governments from successive American administrations. It is this latter dimension which has exacerbated conflict and, from time to time, contributed to strains in US–Caribbean relations. These strains in turn reflect somewhat differing evaluations of the relevance of traditional concepts of sovereignty in the context of contemporary realities as well as divergent assessments of the main threat of Caribbean sovereignty – transnational drug cartels or assertions of US power.

## The international framework and US policy

The dominant line of CARICOM–US cooperation has expressed itself in mutually reinforcing policy initiatives and law enforcement efforts, mainly giving expression to the requirements of the 1988 UN Convention Against Illicit Traffic in Narcotic Drugs and Psychotropic Substances. In this respect, it is worth noting that at the treaty signing ceremony in Vienna on 20 December 1988, among the 43 initial signatories was the United States and one CARICOM State, the Bahamas. Since that time all the Caribbean states have not only signed but also ratified the Vienna Convention.

In the context of the US–Caribbean relationship, it is worthwhile recounting the recognition in the 1988 Convention that 'the links between illicit traffic and other related organized criminal activities...

**Table 9.1**   United Nations Conventions on Drugs and Commonwealth Caribbean Adherence

| Country | UN Single Convention on Narcotic Drugs, 1961 | UN Convention On Psychotropic Substances, 1971 | UN Protocol Amending the 1972 Convention | UN Convention Against Illicit Traffic in Narcotic Drugs & Psychotropic Substances, 1988 |
|---|---|---|---|---|
| Anguilla | E | E | E | – |
| Antigua | P | P | P | P |
| Bahamas | P | P | P | P |
| Barbados | P | P | P | P |
| Belize | – | – | – | P |
| Bermuda | E | E | E | – |
| British Virgin Islands | E | E | E | – |
| Cayman Islands | E | E | E | – |
| Dominica | P | P | P | P |
| Grenada | – | P | – | P |
| Guyana | – | P | – | P |
| Jamaica | P | P | P | P |
| Montserrat | E | E | E | – |
| St Kitts/Nevis | – | – | – | P |
| St Lucia | P | P | – | P |
| St Vincent | – | – | – | P |
| Trinidad | P | P | P | P |
| Turks & Caicos Is. | E | E | E | – |

*Notes:* E – Extended to the country as a British Dependency;
P – Party to the Convention.
*Source:* Jefferson O'Brien Cumberbatch, *The UWI/UNDCP Drug Control Legal Training Program: Legislation Compilation Consultancy Report*, Barbados, November 1994.

threaten the ... sovereignty of States'.[1] Moreover, among the Convention's terms is the requirement for each signatory state to criminalize the possession, trafficking and consumption of illicit drugs, as well as to provide for (a) forfeiture of proceeds from illegal narcotics activity, (b) extradition arrangements, (c) mutual legal assistance treaties in respect of drug related offenses, (d) enhancement of law enforcement effectiveness, (e) eradication of narcotics producing crops, and (f) suppression of illicit traffic by sea. Finally, countries subscribing to the Convention are required to furnish information on its operation to the Commission on Narcotics Drugs of the United Nation's Economic and Social Council which may in turn make appropriate recommendations to signatory states and to the UN. In this sense, the US–CARICOM drug connection takes place within a definite framework of international obligations.

Needless to say, these obligations reflected the perceptions and policy orientations of successive US administrations, which in turn influenced international consensus on the narcotics issue. Two years before the text of the 1988 Vienna Convention was finalized, the 'drug war' initiated by President Nixon at the end of the 1960s achieved new legislative heights. Later, strong federal statute against money-laundering was placed on the American law books, President Reagan issued a directive making the struggle against illicit drugs a national security issue; Congress passed the Anti-Drug Abuse Act (1986) mandating heavy minimum sentences for first offense street-dealing. Moreover, an Amendment to the Foreign Assistance Act was passed requiring the president to identify major drug producing/transit territories and to certify whether such countries are cooperating with the United States in the anti-narcotics struggle.

These legislative and policy initiatives formed part of a crusade which the US extended into the United Nations system and which saw the federal anti-narcotics budget grow from $69 million to $15 billion between 1969 and 1996. In institutional terms, the DEA was created in 1973 during the Nixon Administration, and agencies such as the CIA, the FBI, the US Customs Service, the US Coastguard, the US military, the Office of National Drug Control Policy and the National Drug Intelligence Center were brought successively into the 'war against drugs'. By the 1990s, over $100 billion had been spent on this war by six different presidents and over 50 federal agencies were involved in the anti-narcotics struggle.[2]

The priority attached to drugs and the emphases of the crusade varied from time to time. For example, in the Reagan–Bush era the drugs issue was among the top three items on the national security agenda, while it dropped to number 29 of 29 items under the Clinton Administration. Nevertheless, there has been evident a fundamental consensus across Democratic and Republican Administrations. A principal element of this consensus has been the emphasis on supply control rather than demand reduction and the corresponding treatment of the drugs issue as a law enforcement rather than a public health problem. The budget requested by the president for fiscal year 1997 reflects this orientation and proposes over 60 per cent allocation to domestic law enforcement and interdiction as against one-third to demand reduction.[3] Within this framework two of the Clinton Administration's strategic goals and a number of supporting objectives have direct relevance to the US–Caribbean drug connection.

The first of these is goal number 4: 'Shield America's air, land and sea frontiers from the drug threat'.[4] Towards this goal, the Clinton Administration laid down objectives of 'bilateral and multilateral intelligence sharing' and 'flexible interdiction in the transit zone to ensure effective use of maritime and aerial interdiction capabilities'.[5] Goal number 5 is to 'break foreign and domestic drug sources of supply'. In this context objectives include 'seizing...drugs and assets' of leaders and associates of major trafficking organizations; crop eradication; attacks on money-laundering; building the institutional capability of host nations to conduct successful interdiction; 'more effective drug control efforts on their own and withstand the threat narcotics trafficking poses to sovereignty, democracy, and free-market economies'. Most relevant from the point of view of the dynamics of the US–Caribbean drug relationship is the US aim to 'increase the political will of countries to cooperate with the United States on drug control efforts through aggressive diplomacy, certification and carefully targeted foreign assistance'.[6] There can hardly be any doubt that such an aim clearly envisages, or at least legitimates, carrot-and-stick tactics by inducing foreign states to fall in line with and to advance US policy on the drugs question.

The US temptation to use pressure in the Caribbean as elsewhere is considerable. In the first place, opinion surveys in the United States establish conclusively that an overwhelming majority of the American public regard stopping the flow of drugs into the US as the number one foreign policy issue.[7] Secondly, the obvious and overwhelming asymmetry of power between the United States and the Caribbean narcotics transit and producing states invites an imposition of will. Thirdly, once the drugs issue is conceptualized as war (and not a cancer, for example), perceived failure to achieve objectives leads easily to the view that states allied in the war effort are not pulling their weight, especially against the background of budgetary constraints on the US itself, the major partner in the crusade. In this context, it can hardly be denied that the perception of failure is underpinned by much of the reality of the anti-drugs war. Instead of diminishing the size of the illegal drugs market in the US, that market has grown from $2 billion to $100 billion; the number of major money-laundering countries and territories has grown from seven to 33 and the number of major drug producing and transit countries from 24 to 31 during the two-and-a-half decades of the anti-drugs war.[8]

Despite these indicators of failure, the US has hardly 'put its money where its mouth is', certainly in regard to the external dimension of the war against drugs. Given the huge size and sophistication of the resources available to the transnational criminal organizations, the international component of the US anti-narcotics budget has been, to say the least, inadequate. Moreover, as Table 9.2 shows, the Congress consistently denies and on occasion, significantly cuts presidential funding requests for international and interdiction drugs programs. Within recent years this has been particularly apparent in relation to the Caribbean transit zone through which 30 per cent of the cocaine entering the United States is estimated to pass. Tables 9.3 and 9.4 show that between 1991 and 1995, counter narcotics funding by the US in this zone decreased by almost 50 per cent and maritime assets devoted to the area declined while, at the very same time, evidence suggests a significant shift from air to sea trafficking in illicit drugs (see Table 9.5). The reduction in resource allocation to the Caribbean transit zone has been reflected in such things as reduced radar coverage, reduced flight hours

Table 9.2   President's Request versus Congressional Action ($m)

|  | Interdiction | | International | |
| --- | --- | --- | --- | --- |
|  | President's Request | Congress Enacted | President's Request | Congress Enacted |
| FY 1992 | 2,109 | 2,217 | 779 | 763 |
| FY 1993 | 2,220 | 1,746 | 768 | 538 |
| FY 1994 | 1,765 | 1,300 | 490 | 351 |
| FY 1995 | 1,206 | 1,293 | 428 | 310 |

*Source*: Congressional Research Service, 1996.

Table 9.3   Counter Narcotics Funding in the Transit Zone, Fiscal Years, 1991–95) ($m)

| Agency | 1991 | 1992 | 1993 | 1994 | 1995 |
| --- | --- | --- | --- | --- | --- |
| DOD | 407.1 | 504.5 | 426.0 | 220.4 | 214.7 |
| Coast Guard | 565.2 | 443.9 | 310.5 | 314.4 | 301.2 |
| Customs | NA | NA | 16.2 | 12.5 | 12.8 |
| DEA | 26.2 | 28.8 | 29.1 | 28.7 | 29.6 |
| State | 35.9 | 36.2 | 14.0 | 7.9 | 10.6 |
| Total | 1,034.4 | 1,013.4 | 795.8 | 583.9 | 568.9 |

*Notes*: NA – not available; DOD – Department of Defense.
*Source*: US General Accounting Office, *Drug Control – US Interdiction Efforts in the Caribbean*, April 1996.

**Table 9.4**   JIATF–East Maritime Assets, Fiscal Years, 1991–95 (No. of Ship Days)

| Ship type | 1991 | 1992 | 1993 | 1994 | 1995 |
|---|---|---|---|---|---|
| Logistic | 128 | 287 | 71 | 40 | 0 |
| Cruiser | 524 | 558 | 753 | 742 | 488 |
| Destroyer | 909 | 699 | 602 | 118 | 224 |
| Frigate | 1,874 | 2,008 | 1,441 | 785 | 727 |
| Amphibious | 51 | 87 | 188 | 9 | 0 |
| Coast Guard | 0 | 0 | 138 | 0 | 401 |
| Other | 750 | 533 | 1,255 | 974 | 1,005 |
| Total | 4,236 | 4,172 | 4,448 | 2,668 | 2,845 |

*Notes*: JIATF–Joint Inter-Agency Task Force.
*Source*: *US General Accounting Office, Drug Control-US Interdiction Efforts in the Caribbean*, April 1996.

**Table 9.5**   Air and Maritime Drug-trafficking Events and Results, 1992–95

| Year | Air | | Maritime | |
|---|---|---|---|---|
| | Events | Results | Events | Results |
| 1992 | 344 | 66 | NA | NA |
| 1993 | 217 | 71 | 174 | 122 |
| 1994 | 154 | 45 | 223 | 172 |
| 1995 | 125 | 26 | 249 | 135 |

*Notes*: Traffickers' aborts were not counted in results; NA – not available.
*Source*: US General Accounting Office, *Drug Control – US Interdiction Efforts in the Caribbean*, 1996.

flown and reduced allocations to the US Customs Marine Law Enforcement Program, etc. At the same time, the anticipated shift in funding to source countries in accordance with the 1993 Clinton Administration policy decision, has not materialized (see Table 9.6). Not surprisingly in these circumstances, both air and surface cocaine seizures have fallen significantly in the Caribbean transit zone since 1992.

This situation has had a number of implications for the US–Caribbean drug relationship. One is the fuelling among strategic US élites of the position that in getting more from the US counter-narcotics tax dollar and in the drive to make US neighborhoods more drug free, concerns for the sovereignty of source countries and transit states should be of secondary importance. For example, Dan Burton, Chairman of the House Sub-Committee on the Western Hemisphere typifies this conservative tendency. In a recent sub-committee hearing Burton said 'to

Table 9.6  Counternarcotics Funding in Source Countries, Fiscal Years, 1991–95 ($m)

| Agency | 1991 | 1992 | 1993 | 1994 | 1995 |
|--------|------|------|------|------|------|
| DOD | 76.1 | 120.7 | 154.9 | 144.5 | 148.7 |
| Customs | NA | NA | 6.0 | 3.9 | 5.2 |
| DEA | 18.4 | 21.5 | 21.0 | 20.7 | 21.3 |
| State | 160.7 | 123.6 | 105.1 | 55.2 | 54.8 |
| Total | 255.2 | 265.8 | 287.0 | 224.3 | 230.0 |

*Note*: NA – not available. DOD – Department of Defense;
*Source*: US General Accounting Office, *Drug Control-US Interdiction Efforts in the Caribbean*, 1996.

the President of the United States, let's pull all the stops.... Tell the Presidents of Peru and Bolivia at 5 o'clock in the morning that we have got some aircraft carriers and we are coming down through those coca-filled valleys, and we are going to ... eradicate the coca plants once and for all.... We need to tell those government officials we are going to get rid of the drug crops. Either you help us, or we will do it without you'.[9]

Particularly in relation to the Caribbean, Elliott Abrams, former Assistant Secretary of State for Inter-American Affairs during the Reagan administration reflects a similar tendency. He specifically advocated surrender of sovereignty by Caribbean states in return for more effective US security assistance and economic aid. 'Full colonial status', Abrams conceded 'may be a non-starter, but a voluntary, beneficial erosion of sovereignty should not be'.[10] In this context, the author cited as one example of this new model 'shiprider agreements' signed in 1995 between the United States and six of the smallest Eastern Caribbean States which 'permit US Navy vessels full freedom of action in their territorial waters, calculating no doubt that it is better to have their sovereignty invaded by Americans under treaty than by drug runners at will'.[11] It is this line of thought and of corresponding action, evident to varying degrees in successive US administrations, that has elicited both cooperation and conflict from the Anglophone Caribbean.

## Caribbean responses to US drug policies

On the cooperation side, all Caribbean governments, with the exception of Barbados and Jamaica, signed 'Ship-rider Agreements' presented to them by the Clinton Administration, without significant negotiation or amendment.[12] These agreement in effect accepted the right of the United States to enter the territorial waters and air space of Caribbean states as well as provided blanket authorization for such incursions in pursuit of drug traffickers. The Panday government in Trinidad and Tobago was most forthright in the justification of these agreements as reflecting recognition that the primary threat to Caribbean sovereignty derives not so much from foreign states as from non-state actors in the form of the transnational gangs. Indeed, Prime Minister Panday has been quite explicit in stating his belief that 'we have to revisit the concept of sovereignty in the light of the might and power of some of these drug lords'.[13]

Consistent with this perspective, Panday's Attorney General, Ramesh Maharaj, in defending the Shiprider Agreement signed by Trinidad and the US in March 1996, regarded it as protecting 'the country's sovereignty rather than undermining it'. 'We cannot', Maharaj continued, 'be constrained and impeded by political and geo-political limits if we are to stop these transnational criminal organizations and eradicate the drug trade'.[14] This reconfiguring of traditional concepts of sovereignty naturally attracted fullsome praise and some practical aid from the US administration, but as well, has found some resonance from with the Caribbean scholarly community.[15]

Moreover, in practice, cooperation with the US arising out of US pressure as well as Caribbean perception of interest convergence in the anti-drugs war has been comprehensive and consistent. The majority of states signed the shiprider agreements in the form and terms proposed by the United States, not least of all because of the inadequacy of resources available to the Caribbean mini-states (see Table 9.7). In addition, they have as well entered into mutual legal assistance and extradition treaties, passed money laundering and asset forfeiture legislation and been aggressive in drug law enforcement in terms of crop eradication, seizures, arrests and conviction of offenders. The 1997 State Department *International Narcotics Control Strategy Report* (INCSR) reflects conclusions typical of previous reports and records US recognition of Caribbean cooperation. For example, it notes:

- 'US and Bahamian law enforcement officials worked closely together to apprehend drug traffickers.'[16]
- 'The GOG (Government of Guyana) has requested more intensive coordination with the US on bilateral counter narcotics efforts.'[17]
- 'According to DEA, Jamaican police counter narcotics cooperation in 1996 remained at the high levels of 1995.'[18]

- 'Counter narcotics cooperation between the GOTT (Government of Trinidad & Tobago) and the US reached new heights in the 1996 with the signing of an extradition treaty, a mutual legal assistance treaty and a maritime counter-drug cooperation agreement.'[19]

In relation to the seven countries of the Eastern Caribbean–Antigua and Barbuda, Barbados, Dominica, Grenada, St Kitts and Nevis, St Lucia and St Vincent and the Grenadines – regarded as the 'second largest cocaine gateway to the U.S', the report noted operational cooperation with US authorities and agencies is generally excellent'.[20] Finally, in relation to the Caribbean Dependent Territories, the INCSR report records 'close anti-drug cooperation with the U.S'.[21]

This is not to say that the State Department did not indicate areas of concern from the US point of view. These included policy issues, most notably the inadequacy, in the American view, of some Caribbean anti-narcotics legislation (e.g. the Jamaican money-laundering legislation passed in December 1996) as well as the slowness of Barbados and Jamaica to conclude maritime counter narcotics cooperation agreements.[22] US dissatisfaction also expressed itself in relation to weakness in Caribbean law enforcement, particularly in respect of securing convictions, seizure of assets and confiscation of property of drug traffickers. More generally, US officials have expressed the view that 'corruption is still widespread throughout the region' and that this hampers

Table 9.7  Selected Eastern Caribbean Host Nation Maritime Interdiction Assets

| Nation | Interdiction assets |
| --- | --- |
| British Virgin Islands | 6 patrol boats and 1 aircraft |
| Anguilla | 2 boats |
| St Martin, Guadeloupe and Martinique | 3 patrol boats, 6 fixed-wing aircraft, 4 helicopters |
| Antigua-Barbuda | 3 boats |
| St Kitts-Nevis | 4 boats |
| Montserrat | 1 patrol craft |
| Dominica | 4 boats |
| St Lucia | 4 boats 2 of which are damaged |
| St Vincent & the Grenadines | 4 boats |
| Barbados | 5 boats, 1 possibly damaged |
| Grenada | 4 boats |
| Trinidad and Tobago | Large, medium, and small platforms |

*Source*: US General Accounting Office, *Drug Control-US Interdiction Efforts in the Caribbean*, 1996.

US–Caribbean cooperation, particularly in areas of intelligence sharing and information exchange'.[23] There can be no question, however, that despite these negatives, successive US administrations confirm that cooperation has been the dominant element of US–Caribbean relations on the issue of illicit drugs.

From the point of view of the Caribbean, this cooperation has undoubtedly grown, at least in part out of a recognition of regional self-interest. The West Indian Commission report of 1992 recorded the view of strategic elites and interested publics within the region: 'Nothing poses greater threats to civil society in CARICOM countries than the drug problem ... in our consultations in country after country the anxiety of citizens about these dangers ... have been raised consistently'.[24] Similarly, the Commission took the position that 'CARICOM countries are threatened ... by an onslaught from illegal drugs as crushing as any military repression'.[25] Prior to the West Indian Commission's assessments, CARICOM Heads of Governments had in 1987 'agreed to the development and implementation of a regional programme designed to complement the efforts being made at national levels to control the traffic in and abuse of narcotic substances'.[26] Two years subsequently, regional heads endorsed proposals, later put to the UN by Prime Ministers Manley of Jamaica and ANR Robinson of Trinidad and Tobago, respectively, that the international community should cooperate in the establishment of a multi-lateral strike force and an International Criminal Court to deal with issues of narcotics interdiction and adjudication, very often beyond the capabilities of individual states.

By the mid-1990s, the Caribbean states and territories, at least in large measure from their own experience of the growth in danger of the drug threat, were deepening their own analysis of regional self interest in the issue and developing much more comprehensive Plans of Action. Caricom's Fifth Special Meeting of the Conference of Heads of Government held in Barbados in December 1996 'recognised the fundamental coincidence of interests of CARICOM Member States and the United States'[27] in dealing with the drugs issue. Prior to this, the UNDCP convened a regional meeting on Drug Control Cooperation in the Caribbean, attended by 26 Caribbean states and territories, in May 1996 in Barbados. This meeting produced a comprehensive report endorsing recommendations for action in relation to national drug bodies, anti-narcotics legislation, law enforcement, demand reduction and maritime cooperation.[28] While there can be little doubt, as Anthony Maingot has pointed out,[29] that there was limited official articulation of the importance of the drug threat in the Caribbean before the end of the 1980s (though there were 'pioneering,' if isolated cases, of Caribbean–US cooperation in the 1970s)[30] to this, the awareness of regional self-interest in this area certainly took root in the 1990s.

## Caribbean concerns regarding sovereignty

Cooperation with the United States in advancing this self-interest did not develop, however, without serious concern in the Caribbean that mutually beneficial collaboration with the United States should not be at the expense of the sovereignty of the Caribbean states. One of the earliest and strongest expressions of this anxiety came out of the 1988 Ninth Conference of CARICOM Heads of government in a letter written on behalf of the Conference by its chairman, Vere Bird, Antigua's Prime Minister, to President Reagan. The letter expressed concern at, among other things, 'attempts to extend domestic United States authority into neighbouring countries of the Region *without regard for their sovereignty* and independent legal systems of those countries'.[31] These attempts took the form in particular of 'hot pursuit', interdiction and seizure of suspected drug traffickers within CARICOM territorial waters. The CARICOM states indicated to Reagan that this matter 'threatens to create discord and division between the friendly nations of the Region on the one hand and the United States on the other'.[32]

This concern of the CARICOM leaders was reflected in resentment from important elements of civil society at the relationship with the US on the drugs issue. In June 1990, for example, a Conference of Bishops and Pastors from the Caribbean and Latin America organized by the Caribbean Conference of Churches spoke of policies relating to the drug issue 'not derived from a Latin American and Caribbean diagnosis of the problem but from the United States approach to the topic'. 'We are once again', the Churchmen stated 'faced with the imposition of unilateral policies and ideas whereby one country determines what others should do without taking into account their problems and real needs'.[33]

This conclusion was largely shared by other Caribbean scholars. Cumberbatch and Duncan argued, for example, that the United States strongly influences, if not controls, Caribbean governmental response to the drug trade.[34] Ramharack recalled that under the CBI, beneficiary states must cooperate with US anti-drug efforts and concludes that Caribbean states are often pressured by the US to cooperate in anti-drug efforts.[35] The West Indian Commission Report itself records that 'Caribbean governments have been subject to more that a little coercion by US agencies'[36] in narcotics-related matters. In this context, what has been the response of Caribbean governments?

Three tendencies have been apparent: willing acquiescence, reluctant acquiescence and negotiated cooperation. These tendencies manifested themselves most dramatically in relation to the maritime counter-narcotics agreements (the 'Ship-rider' agreements) proposed to regional states on bilateral bases by the US from 1995 onwards. The tendency of willing cooperation was most effectively articulated by the Panday government of Trinidad and Tobago. For that administration, the Shiprider Agreement was not so much an imposition but a necessary and legitimate recognition that traditional sovereignty *vis-à-vis* the US has to be sacrificed in order to more effectively cope with the greater threat posed to national statehood by transnational drug-trafficking groups. This view was most clearly expressed by Trinidad and Tobago Attorney General, Ramesh Maharaj, who in January 1997, called on CARICOM to 'sacrifice sovereignty for drug war... cooperation was especially vital to the Caribbean which is under escalating threat from the international drug cartels'.[37]

The second tendency of reluctant acquiescence to US demands frequently expressed itself in comments by officials of the government of St Vincent and The Grenadines. In March 1995, St Vincent's Deputy Prime Minister and Attorney General stated 'short of handing St. Vincent and the Grenadines over to the Americans to administer, I do not know what else the government could lawfully do to combat drugs'.[38] A year and a half later Prime Minister James Mitchell was quoted as saying 'We have surrendered our sovereignty. We've given the US all the cooperation in the world – what else do they want?'.[39]

The third line in the region – negotiated cooperation – reflected itself most of all in the response of the Patterson and Arthur governments in Jamaica and Barbados, respectively, to the American proposals for ship-rider agreements. In the Jamaican case, the government, with the support of opposition parliamentary parties and influential opinion makers,[40] refused to sign the standard agreement produced by the Americans on the grounds that some of its provisions required an unacceptable erosion of national sovereignty. Among these was the article through which the standard ship-rider agreement signed by other CARICOM states 'constitutes permission... [for the] United States vessel [to] enter... waters in order to investigate any suspect aircraft or board and search any suspect vessel'.[41] The Jamaican position upheld the anti-narcotics trafficking goal but in contradiction to the stance of the Panday government, 'was not prepared to sacrifice... sovereignty in the process'.[42]

The initial divergence of positions between the US, on the one hand, and Barbados and Jamaica on the other, led to protracted negotiations which ultimately concluded in agreements with both CARICOM states. These agreements were however different from the standard document in ways which showed greater regard for the sovereignty of Jamaica and Barbados particularly in respect of the need for US authorities to obtain case by case authorization to enter the territorial waters of either state. Moreover, they were not concluded without definite regional perceptions of efforts on the part of the US to put pressure on Barbados and on Jamaica to sign the standard agreement. Such were the dynamics of this conflict that the perception of US pressure triggered renewed efforts on the part of CARICOM states to reduce bi-lateralism in relations with the US and to formulate a common position on the basis of which to renew cooperation with the US on narcotics issues.

## From bilateral to multilateral relations with the US

This effort took the form of the fifth special meeting of the conference of heads of government, convened primarily on the initiative of the government of Jamaica. It is out of this conference that there emerged the explicit recognition of the 'fundamental coincidence of interests of CARICOM member states and the United States in a peaceful, stable and prosperous Caribbean'.[43] But the conference reaffirmed that the pursuit of these interests and the attainment of harmonious relations had to be on the basis of 'dialogue, partnership and *mutual respect for each other's sovereignty*, constitutions, institutions and judicial systems'. [Emphasis mine.]

Moreover, obviously mindful of the perceived pressures on Jamaica and Barbados to sign the standard ship-rider agreement, the CARICOM states 'rejected any threat or suggestion of coercive measures as a means of securing compliance with pre-determined policies'. They 'reaffirmed ... commitment ... to strengthen cooperation with the United States' but on a basis of working through differences rather than pressure to secure compliance in situations where conflicts emerged. The Fifth Special Meeting was also significant in its explicit self-criticism in recognising that prior to then the CARICOM member states had not adopted a sufficiently collaborative approach. In remedying this deficiency the conference agreed 'to establish an Inter-governmental Task Force (IGTF) charged with the responsibility of formulating an integrated *regional counter-narcotics policy ... and a regional approach to the conclusion of treaties with Third States in counter-narcotics matters*'. [Emphasis mine.]

From the standpoint of CARICOM–US relations on drugs issues, two other points were of significance at this meeting. One was the explicit linkage between the success of the counter-narcotics struggle and the development of harmonious relations with the United States and issues such as NAFTA Parity, the marketing of bananas and gun smuggling. While there had been invariably an appreciation for the connection between drugs issues and matters of economic development, a new urgency attached to dealing with this linkage in the context of liberalization of global trade regimes, the ruling of the WTO against preferential access for Caribbean bananas in the European market and the unacceptable high levels of gun crime, particularly in Jamaica, related to illegal trafficking in arms from the United States. The second point of particular significance was the call 'for the convening of a CARICOM–US Summit at the earliest possible opportunity in 1997'. This Summit, which eventually took place on 10 May 1997, itself epitomized much of the conflict–cooperation dynamics of the CARICOM–US relationship on the narcotics issue.

In the first place, the Summit was convened, at least in part, because CARICOM leaders perceived elements of conflict or at least of differences of tactics with the US administration in the approach to the drug problem. In contradiction to the CARICOM governments, the US tendency was to separate the narcotics/ security problem from economic issues, to delink drugs from arms-trafficking and to show little regard for Caribbean sensitivities on matters relating to sovereignty. In that last regard, the issues of Jamaica being decertified by the US arose in the context of the Jamaican government's reluctance to sign the ship-rider agreement in the form proposed by the US.[44] It was out of these differences that the Summit materialized as a means of conflict-resolution and of renewed cooperation. The conclusion of the summit in turn reflected the extent to which these differences were resolved.

By and large the language of both the Declaration of Principles as well as the Plan of Action deriving from the Barbados meeting went some distance in addressing Caribbean sensitivities and concerns. In this regard the US along with the Caribbean leadership affirmed 'a spirit of partnership and mutual respect...', and specifically, 'respect for the sovereignty of states'. [45] The Declaration of Principles further recognizes 'The inextricable link between trade, economic development, security and prosperity' and therefore the need to create 'stable and prosperous economies' as 'bulwarks against the forces of transnational crime'. Moreover, the United States along with other summit participants declared their resolve 'to collaborate in combatting...the threat posed to our peoples and the foundations of our nations by illegal firearms and ammunition trafficking'. There can be little doubt that in these and other ways the language of the Bridgetown Declaration spoke to the concerns of the Caribbean leadership and provided an improved framework for less conflict with the US on drug related issues.

The Plan of Action also reflected this framework. It incorporated areas related to Justice and Security as well as Trade, Development, Finance and the Environment. In regard to the former, the plan reiterated acknowledgement of the 'threat posed by illegal trafficking in arms', a threat 'compounded by its linkage to the illicit traffic in drugs'.[46] Among the number of steps proposed to deal with this threat were the following: examination of 'the adequacy of existing legislation to combat the illegal manufacture and traffic in arms, ammunition explosives and other similar materials and strengthening such laws where necessary'; 'continued provision by the United States of technical and other assistance to assist law enforcement agencies in the control of illicit traffic in arms'; finally, the US along with Caribbean States committed itself 'to work towards the early adoption of an international agreement against the illicit manufacturing and trafficking in arms, ammunition, explosives and other similar materials'.[47]

In addition to this particularly controversial area of arms trafficking, the Plan of Action covered less contentions areas such as enhanced demand reduction, strengthening criminal justice systems, combatting attempts to corrupt officials, combatting money laundering, strengthening combined and cooperative interdiction efforts. The summit further agreed that the recommendations for action would be monitored and reviewed by a Joint Committee on Justice and Security: 'to facilitate an increasing and effective level of communications, coordination and follow-up among our governments'. Arguably, the establishment of this institutional mechanism, along with a similar arrangements for development, finance and environmental issues, was among the most important outcomes of the summit. Equally, it cannot be denied that despite these declarations of intent, the CARICOM governments in general and the Jamaican government in particular failed in large measure to persuade the Clinton Administration take urgent and meaningful practical action on the critical issue of arms smuggling from the US into the Caribbean.

This deficit in practical action, despite elaboration of common principles, was also evident in respect of central trade and economic matters. On the vital question of US opposition to duty free, preferential access by CARICOM bananas to the European Union, the US made no meaningful concessions. A hardly satisfactory substitute was the pledge by the Clinton Administration to continue 'to work with all concerned parties to achieve mutually satisfactory marketing arrangements for Caribbean bananas, recognising the critical importance to Caribbean countries of the continued access of Caribbean bananas to the traditional markets of the European Union'. In this context, not surprisingly one Eastern Caribbean Prime Minister quoted on condition of anonymity concluded: 'We got nothing substantial on bananas.' We may conclude therefore that the summit, a result of conflict elements in the relationship, produced enhanced principles and mechanisms for co-operation but little practical results in anti-drugs collaboration.

## Conclusion

From this analysis, a number of points maybe concluded:

- The United States drug policy in the Caribbean, consistent with policy elsewhere, places emphasis on law enforcement and supply interdiction over and above demand control.
- United States policy has in some measure coincided with 'autochthonous' Caribbean positions but where there have been divergencies, the United States has put significant pressure on Caribbean governments to conform to US demands.
- Caribbean states have by and large cooperated with the US as a result of three factors: perceived coincidence of interests, the search for aid more often than not on a bilateral basis, and the sense that, arising out of asymmetries of power, there is no alternative to compliance with US requests.
- Where divergencies have arisen over specific drug related issues, there has been more room for manoeuvre and for negotiating compromise agreements with the United States than either dependency theory or world systems analysis might suggest.
- In the context of such compromises where outcomes differ from initial positions of Caribbean and US partners, the terms of negotiated settlements nevertheless reflect the preponderance of US power and the imperative of combatting threats to national sovereignty from transnational criminal organizations.
- The Bridgetown Declaration of Principles and Plan of Action provides an improved framework for managing US–CARICOM differences, strengthening cooperation, and for making the anti-narcotics struggle more effective.

# Notes

1   UN, *Convention Against Illicit Traffic in Narcotic Drugs and Psychothropic Substances* [Done at Vienna, 20 December 1988], Preamble.

2   Douglas W. Payne, 'Drugs into Money into Power', *Freedom Review*, Vol. 27 No.4, July–August 1996 pp. 28–44.

3   Barry R. McCaffrey, *Reducing Drug Use and Its Consequences in America,*1996, pp. 6–7.

4   Ibid., pp. 4, 12.

5   Ibid., p. 5.

6   Ibid. emphasis added

7   One survey, referred to by Benjamin A. Gilman, Chairman, House Committee on International Relations, found that '85 per cent of the respondents stated that the most important foreign policy issue today, even more important than protecting jobs, is stopping the flow of illegal drugs into our nation'. See *Hearing Before the Subcommittee on the Western Hemisphere of the Committee on International Relations,* House of Representatives, 104th Cong., 2nd Session, 7 March 1996, p.8.

8   Payne, op. cit., pp.18–20.

9   *Hearing...* op. cit., p. 15.

10   Elliott Abrams, 'The Shiprider Solution: Policing The Caribbean', *The National Interest,* Spring 1996, p. 90.

11   Ibid.

12   See the Caribbean section of United States Department of State, *International Narcotics Control Strategy Report,* March 1997.

13   *Caribbean Week,* July–August 1996.

14   *The Daily Gleaner,* March 1997.

15   See, for example, Anthony P. Maingot, *The United States and The Caribbean* (London: Macmillan, 1994), pp. 228–47.

16   *International Narcotics Control Strategy Report,* op. cit., p.5.

17   Ibid., p. 11.

18   Ibid., p.15.

19   Ibid., p. 23.

20   Ibid., p. 26.

21   Ibid., p. 35.

22   Ibid., pp. 15, 19, 29.

23   US General Accounting Office, *Drug Control–US Interdiction Efforts in the Caribbean,* April 1996, p.11.

24   West Indian Commission, *Time For Action: Report of the West Indian Commission* (Black Rock: Barbados, West Indian Commission, 1992), pp. 303–4.

25   Ibid., p. 351.

26   Ibid., p. 350.

27   *Summary of Conclusions Fifth Special Meeting of The Conference of Heads of Governments,* held in Barbados on 16 December, 1996, Annex 1 US – CARICOM Relations (Agenda Item 4).

28   *Report of the Regional Meeting on Drug Control Cooperation in the Caribbean,* convened by the UNDCP in Barbados on 15–17 May 1996 (mimeo).

29   Maingot, *The US and the Caribbean,* op. cit., p. 151.

30   For example, the cooperation between the Michael Manley government and the DEA on Operation Buccaneer in 1974. See Horace Campbell, *Rasta and Resistance: From Marcus Garvey to Walter Rodney* (London: Hansib, 1985), pp. 112–15.

31   West Indian Commission, *Time For Action*...op. cit., p. 348.

32   Ibid., pp. 349.

33   Ibid., pp. 347–8.

34   See Janice Cumberbatch and Neville Duncan, 'Illegal Drugs, USA Policies and Caribbean Responses: The Road to Disaster', *Caribbean Affairs*, Vol. 3, No.4, 1990, pp. 150–1.

35   Baytoram Ramharack, 'Drug Trafficking and Money Laundering in the Caribbean Mini States and Dependent Territories: The US Response', *Latin American Studies of Japan*, Vol. 14, 1995, pp. 1–27.

36   West Indian Commission, *Time For Action*...op. cit., p. 338.

37   *The Daily Gleaner*, 30 January 1997, p. 2.

38   *Caribbean Week*, Vol. 6, No.12, 1995, p. 16.

39   Ibid., Vol. 7, No. 25, 1996, p. 2.

40   See, for example, *The Daily Observer*, 17 October 1996, p.230.

41   See *Agreement Between the Government of the Republic of Trinidad and Tobago and the Government of the United States of America Concerning Maritime Counter-Drug Operations*, Art 8 (c), March 1996, p.3.

42   *The Daily Gleaner*, 4 February 1997.

43   *Summary Fifth Special Meeting* (NB:Quotes which follow in this paragraph and the one that follows are from the same document.)

44   *The Daily Gleaner*, 15 December, 1996.

45   Caribbean/United States Summit, *Partnership For Prosperity and Security in the Caribbean* Bridgetown, Barbados, 10 May 1997, p.1.

46   Ibid., p.21.

47   Ibid., p.23. The majority of CARICOM states, of course, have National Drug Councils which deal primarily with demand reduction issues.

# PART III

# Coping Strategies and Countermeasures

# 10
# Drug Prevention and Rehabilitation in the Caribbean

*Sonita Morin Abrahams*

Recent socioeconomic developments in the Caribbean have resulted in profound effects on at-risk populations. Some of these effects include an increased vulnerability to poverty; a higher proportion living in single-headed households; increased pressures to supplement family incomes; and declining socialization capacity of families, schools and community institutions. A large number of these people live in marginalized neighborhoods characterized by economic problems, crime and the disintegration of traditional forms of social cohesion.[1] These conditions provide the ideal climate for the increase of substance abuse and drug trafficking.

## Prevention strategies

In reference to demand reduction strategies, research and experience have demonstrated that investing early in primary substance abuse prevention programmes for children and younger adolescents is the best strategy to adopt, before the onset of antisocial behavior patterns which then become exceedingly difficult and costly to reverse. Investing in this population leads to high returns for the individuals, the families and the society. In these early and impressionable years, critical decisions are taken which will determine future well-being. The importance of integrated early childhood interventions in improving school readiness, increasing returns to education, reducing social welfare costs and stimulating community development has been too well documented to require elaboration here. Prevention measures are a combination of regulatory and social measures and both are required in any effort to contain, reduce or prevent substance related problems. Worldwide evidence has shown that assisting youth to remain in school and receive quality education is probably the single most important measure that governments and communities should concentrate on since it will pre-empt many negative outcomes, such as delinquency, drug addiction and teenage childbearing. When resources are limited, special focus should be placed on targeted prevention efforts with at-risk youth. [2]

In the Caribbean, primary and secondary school enrolment is as high as 93 per cent and 54 per cent respectively,[3] so that school-based programmes will make an important contribution. A strategy document for a Health and Family Life Education (HFLE) intervention in schools called *Enhanced Teacher Training in Family Life Education* has been developed as a multi-agency project. The overall responsibility for its coordination is vested in Caribbean Area Office of the United Nations Children's Fund (UNICEF) on behalf of the CARICOM Secretariat. The Pan American Health Organization (PAHO) and the WHO office in Barbados, in collaboration with the University of the West Indies Advanced Training and Research in Fertility Management Unit (FMU) at the Mona campus in Jamaica, will be responsible for the coordination of the technical aspects of the project. Key partners include UNDCP, United Nations Programme on AIDS (UNAIDS), United Nations Association for International Service (UNAIS), United Nations Educational, Scientific and Cultural Organization (UNESCO), and United Nations Development Fund for Women (UNIFEM). The project will be implemented in three phases: the setting up of national coordination teams; implementation of specific country programmes; and the evaluation and modification of national programmes. The estimated cost of implementation is US$400,000, and the project will have a two-year duration.

The main objective of the HFLE is to enhance the capacity of the school system to deliver skills-based HFLE programmes which have the potential to promote behavior development and change among young people, as a response to many of the social problems they face. The drug control objective of this project is to reduce the demand for illicit drugs among adolescents from pre-primary through secondary schools in CARICOM countries. Although the main focus of the project will be in-school youth, activities will also be extended to reduce demand among out-of-school youth through the training of outreach workers.[4]

Among successful prevention programmes in the Caribbean is Servol, an internationally known community development programme in Trinidad and Tobago. Since 1980, Servol has worked nation-wide in Trinidad and Tobago in assisting low-income children and youth, and regionally by training youth-serving professionals throughout the

Caribbean. They are funded mainly by the EU and the Bernard Van Leer Foundation.[5] They anticipate receiving funding from the Inter-American Development Bank for a new computer training program that will offer vocational education to 1400 youth. Servol insists that all students contribute to the cost of their education in order to improve their understanding of the worth of the training and to avoid dependency. These fees combined with local income generation activities enable Servol to finance a large portion of the costs of training.

The main activities of the project are: an early child development program which includes 250 early child care centers in the country; a parent outreach program; the Adolescent Development Programme; and a Junior Life Center which assists out-of-school youth, ages 13–15 years. Their main accomplishments are achieving island-wide coverage which includes 31 centers in operation, training over 2000 youth at any one time. A high percentage of youth find jobs after training and a growing number start their own businesses. Servol's combination of vocational training, income generation through micro-enterprise loans and life skills training is a replicable model and already provides training for any Caribbean organization that is interested in adopting the model.[6]

A programme which has demonstrated a positive change in attitudes and a decrease in drug use and abuse among at-risk adolescents is operated by Addiction Alert Organization, a non-governmental organization in operation in Jamaica since 1990. Selected youth, aged 12–18 years, are given extensive training in life management skills such as drug education/refusal skills, conflict resolution, STD/HIV prevention, decision-making, problem-solving, personal development, coping with crime and violence, dealing with relationship issues, and assertion skills. In addition, they receive communication skills in order to give creative presentations to their fellow peers in the wider communities. Of the younger cohort 140, called peer educators, are trained for a period of two years. They receive 172 hours of training and presentation experience with the assistance of support groups set up in their respective high schools to ensure sustainability.

A new programme that began in September 1997 involves 30 older youth, called adolescent facilitators, who will be trained more extensively on a full-time basis (1076 hours of training over two years). Their training, in addition to the above mentioned topics will include remedial Math and English, computer training, vocational preparation and life management skills. Both programmes are designed to promote a healthy, drug free life style and prevent life long cycles of self destructive behaviors among high-risk youth. Intervention counseling is also offered for students suspended from school for drug use. The aim of this intervention is to work with the guidance counselors and parents in order to get these students back into school drug free. One of the strengths of these programmes, according to an evaluation prepared for the World Bank in 1996,[7] is that youth are more likely to listen and internalize messages related to health promotion if received from their own peers. In addition, many of these trained adolescents become positive role models for their fellow peers.

Other prevention initiatives in the region that are executed or funded by the UNDCP include school-based programmes in the Dominican Republic, The Bahamas, Anguilla, Dominica, St Vincent and the Grenadines, the British Virgin Islands and the Turks and Caicos Islands. Moreover, a National Drug Resource Center was officially opened in Barbados in November 1996. It focuses on the implementation of the government's national demand reduction project, and includes coordination and research, schools prevention, community prevention, treatment and rehabilitation.

In response to the increasing problem of drug abuse in the region, most Caribbean states have a national drug council or similar statutory board that is empowered by law to coordinate the government's efforts. However, in some cases, financial constraints and unclear mandates have limited their role essentially to an advisory one. According to surveys conducted by the secretariat of the CICAD, and the UNDCP, some limitations which prevent councils from being more effective include a lack of organizational weight and political backing internally. This often comes from the absence of comprehensive national drug control policy frameworks, with the result that concrete and realistic terms of reference are lacking. In other instances, policy-making and policy-implementing roles are not sufficiently differentiated, the capacity to coordinate, organize, and plan activities may be weak, and offices may be under-equipped and under staffed, or may rely heavily on volunteers. Suggestions for improvement offered by these organizations included the need for legislative reform, the improvement of the councils' organizational structure through a process of self-analysis and self-management, and the identifying of sources of direct financing other than from governments.

On the international front, there is a perceived lack of coordination and cooperation by the national authorities and by experts in the field. Especially problematic, they feel, is the desired objectives, especially the exchange and processing of information, which requires a high degree of national and international integration and organizational development. Some obstacles to closer cooperation in the region include language barriers, different legal systems, cultural differences, a lack of knowledge of other governments' drug control structures and capabilities, and the absence of personal contact among drug control officials. There are several international and regional organizations involved in drug control in the region. These include CARICOM, the UNDCP, CICAD, the EU, PAHO, the Commonwealth Secretariat, the Mini-Dublin Groups and others. Unfortunately, overlapping mandates sometimes cause difficulties for National Drug Councils; they may also become overloaded with tedious reporting requirements. Mechanisms for closer regional and international coordination and cooperation, and the strengthening of these agencies mentioned above, is to be established by the EU, pursuant to the conclusions of a meeting of the European Council held in Madrid, Spain, in December 1995.

At a UNDCP sponsored regional meeting on Drug Control Coordination and Cooperation in the Caribbean, which was held in Barbados in May 1996, a Plan of Action for drug control coordination and cooperation in the Caribbean was drafted and included the following important recommendation: the development of Master Plans with the intention of producing in each case a single, government-approved document that summarizes national drug-control policy, sets priorities and identifies resources based on realistic estimates, assigns responsibilities and encourages multi sectoral collaboration. These Plans would be public statements of national priorities in the area of drug control which highlight strategies to be adopted in order to fulfill these priorities. Among the objectives of the Master Plan is more effective coordination of drug control programmes, and more constructive regional dialogue and international cooperation by directing external resources towards one national strategy.

CICAD and UNDCP are planning a series of workshops with the view of strengthening the capacities of the national drug bodies through organizational development, and by engaging in a strategic planning process aimed at identifying strengths and weaknesses. Plans will then be formulated for appropriate action which will be more effective in dealing with the problem of narcotic drugs and related matters. Other assistance from CICAD includes the provision of communication equipment and technical assistance to enhance the telecommunication capabilities of the Councils to enable more rapid and economical communication with their counterparts in other countries, as well as accessing local, regional and international databases, electronic mail and Internet services.

In Jamaica, the National Council on Drug Abuse is committed to an integrated demand reduction approach to preventing and controlling drug abuse. The mechanism in place to achieve this integration comprises a Cabinet Inter-ministerial Committee on Drug Abuse, community and parish organizations, eight sub-committees, and a board of management which is supported by the country's Drug Abuse Secretariat. The Integrated Demand Reduction Programme (project IDER) is a UNDCP-sponsored project, where 22 communities across the island have been mobilized to write action plans and programmes of drug abuse prevention. Each community has formed a Community Development Action Committee (CODAC) that has the responsibility for examining its problems and selecting those which would most likely lead to drug abuse within the relevant area. A two year development action plan was then compiled to counteract those problems. One of the goals of these CODACs is to become legal entities as non-governmental organizations. Parish Drug Awareness Committees (PARDACs) were also formed in each parish to promote specific prevention, treatment and rehabilitation services. The major strength of this programme is that it is community-based and -driven. A weakness, however, has been the inability to sustain many of the projects established once the funding ends.

Programmes that offer law enforcement and drug prevention training in the Caribbean region include:

- The Regional Counter-Narcotics Law Enforcement Training Center (REDTRAC) in Jamaica, intended to meet the needs in anti-narcotic training identified by the governments of 18 English-speaking Caribbean countries. It also aims to strengthen national and regional anti-narcotic law enforcement capabilities and efforts in the region.
- The Interministerial Drug Control Training Center in Martinique.
- The Police Training College in Barbados, opened in 1956 and catering to the training of police officers at all levels for forces within the Caribbean.
- The Caribbean Institute on Alcoholism and other Drugs (CARIAD) operates a two-week drug educational summer course in Tobago every year. As of June 1997, the Institute which is accredited by the Continuing Studies Department of the University of the West Indies at St Augustine, held its 24th training course. Approximately 2000 professional and voluntary workers have been trained, each at a cost of US$950 which covers tuition, lodging and books.
- The School of Addiction Studies at the University of the West Indies campuses of Cave Hill (Barbados), Mona (Jamaica) and St Augustine

(Trinidad and Tobago). This programme targets educators, public health professionals, nurses, doctors and law enforcement officers, among others. The main aim is to ensure quality in the development and implementation of drug abuse prevention and treatment/rehabilitation programmes across the region. It is jointly executed by the University of the West Indies and the Addiction Research Foundation of Canada.

- The James Hendricks Memorial Drug Prevention and Treatment Workshops, co-funded by CICAD, offers training for drug treatment counselors, teachers, social workers and others. Approximately four courses are held every year in different Caribbean countries.

A critical area in need of improvement is the evaluation component of existing treatment and prevention programmes, as well as data collection and the dissemination of information. Many Caribbean countries collect data on drug abuse, but often not in a consistent or systematic manner. Although many data sources exist, information available from these sources is rarely consolidated and made available to others, although the UNDCP Regional Office for the Caribbean, based in Barbados, is working on this. Recommendations from the Plan of Action for Drug Control Coordination and Cooperation in the Caribbean include the importance of collecting timely, comparable, and reliable data on substance abuse, both nationally and regionally; the necessity for training and the provision of necessary technology for the collection, analysis and dissemination of epidemiological information; the formation of research teams in each country trained in epidemiology, research methods and data analysis; the refinement of instruments and methods to ensure comparability; and the provision of computer hardware and software for data analysis to national drug commissions.

These are all important recommendations that need to be put in place if the region wants to be in a position to state with authority and legitimacy the extent of the drug problem and the efficacy of the existing treatment, prevention and training programmes. In order to facilitate and improve coordination in these efforts among Caribbean countries, a good suggestion at this meeting was for the appointment of Caribbean Drug Liaison Officers to ensure that these efforts are properly executed.

The following elements were found to be common to successful Latin American and Caribbean prevention programs: early intervention, small school size, individualized attention; identification, sustained counseling and monitoring of youth; programme autonomy and flex-ibility; and parental involvement. The survey also indicated the follow-ing ingredients for success: proper case management, community-wide multi-agency collaborative approaches, a mix of public/private funding, youth participation in the design, implementation and evaluation of programs, replicability and sustainability.[8] Recommendations high-lighted the importance of constructive occupation and educational attainment as the two most important factors for empowering and assisting at-risk youth, especially when these interventions are com-bined with individual and group counseling, or other interventions which meet the personal development and psychosocial needs of these at-risk youth.

At the regional meeting of Drug Control Coordination and Coopera-tion in the Caribbean, in the area of demand reduction, recommenda-tions included the importance of taking into account language and cultural differences, the need for a comprehensive, balanced and integ-rated strategy, inter-regional cooperation, programme evaluation and the importance of obtaining timely, reliable data to ensure appropriate policy and programme development and evaluation. Emphasis was placed on the need for drug education to take place in the context of a skills-based approach to health and family life education in Caribbean schools, and endorsed the inter-Agency Health and Family Life Educa-tion project in the CARICOM States. Special attention was to be paid to critical target groups such as out-of-school youth. The training of teachers, guidance counselors, school administration and policy-makers was also recommended. So too was the strengthening of partnerships between the business community and Government in addressing drug problems.

## Treatment approaches

Caribbean people use both licit and illicit drugs for a variety of reasons. It is important to have an understanding of these reasons as they have implications for drug treatment and prevention.

The main drugs of abuse in the region are alcohol, tobacco, marijuana, crack cocaine, prescription drugs among women, and inhalants among adolescents. Heroin abuse has been reported in Bermuda, French Gui-ana, Martinique and Puerto Rico; while LSD, ecstasy and other hallucin-ogens use is reported in some territories. In the Caribbean, drugs are used by all social classes. However, marijuana use is more prevalent among the working class, the Rastafarian sect and adolescents; alcohol abuse is high among the Trinidadian East Indian population, and the middle and upper classes; and crack cocaine is growing among various social classes and groups.

Alcohol plays an important role in Caribbean culture, from the production of rum and beer in order to satisfy the local, tourist, and export market, to being the focal point of most joyful as well as sad occasions. The young Caribbean male has to learn to *hold his liquor* when becoming a man, almost as a 'rite of passage'. Studies indicate that alcohol is the number one drug of abuse in the region and plays a major role in many traffic accidents, low job productivity, domestic violence, and serious health problems.[9]

Marijuana, or ganja as it is popularly called in the Caribbean, was introduced during the nineteenth century by indentured laborers from India. The 'herb is produced for local and foreign consumption with a high demand in tourist resort areas. Jamaica is one of the major suppliers to the other Caribbean countries, followed by St Vincent and the Grenadines. Marijuana is used for a variety of reasons: for relaxation, to heighten feelings and sensations, to relieve boredom, cure illnesses, and to enhance spiritual experiences. It is also frequently used in combination with other drugs, mainly tobacco, alcohol and crack cocaine. Despite the fact that marijuana is illegal, its use is widely tolerated in many of the Caribbean territories, and its reputed high quality and potency make it a sought after commodity by North Americans and Europeans. In Jamaica the heaviest users are the Rastafarians, a religious group that use marijuana as part of their religious practice. Use of the herb is also widespread and traditional in rural areas and has been glamorized by music celebrities like Bob Marley and Peter Tosh.

A concern for health personnel working in drug treatment and prevention is the increased potency of marijuana, and the mixing of the herb with crack cocaine or other substances. In a bid to compete with US grown marijuana produced by technologically advanced cultivation methods, Caribbean growers have developed a product with a THC (tetrahydrocannabinol – one of the psychoactive compounds found in marijuana) reputed to be significantly higher than was available in the 1960s and 1970s. This could be a factor in the increased appearance latterly in Jamaica of psychiatric unit admissions for 'dual diagnosis', referred to as 'cannabis-related psychotic episode' or 'ganja induced psychosis'.

One of the difficulties encountered in conducting effective prevention programmes is dealing with the perception of the youth who grow up in a culture where the acceptance of marijuana use is widespread. In

Jamaica, the practice exists in some rural and urban inner city communities where marijuana is brewed as tea or cooked in food, with the belief that this practice will make the children 'wise'.

Cocaine started to become popular in some territories from the late 1970s, and was sniffed in powdered form, but this was limited to a small minority, due to its high price. A new way of preparing the drug was soon discovered which made it more potent and inexpensive yet highly addictive. Hence the emergence of crack cocaine. Today crack is widely available and is the drug of choice for a large percentage of people entering drug treatment in Jamaica and several other Caribbean islands. The highly addictive properties of crack creates a high demand among its users, a total disregard for law and order, widespread violence and prostitution, and ultimately creates havoc in families and communities.

Drug abuse is undeniably linked to drug production and trafficking. The Caribbean islands, sandwiched between the producing countries of South America and the high consuming countries of North America, are particularly vulnerable to trafficking. According to the January 1997 issue of the UNDCP's *Focus On Drugs* and the agency's activities report for 1997, an estimated 40 per cent of all cocaine entering the United States market passes through the Caribbean. In the first six months of 1996, more heroin appeared on a regular basis in the Caribbean than any time before. The spillover of in-transit drugs has resulted in a rapid increase in illegal drug consumption. This correlation becomes apparent when both increases in drug trafficking and drug consumption are tracked over time. In addition, weak institutional and economic structures of some Caribbean countries make them particularly vulnerable to outside pressures and influences.

Before drug treatment centers were established, abusers were treated either privately by physicians, or in the psychiatric wards of hospitals. This practice continues even today especially in some of the smaller islands where there are limited resources; in other instances where the treatment centers are full, or when the patient is diagnosed with a dual disorder. Regular participation in the 12-step programs of Alcoholics and Narcotics Anonymous has also provided the opportunity for abusers to get 'clean and sober' outside of formal treatment, and this continues to play an important role in the long term abstinence from alcohol and other drugs. In Trinidad, perhaps due to the excessive use of alcohol by the East Indian population, there is a proliferation of Alcoholics Anonymous groups. This process might have been assisted by the early recognition of the problem and actions taken since the 1950s.

Many drug treatment programs are located in hospitals, which although convenient, are not without problems. In many instances doctors and nurses are not specially trained in the area of chemical dependency, which can create frustration and resentment, both for the patient and health-care provider, often-times leading to unsuccessful treatment. Most existing treatment programs accept both males and females upwards of 18 years, and offer treatment for all forms of drug abuse. This creates many challenges as experience has taught us that people addicted to different drugs present peculiar problems that need to be addressed separately. If possible, women and men should be separated in treatment, or at least have separate group sessions, as it is sometimes very difficult to share painful experiences in the presence of the other gender.

Reports received from some Caribbean countries indicate that the profile of the person entering treatment is typically male in the 20–39 age group, unemployed or underemployed, and with crack cocaine as the drug of first choice. But it may also be alcohol, marijuana and/or tobacco. Alcoholics are usually in the older age group and many, if they are ready to become sober, can do so with short-term hospitalization or rehabilitation, and/or by attending regular Alcoholics Anonymous meetings. Persons entering treatment for marijuana abuse are few, and mostly in the 18–25 age group. However, as mentioned earlier, some do end up in psychiatric wards because of psychotic episodes. Persons referred to as polyabusers use a combination of drugs, and tend to have an extremely difficult time remaining drug free. The male/female ratio of persons entering treatment is approximately four to one.

Women have a much lower prevalence of drug use and abuse, although trends are beginning to show an increase in alcohol, crack cocaine, and inhalant use in some territories. The low numbers of women accessing treatment, however, may not be a true indication of the actual prevalence of drug abuse in this population as there are factors unique to women which deter them from accessing treatment. For example, they may have small children at home with no one to care for them while in treatment, or they may fear their children being taken away; they may also become prostitutes to maintain their drug habit, or as a result of shame, guilt or denial associated with their drug use, may be able to hide their problem for a long time. Family members may be guilty of covering up the drug problem for the same reasons.

The types of treatment programs available in the Caribbean are:

- Outpatient day programmes which may be structured for a set period of time, for example a four-to-six-week programme, or those that operate with more flexibility as 'drop in' centers.
- In-patient facilities can either be short term, for example a four-to-six-week short-term rehabilitation program, or long-term, as in a therapeutic community, lasting from three months to one year. Many in-patient programmes in the Caribbean are attached to hospitals, follow a medical model, and are staffed by nurses and consulting physicians. In some instances, detoxification is carried out in hospitals, especially for alcoholics who are then referred to treatment programmes.
- Halfway houses offer live-in facilities in a semi-protected environment for those who have completed treatment but who are not yet ready to return to their communities. These exist in few of the islands, for example Trinidad and the US Virgin Islands.
- Some islands offer programmes specifically geared to a particular target group. For example in Santo Domingo and the Bahamas, programmes exist for adolescent males, and in Barbados and Grenada, there are remand homes for first-time offenders. In Curacao, Santo Domingo and Guadeloupe, residential programmes are operated for women, while several islands have facilities for males only.
- Of interest is the sixty-bed facility in St Croix, US Virgin Islands, which also accommodates children; the many facilities reportedly existing in the Dominican Republic (17 centers with 580 beds in total); and the comprehensive, well staffed in-patient 24-room rehabilitation programme in Holguin, Cuba.

Drug treatment and rehabilitation are very complex issues. Although a government or community may recognize the urgent need for treatment services, it is not just a simple task of providing these services by making the resources available. Chemical dependency is a poorly understood illness, in terms of what causes it, who has it, and how to treat it. One of the major features is denial, which usually enables prolonged destructive behavior and interferes with the abuser and family members admitting or addressing the problem until a crisis occurs. The shame and guilt that accompany the illness only serve to exacerbate the problem. In order to break this denial and heighten awareness, the following steps need to be taken:

- Widespread public education which includes the signs and symptoms of substance abuse, and how to access available referral, treatment and follow up services.

- Effective data gathering and research projects in order to determine the true prevalence and incidence of substance abuse.
- Workplace and school programmes to identify affected employees and students, and mechanisms for these persons to access help.
- Compulsory drug testing and follow up services for people involved in law enforcement and the transportation industry.
- Enlightened justice agencies that will entertain the option of referring first time offenders to treatment and community service rather than incarceration.
- The establishment of 12-step groups and treatment programmes in prisons.
- Health care providers and religious counselors to receive additional training in early detection, assessments, referrals and treatment of substance abuse.
- Recognition by companies and the health insurance industry of the importance of providing benefits for drug and alcohol treatment, rather than bearing the cost of many years of low productivity, motor vehicle and job related accidents, high disability payments, and in the long run, significantly higher health care costs borne by companies and taxpayers.

Research has shown that for people with drug problems, health care costs rise dramatically, not only for the abuser but also for the family, and ultimately the entire society. On the other hand, treatment interventions have been shown to have a significant beneficial impact on these health care costs. What is necessary is the formulation and implementation of appropriate policies and properly designed treatment programmes which are clinically effective and financially efficient. In order to achieve this, creative and multi disciplinary approaches to epidemiology are required. Existing treatment programmes need to be properly evaluated to determine the efficacy of treatment, financial sustainability, and whether the programmes are meeting the needs of the communities they serve.

A review of successful treatment programmes conducted in the United States by a Committee on Treatment Benefits (COB), under the auspices of the National Council on Alcoholism and Drug Dependence, indicated the following:

- The longer the treatment, the better the outcome.
- Treatment pays for itself in terms of cost savings in other medical care, reduced motor vehicle accidents, fewer arrests, and increased vocational productivity.

- The 12 step groups (e.g. Alcoholics Anonymous) provide one of the most cost-effective 'continuing care' strategies.
- Different types of treatment may work better for different clients, so clients should be matched to different types of treatment if at all possible.[10]

## Conclusion

In reviewing the treatment services available in the Caribbean and taking into consideration the cost of providing these services, this writer recommends the development of a treatment model which includes short-term detoxification, intensive inpatient, intensive outpatient, and day treatment. This basic model could be structured in such a way that the initial treatment would not exceed six weeks, but would be followed by a well-structured continuing care programme of two years. This would include support group meetings and community involvement. It is necessary also to have separate facilities for females, males and adolescents and if possible, facilities that concentrate on treatment for particular drugs, especially crack cocaine and alcohol; these could be offered at a regional level. Self-sufficient half-way houses would be helpful for clients who are not ready to return to their own communities. Well trained staff and a properly developed and implemented treatment programme would be critical to the success of such a model. In addition to the above, regional long term facilities (for example therapeutic communities) for those clients in need of long term treatment could be set up with shared resources and be made available to the other territories.

## Notes

1   See *They Cry 'Respect!': Urban Violence and Poverty in Jamaica* (Kingston: University of the West Indies, 1996); and M. Schneidman, *Targeting At-risk Youth: Rationales, Approaches to Service Delivery and Monitoring and Evaluation Issues*, 1996.
2   Gary Barker and Miguel Fontes, *Review and Analysis of International Experience with Programs Targeted on At-Risk Youth*, August, 1995.
3   *Focus On Drugs*, Vol. 2, May, 1996.
4   Data from Christine Norton, HFLE consultant, UNICEF Caribbean Area Office, Barbados.
5   The Bernard van Leer Foundation is a private institution based in The Netherlands. It was created in 1949 for broad humanitarian purposes and now

concentrates its resources on the support for early childhood care and development.

6 See Barker and Fontes, op.cit.
7 Schneidman, op.cit.
8 Ibid.
9 Sonita Morin Abrahams, 'Project Proposal to Reduce Substance Abuse in Jamaica by Identifying High-Risk and Protective Factors in Order to Plan Appropriate Prevention Programs', Hubert H. Humphrey Fellowship Program, Johns Hopkins University, 1993; and G. Cole, 'Issues For Consideration in the Treatment and Rehabilitation of Drug Addicts in the Caribbean', unpublished paper, 1995.
10 The COB Project commissioned Norman G. Hoffman (Brown University) and Sara S. DeHart (University of Minnesota) to conduct a five-year review of the scientific literature regarding addiction treatment outcomes. A total of 350 studies were analysed.

# 11
# Fighting the Dragon: the Anti-drug Strategy in Central America

*Gabriel Aguilera Peralta*

Drug trafficking did not pose an important security problem in the Central American region (considered for the purposes of this chapter as the old Central American Federation countries, i.e. Guatemala, El Salvador, Honduras, Nicaragua and Costa Rica, plus Panama) until the decade of the 1980s. And even from that time, penetration of the diverse dimensions of the drug problem was different for the various countries in the area, being influenced not only by natural characteristics of the phenomenon and the way the states and societies were organized, but also the internal and external military–political conflicts that affected all the nations in the Isthmus.

Thus, throughout the fore-mentioned decade, drug trafficking was perceived as a secondary problem in the security agendas of Central American countries, which had other priorities. Otherwise, it was analysed as linked with other security elements, such as its relation with the low intensity war, particularly allegations that conflicting parties in some countries participated in drug trafficking activities to finance their activities. During the same period, the major incident related to the subject was the conflict between the US government and the Panamanian regime of Manuel Antonio Noriega; although their differences had various origins, the allegation against the Central American ruler, of using the government for drug trafficking, was the one that weighted the most during the Bush administration, leading to the invasion of Panama by US troops and the toppling of Noriega on 20 December 1989.

The Central American regional crisis ended as a result of regional efforts to pursue negotiations and democratization. These started with the Contadora initiative, which was secured through the Esquipulas procedure. As a result, tensions among countries in the area as well as with foreign powers ended, giving place to negotiated solutions to internal conflicts in Nicaragua, El Salvador and finally, Guatemala. The new situation enabled the policy-makers of various countries to make progress in the Central American integration process and to redesign the security agenda, placing drug trafficking high on that agenda. Similarly, several actors that are influential in Central America, such as the US government, which had placed a high priority on the promotion of its interests within the framework of the conflict and in the logic of the Cold War, began to define the war against drug trafficking as one of their most important security objectives in the region.

## Drug production in the region

Due to its natural conditions, Central America potentially may serve for the production of the various plants that give origin to natural narcotics. However, with the exception of cannabis, production on a significant scale has not occurred in most of the countries, partially due to the forementioned armed conflict. Internal struggles, which to a good extent were fought in rural areas, made planting risky and transportation of the product quite uncertain.

A portrait of the present situation reveals that in Guatemala the planting of poppy from which opium is derived was maintained, albeit on a small scale, in spite of the armed conflict. The plant is common to certain provinces, but its large-scale exploitation began in the early 1990s, as a consequence of inputs from the Mexican cartels which were being persecuted by the government. Thus the so-called doughboy effect occurred, by which drug trafficking can be easily moved from one country to another, in procurement of more favorable conditions. This situation resulted in the transfer of improved varieties of seeds, new planting and harvesting techniques and hiding the plantations, primary processing of opium and mainly, an immediate marketing of the product.

The acreage that was planted increased substantially, going from around 212 hectares in 1985 to 1145 in 1991, with a corresponding increase in the yield capacity of opium of 2.1 tonnes to 11.5 tonnes in the same period, becoming the world's seventh largest producer of the substance.[1] Planting, mainly in the provinces of San Marcos and Huehuetenango, near the Mexican border, was welcome enthusiastically by small farmers who saw their income grow by nearly 120 per cent from plots formerly planted with corn. The immediate effect was the improvement of living conditions of the growers and a certain local economic boom which was reflected in indexes such as an increase in local trade, an increase in the prices of rural property, and increased real estate values at urban centers in the provinces. Similarly, the local power of growers and intermediaries grew.[2]

The main activity of producers consists in processing the latex extracted from the flower chalice, which when dry becomes a sort of gum packed in small cakes locally known as opium 'bread' or 'cheese', which are transported through smuggling routes to Mexico, where they are processed with heroin chlorohydrate. The poppy fields, generally masked by other crops, are usually located in cliff areas, with elevations of up to 10,000 feet and in small plots, one-fifth of a hectare in size, in order to make its location difficult. Between January and May of any year, experienced growers can obtain up to three crops. Nevertheless, in one of the most successful anti-drug experiences in the continent, the production of poppy was decimated in only four years. Working with the assistance of the DEA, the Anti-Drug Operations Department of the Customs Police, by means of air and land eradication, reduced by 1995 the planted area to 39 hectares with an estimated production of 0.40 tonnes.[3] Poppy cultivation does not exist in any significant way in the other Central American countries.

Cannabis, however, has a wide presence in the region, since it has traditionally been the source of marijuana, produced and used in the countries. However, cultivation of the crop expanded during the 1980s due to the same 'doughboy' effect mentioned earlier. Again, the main production takes place in Guatemala, where the plant is found throughout the territory, but mainly concentrated in the province of Peten, a jungle area bordering Belize. The planted area increased from 215 hectares in 1985 to 450 in 1989 with an equal estimated amount of production. Nevertheless, eradication campaigns reduced production to an estimated 50 hectares in 1995, with a potential yield of 12 tonnes.[4]

In all other countries of the Isthmus, planting is less, with a predominant tendency to produce for local consumption. Understandably, statistics are not precise, but eradication data give a fairly good idea: in 1995 in Nicaragua, 67,000 plants, with a potential of 2,673 kilograms of marijuana,[5] were reported as destroyed, and in Costa Rica, in 1996, 110,002 plants were destroyed.[6] As far as coca is concerned, this plant is present only in Panama, and it has a much smaller impact. Coca planting was introduced probably as an expansion from Colombia. There are no precise figures about the planted area, although in 1996, 105 hectares of coca were reported as destroyed. Also destroyed was a facility for processing cocaine paste. The facility had a production capacity of 700 to 1,000 kilograms of cocaine per week.[7]

## Drug trafficking

The Central American Isthmus has a geographical location which is very appropriate for drug traffickers, since it may be used as a bridge between the centers of cocaine production in South America and the consumer centers of North America. Geography and infrastructure help this purpose, since forest or jungle areas and the abundance of waterways allow for hidden movements. Finally, there are hundreds of informal aircraft landing strips that are not controlled, and the general weakness of the states make controls at borders and transportation means weak as well.

As suggested earlier, during the conflict years, drug traffickers could not travel easily, due to the presence at border posts and in rural areas of the armed forces of those nations at war. But once the conflict ceased, and due to pressure exerted on other traffic routes, the Central American connection became cherished for the transportation of cocaine and, to a lesser extent, of heroin and marijuana, especially from the Colombian cartels. Initially, air means were mainly used, taking advantage of the lack of a radar network covering the whole region. Aircraft often refueled in rural landing strips and in some cases unload their cargo in Guatemala, moving it afterwards overland to Mexico or the United States. However, the use of Central American air force assets for seizures diminished the opportunities for such means of transportation. Consequently, moving the drug by surface and maritime means is now more important. The former operates by means of trailers and other vehicles departing from Panama and the latter by speed boats and hidden in fishing boats, especially from the San Andres and Providencia islands, towards the Nicaraguan coastline or other coasts along the Isthmus.

## Consumption and money laundering

Although drug addiction is both a public health and a security problem, we are not dealing here with the use of hard drugs, its consumption being relatively low, but predominantly, with the use of marijuana, sedatives and stimulants as well as inhaled glue, with a low consumption of cocaine, heroin and its derivatives. In Central America the highest registered drug consumption is for legal drugs such as alcohol and tobacco, the exception being Panama, where high levels of cocaine use have been reported. This suggests that the region is not much sought after by the drug trafficking industry as a market, but rather for its capacity for production, money laundering, and particularly, trafficking. Nevertheless, to the extent that the cartels pay for the services of intermediaries partially in hard drugs, these substances are distributed locally, and progressively the circle of users increases.

In Guatemala, for instance, the most widely used illicit drugs generally are tranquilizers and marijuana, while in detention centers marijuana, tranquilizers and stimulants are used heavily. Cocaine comes up as the second most widely used drug at treatment centers, with only 9 per cent of the addiction cases.[8] In Honduras, a poll among drug users in schools disclosed that 43.4 per cent drank alcohol, 16.7 per cent used tobacco, 2.1 per cent used marijuana, 0.7 per cent cocaine, 1.5 per cent inhaled glue and 17.1 per cent used stimulants.[9]

As regards money laundering, it is estimated that laundering activities for resources coming from drug trafficking take place throughout the region, but hard data are scarce. Panama seems to be one of the countries experiencing this problem very critically because it has an international financial center.[10] However, Costa Rica has also given particular attention to this issue. Money laundering in Costa Rica can be illustrated with the case known as Sentence No. 107.

In that case, the person responsible had established nine investment and distribution corporations, and had opened seven bank accounts which, over a six-month period, had transactions valued at US$40 million, allegedly as the result of his businesses, which nevertheless did not show major activity. Later on, from those accounts, money was transferred to banks in Miami, Panama, Cali and Medellín. In June 1988, the person in question traveled to Los Angeles and came back with US$749,728 in small bills, distributed in three suitcases and hidden under packages containing key chains and stickers for a political campaign, supposedly being met by a customs guard who was part of the conspiracy. Intelligence provided by the DEA led to the capture of the individual and to the disruption of his operations.[11]

The problem of chemical precursors is smaller, because drugs are not processed in the region, but for a very small amount. However, transit of chemicals takes place to processing countries. For instance, reexportation from Guatemala is suspected, since the country in 1996 imported 9538.80 liters of acetone, as well as significant volumes of toluene, hydrochloric acid, methyl-acetone, sulphuric acid and pseudoephedrine.

## The anti-drug strategy

The prominence given by Central American countries to fighting drugs once the regional crisis ended coincided with the resumption and deepening of the Central American integration process. This situation, plus the correct perception that drug trafficking responds essentially to international organized activities, had an influence on the design of an anti-drug strategy in the early 1990s. The strategy was discussed at the regional level and within the framework of the integration structure which was built around the guidelines of the Esquipulas Procedure, mainly following the decisions of the various presidential summits.

It was in that context that the security agenda was redefined and, when in 1991 the general outline of the new integration scheme, called the Central American Integration System (SICA) established in the so-called Tegucigalpa Protocol, the definition of a New Security Model was concluded for the region. This Model identified drug trafficking as one of the region's major threats.[12] This was also reflected and broadened in a document called the Frame Treaty for Central American Democratic Security, agreed to at the 1995 Central American presidential summit, which was held in San Pedro Sula, Honduras. The 1995 document even specifies in one of its articles the components of an anti-drug policy, stating that: 'The parties will promote cooperation towards eradication of drug related activities, illegal trade of chemicals and related crimes in conformity with international, regional and sub-regional agreements to which they are a part or those that may be subscribed on this subject, particularly the Constitutive Agreement of the Permanent Central American Commission for the Eradication of Production, Traffic, Consumption, and Illicit use of Drugs and Psychotropic Substances. For this purpose, expeditious and effective communication mechanisms will be established as well as cooperation among the authorities in charge.'[13]

In 1993, an extraordinary summit of the Central American presidents took place with the Prime Minister of Belize along with observers from Mexico, Great Britain and the United States, in order to agree on actions at the highest level in the fight against drug trafficking. The document issued at the end of that meeting highlighted the need for cooperation in the fight against drug trafficking as well as production and related crimes, among them the laundering of assets and trade of chemicals. It also mentioned the social and economic elements of the problem and the need to strengthen judicial institutions.[14] Thus, this meeting resulted more in an elaboration of principles than in an actual program of action, but it was important inasmuch as it emphasized the regional approach to designing a strategy. Later on, in 1993 an instrument that was being prepared for a long time was concluded. It was called the Constitutive Agreement of the Permanent Central American Commission for the Eradication of the Production, Traffic, Consumption and

Illicit use of Drugs and Psychotropic Substances and Related Crimes (CCP).

The agreement created a permanent structure and defined the following as the main objectives of the strategy:

- modernization and unification of the legislation;
- improvement of judicial action and cooperation;
- perfection of the information networks; and
- training and education of anti-drug police, provided to act in coordination with the Inter-American Drug Abuse Control Commission (CICAD), the United Nations International Drug Control Program (PNUFID) and the Latin American Institute for the Prevention of Crime and the Treatment of Offenders (ILANUD).[15]

One of the results of this approach was the creation of the regional center for juridical development and cooperation in Central America on the subject of control of drug production and trafficking (CEDEJU). The objective of this center is to provide specialized technical assistance for planning, development and execution of programs in harmonized legislation, police training and prevention and treatment programs. Furthermore, work is being done on a Central American draft agreement for the prevention and repression of money laundering and assets and other related crimes, an agreement for international judicial cooperation, and one related to the creation of a Central American Institute for Higher Police Studies.[16]

In addition to CCP, several structures of the Central American institutionality have to do with the design and development of an anti-drugs strategy. Among them are the Central American Security Commission, the Central American Parliament, the Secretariat General of SICA, and the Justice Courts of the Central American States. Among their various activities are those of promoting the training of judges, attorneys and magistrates in the control of drug trafficking and the laundering of money and assets, as well as training programs for drug police corps. Other provisions, such as agreements for the control of stolen vehicles are deemed to be connected with the anti-drug actions.

At the national level, all countries have progressively been adopting specific anti-drug legislation. Among the legislation in question are Guatemala's Law Against Drug Activities (1992), El Salvador's Law Regulating Activities Related to Drugs (1991), Honduras' Law on the Undue Use and Illicit Traffic of Drugs and Psychotropic Substances

(1990), Nicaragua's Law No. 177 (1994), Costa Rica's Law on Drugs, Psychotropic Substances, Drugs of Non-Authorized Use and Related Activities (1991), and Panama's Law No.13 (1990). This legislation covers the following subjects: penal types, sanctions, aggravating circumstances, dimensions, forms of participation and intent, proceedings of delivery under custody, extradition procedures, undercover operations, transfer of prisoners, confiscation of goods, protection of third parties' rights, use of informants, mutual judicial assistance and execution of foreign sentences.[17] This legal scaffolding is expanding into areas not previously covered, such as specific legislation for the control of chemicals and laundering of money and assets, which is being worked on the basis of model regulations issued by CICAD/OAS and other sources. Moreover, all Central American countries have signed the 1988 Vienna Convention on drugs.

Also, in most countries, there are coordination agencies for the efforts on the fight against drugs by the various government agencies and initiatives from civilian society, including with NGOs working in the field. The structures of these entities are varied, but they usually include representation from state institutions that have to deal with some aspect of the subject. In general, the mandates of those centers cover not only illegal drugs, but also the legal ones (alcohol and tobacco). The centers are in:

- Guatemala: Commission Against Addiction and Illicit Drug Trafficking;
- Honduras: National Council Against Drug Trafficking;
- Nicaragua: National Council of Fight Against Drugs;
- Costa Rica: National Drug Council;
- Panama: National Commission for the Study and Prevention of Drug-related Crimes.[18]

Another element in the strategy is the network of information/intelligence centers which operate nationally and are also interconnected at the regional level and with the EPIC network in El Paso, Texas. Their main centers are:

- Guatemala: Joint Anti-drug Information Center;
- Honduras: Anti-drug Information Center;
- El Salvador: Information Center at the Anti-drug Foundation;
- Costa Rica: Joint Intelligence Anti-drug Center;
- Panama: Joint Information and Coordination Center.

In addition to the regional dimension, the Central American states have signed bilateral agreements or joint agreements for coordination and cooperation with Mexico, the Andean states and the European Union. They also keep close coordination and cooperation with the DEA, and they operate within the OAS/CICAD network. The regional strategy started, therefore, by building a legal foundation and a coordinating network for the anti-drug action. It is assumed that the security agencies, based on those legal entities has increased their seizure capabilities, mainly against drug trafficking and, in the case of Guatemala, also against drug production. The executing bodies are specialized units within the security services. They receive many kinds of assistance from the DEA in the areas of training, intelligence, equipment and financing. The agencies in question are:

- Guatemala: Department of Anti-drug Operations of the Customs Police;
- El Salvador: Anti-drug Division of the National Civil Police;
- Nicaragua: Anti-drug Unit of the National Police;
- Honduras: Anti-drug Unit of the Public Security Force;
- Costa Rica: Drug Control Police of the Public Forces;
- Panama: Technical Judicial Police.

Seizure operations frequently involve the collective efforts of several countries, within the framework of the above-mentioned agreements. Among recent collective initiatives have been Operation 'Triangle 95' which was conducted in June 1995 among Mexico, Belize and Guatemala, and Operation 'United' carried out at the end of 1995 among Central America, Mexico and Belize.[19] In Central America the armed forces cooperate in air and maritime seizures since police forces do not have the required resources. Anti money laundering operations as well as precursor chemical control operations, however, are not as organized as those against production and trafficking. This is partially because (a) the necessary legislative and institutional foundations have not yet been built, (b) there is less intelligence on these matters, and (c) therefore a smaller operational capacity to combat them.

On the subject of fighting the laundering of money, in Costa Rica an office of financial investigations was created within the anti-drug police force. In Panama, a presidential-level unit was established to coordinate efforts in that area and a Financial Analysis Unit was created to gather and analyse the necessary information. Moreover, the Technical

Judiciary Police organized a specialized section to deal with the subject.[20] In Guatemala, there was a plan for the Customs Police to organize the Integrated Division of Financial Investigation, devoted to money laundering, with special attention to financial, monetary, fiscal, and customs transactions as well as to locate goods acquired with drug money.

## Conclusion

The reaction to the drug dilemma in Central America has been most significant by the governments, since the subject has assumed great proportions within the integration process as such, has become a part of regional institutionalization. The regional strategy is based on creating a common legal and institutional foundation and on acting within the framework of hemispheric and world-wide efforts to fight drugs. This aspect has undergone a marked development and continues to deepen, as more laws are being adopted and structures continue to be organized.

Nevertheless, it is not possible to make an empirical judgement on the effects of the strategy in fighting the drug powers, in part because statistics continue to be weak. The progress in reducing drug production is obvious, since the main case, that of opium in Guatemala was quite successful, despite having only utilized repressive measures and not significantly, a substitution of crops. It may be that this success is due to the fact that despite the persistence at the time, of the internal armed conflict, the main players in the conflict did not become involved in the production of poppy.

However, on drug trafficking, although there is a high level of seizures, there are signs that the flow continues and that the capacity of the drug dealers to penetrate government structures as well as those of the civilian society is also maintained. The problem of hard drug consumption is still low, but the tendency to pay for services with drugs might expand it. There is little information on the true dimensions of money laundering, which seems to vary from one country to another and actions against it are still, at the regional level, incipient. The same thing may be said about precursor chemicals. Limitations to the anti-drug actions are partially due to misconceptions, because in some countries there is still no clearly defined strategy. They are also due to the organizational and resource limitations of the states, which translates into security and other forces lacking the necessary means for the full execution of their missions. At the level of the civilian society, there is an increased awareness of the risks of drug trafficking. Various initiatives are also carried by a variety of NGOs.

There are two sets of considerations to be kept in mind. On the one hand, the geographical location of Central America, the weaknesses of the security forces and the continuous attraction of the consumer markets in North America will probably continue to facilitate the flow of drug trafficking. Its permanence may spread consumption and even the progress made in fighting drug production may be jeopardized. Certainly, the high priority which the governments have given it is a positive element in dealing with the dilemma. The idea of giving a legal and institutional basis to a regional strategy can provide a very solid foundation for fighting the drug trafficking dragon. However, the practical resources of the states continue to be insufficient, especially at the level of the police corps and of the courts, in addition to the fact that not much has been accomplished on the control of money laundering and of chemicals. It is true that this problem surpasses that of the drugs and some governance questions have not yet been solved. But in order to have substantial accomplishments a central effort must be made to clean up and give professional training to the anti-drug police units as well as in the provision of appropriate equipment and techniques, among which a modern radar network.

In that context, external cooperation – the second consideration – becomes important. The participation of the United States is vital and that of the European Union has become important as well. Central American coordination with the G-3 and other countries in Latin America has to be improved and it is also necessary to get more involvement and better organize the efforts of the civilian society. As with any other delinquent activity, drug trafficking is nourished by poverty and social underdevelopment. An adequate management of social agendas by the governments as well as efforts made towards economic growth which can provide better employment opportunities can have an invigorating effect, in the medium term on the anti-drug governmental actions. All this needs to be done for success in the fight against the drug dragon in Central America.

## Notes

1   US Department of State, *International Narcotics Control Strategy Report*, March 1996. Available at www.usis.usemb.se/drugs/CANMEX/DRGGUA.HTM.

2 Field research carried out by author in Huehuetenango and San Marcos during 1991 and 1995.

3 *International Narcotics Control Strategy Report*, 1996.

4 Ibid.

5 Policia Nacional, *Compendio estadistico 1991–1995*, Managua, 1996.

6 Fuerza Publica, Policia de Control de Drogas, Costa Rica, *Situacion actual de Costa Rica en la lucha anti-drogas*, San Jose, October 1996.

7 *International Narcotics Control Strategy Report*, 1996.

8 Ministerio de Salud Publica y Asistencia Social, *Control y prevencion del uso y abuso de alcohol, drogas y estupefacientes*, Guatemala 27 August 1996.

9 Instituto Hondureño para la Prevención del Alcoholismo, la Drogadicción y la Famacodependencia, *Investigación sobre el uso y el abuso de alcohol y drogas en los estudiantes de escuelas normales de Honduras*, Tegucigalpa, Honduras, June 1996.

10 *International Narcotics Control Strategy Report*, 1996.

11 Patricia Cordero, 'Resumen de la presentación del caso costarricense', in *Ayuda a la Memoria del Primer Taller Subregional, Cooperactión Judicial Internacional en materia de control de la producción y el tráfico ilícito de drogas en los países del istmo centroamericano*, CEDEJU, Costa Rica, 1996.

12 Sistema de Integracion Centroamericana, Secretaria General SICA, *Informe sobre actividades contra el narcotráfico en el contexto del tratado marco de seguridad democratica centroamericana*, IF/D/96/057, San Salvador, El Salvador, September 1996.

13 *Declaracion de la conferencia antidrogas de jefes de gobierno de Centroamerica celebrada en la ciudad de Belice el 19 de febrero de 1993.*

14 *Convenio Constitutivo de la comision centroamericana permanente para la erradicación de la producción, trafico, consumo y uso ilicito de estupefacientes y sustancias psicotropicas y delitos conexos*, Guatemala, 1993.

15 Sistema de Integracion, *Informe sobre actividades contra el narcotráfico en el contexto del tratado marco de seguridad democrática centroamericana.*

16 Patricia Cordero, *Estudio comparativo de las legislaciones y reglamentacion vigente en materia de control de la produccion y el trafico ilicito de drogas en 6 paises de la sub region centroamericana*, CICAD, Costa Rica, 1995.

17 Ibid.

18 Ibid.

19 Gobierno de Guatemala, Ministerio de Gobernacion, *Informe sobre las actividades del gobierno guatemalteco en su lucha contra la narcoactividad y propuestas de cooperacion*, Guatemala, febrero de 1997, US Department of State.

20 Fuerza Publica, Policia de Control de Drogas, op.cit.

# 12

# Multilateral Narcotics Interdiction Measures in the Caribbean

*Captain Richard R. Beardsworth*

In the 1970s, maritime interdiction of drugs in the Caribbean was purely a unilateral effort on the part of the United States. By the mid-1980s the US would occasionally cooperate in *ad hoc* bilateral efforts to interdict illegal narcotics. At the same time these nascent bilateral approaches were occurring, the US, the Bahamas, and the United Kingdom entered into the first, and highly successful, multilateral arrangement to interdict maritime shipments of narcotics – OPBAT, which came into force in June 1982. By the early 1990s, as a result of the 1988 United Nations Convention Against Illicit Traffic in Narcotic Drugs and Psychotropic Substances, the US and many of its Caribbean neighbors had begun to enter into cooperative bilateral arrangements to interdict and disrupt maritime narco-trafficking.

As these bilateral arrangements were refined, exercised, and formalized into agreements, the US and Caribbean countries realized that cooperation could indeed be effective against narco-trafficking. Hence, in June of 1995, for example, the US and the Netherlands, and later the United Kingdom and the countries of the RSS joined together in a multilateral operation in the Eastern Caribbean dubbed Caribe Storm. The subsequent operations have been named Caribe Venture. In June 1997, the ACCP executed a successful, Caribbean-wide operation called Summer Storm. While certainly not the only examples of successful multilateral interdiction efforts, these three efforts – OPBAT, Caribe Venture, and Summer Storm – illustrate that multilateral efforts can be successful, but at certain costs.

The last two decades have witnessed a progression from unilateral interdiction efforts through bilateral interdiction efforts to, most recently, multilateralism. Obviously, multilateral initiatives have not precluded bilateral ones, and while this chapter focuses on multilateral initiatives, a brief comment on some of these bilateral initiatives is warranted.

## Bilateral, maritime counternarcotics agreements

Often inappropriately referred to as 'Shiprider' agreements, these bilateral agreements are correctly entitled Cooperative Maritime Counternarcotics Agreements. For the most part they have their basis in the mandate of Article 17 of the 1988 United Nations Convention Against Illicit Traffic in Narcotic Drugs and Psychotropic Substances. Prior to the adoption of this convention, the US had signed two Maritime Cooperative Agreements in the region.

The first such agreement was the Grey Agreement. While not originally designed as a counternarcotic agreement, the Grey Agreement was clearly an agreement between the US and the Bahamas that granted standing permission for the US to enter Bahamian territorial seas for very specific purposes. Signed in 1964, the original Memorandum of Understanding between the Bahamian Governor Sir Ralph Grey and Rear Admiral I. J. Stephens, the US Coast Guard's Seventh District Commander at the time, allowed the Coast Guard to enter Bahamian waters and overfly Bahamian territory for search and rescue or to investigate the 'irregular presence' of persons or vessels. In 1988 a common understanding about the Grey Agreement and about Diplomatic Notes exchanged subsequent to Bahamian independence in 1973 allowed US Coast Guard vessels to enter Bahamian waters to investigate US or stateless vessels for the purpose of enforcing US law. This authority under the Grey Agreement extends only to investigating the vessel; if the US then desires to take law enforcement action, the US must seek permission from the government of the Bahamas.[1] The fairly narrow scope of this agreement along with subsequent agreements with the Bahamas and the excellent present cooperation between the Bahamas and the US make the Grey agreement nearly obsolete today.

The other pre-1988 agreement, signed between the U.S. and the United Kingdom in 1981, permitted the US Coast Guard to board any private UK-registered vessel in the Gulf of Mexico, the Caribbean, the region of the Atlantic south of 30 degrees north latitude and west of 55 degrees west longitude, and anywhere within 150 nautical miles of the US coast only if the US authorities had reasonable suspicion that the vessel might be carrying drugs. This agreement applies not only to vessels registered to the UK, but also to vessels registered in any of their six dependent territories of Anguilla, British Virgin Islands,

Bermuda, Cayman Islands, Montserrat, and Turks and Caicos Islands. Once aboard the vessel, US authorities may address inquiries, examine papers, and, when these measures suggest a violation of US law relative to narcotics, search and seize the vessel.

After the ratification of the 1988 UN convention, the US Coast Guard and the US State Department embarked on efforts to develop Cooperative Maritime Counternarcotics Agreements with the Caribbean countries. By the early 1990s these efforts had evolved into proposing standard or 'model' agreements. The initial standard agreements had four operational provisions or parts which were shiprider, shipboarding, pursuit, and entry to investigate.

The shiprider provision allows a nation to place a shiprider aboard a US law enforcement vessel with the authority to exercise jurisdiction over that nation's flag vessel in international waters. It also allows the shiprider to exercise jurisdiction from the US law enforcement vessel within that nation's territorial seas. This provision essentially allows the nation to borrow and use a US law enforcement vessel along with its sensors and trained law enforcement officials. In the absence of a shiprider, the shipboarding provision permits a US law enforcement vessel to board that nation's flag vessels, on their behalf, in international waters, but only if the US law enforcement vessel has reasonable suspicion that the vessel is carrying illegal narcotics. If illegal narcotics are found, the flag state decides the disposition of the vessel and crew. The nation may have the vessel brought into its port for prosecution, or it might waive prosecution, thus allowing the US to prosecute. However, it may decide to prosecute all the crew or only its citizens.

Again, in the absence of a shiprider, the pursuit provision allows a US law enforcement vessel to pursue a suspected smuggler into that nation's territorial seas where it may stop, board, search, and seize the vessel on behalf of the nation, if drugs are found. The disposition of the vessel and crew remains with the nation. The final provision – entry to investigate – grants, in the absence of a shiprider, permission to a US law enforcement vessel to enter the nation's territorial seas in order to investigate a suspicious vessel. Further, the US law enforcement vessel may stop, board, search, and even seize the vessel on the nation's behalf if drugs are found. Again, the disposition of the vessel and crew remains with the nation.

Subsequent standard agreements seek two additional provisions, overflight and order-to-land. The overflight provision allows US law enforcement aircraft to overfly territorial airspace to pursue or to investigate suspicious aircraft. The order to land provision allows US law enforcement aircraft, on behalf of the nation, to order suspicious aircraft to land so that the nation's law enforcement authorities can investigate. This provision does not include any authorization to use force to secure compliance.

Due to the tremendous efforts of the State Department negotiators led by Ash Roach and the personal efforts of Ambassador Jeanette Hyde, nine of these standard agreements were signed in fairly short order. Belize signed in December 1992; the other eight nations signed between April 1995 and March 1996. These nine agreements are with Belize, the Dominican Republic, St Lucia, Dominica, St Kitts and Nevis, Antigua and Barbuda, St Vincent and the Grenadines, Trinidad and Tobago, and Grenada. Since then three nonstandard agreements have been signed, with Columbia, Jamaica, and Barbados. As of Summer 2000 agreements were being negotiated with Nicaragua, Honduras and Guatemala and preliminary discussions had begun with other countries in the region. In total there are 19 Cooperative Maritime Counternarcotics Agreements.[2]

While the standard agreements are fairly easy to understand and implement from an operational perspective, the older agreements and the newer nonstandard ones are more problematic in that there are significant differences in what is authorized. Issues such as reciprocity, expedited authorization, and third party ships vary from country to country. A brief, real life example would serve to illustrate some of the legal and operational challenges involved.

A US Coast Guard Law Enforcement Detachment (LEDET) deployed aboard a Dutch frigate operating in international waters near Trinidad and Tobago comes across a suspicious go-fast heading into Trinidad and Tobago territorial seas. If the go-fast is a Dominican Republic vessel the US Coast Guard LEDET could board the vessel because the US has a standard agreement with the Dominican Republic and the Dutch frigate is considered a US law enforcement vessel due to the Coast Guard LEDET presence. If the go-fast is Colombian, the operational commander, in this case of the US Coast Guard Commander in Miami, would use an expedited procedure to ask permission directly from the Colombian Navy to board the go-fast. Once authorized by the Colombian Navy, the LEDET could board the go-fast. However, if the vessel is Venezuelan, the operational commander would ask the Venezuelans for permission to board through US Coast Guard Headquarters in Washington, DC and through the US State Department. Until summer 1997, the Venezuelans would have said 'no', because they did not consider the Dutch frigate with an embarked US Coast Guard LEDET to be a US law enforcement vessel.[3] Finally, if the go-fast made it into Trinidad and Tobago's territorial seas, the Dutch frigate could pursue, stop, and search the vessel because of the pursuit provision in the standard agreement with Trinidad and Tobago.

The above example illustrates some of the differences among the agreements. The agreement with Colombia provides for an expedited verification of registry and permission to board a Colombian vessel in international waters; it also provides for direct communication between the US Coast Guard and the Colombian Navy. The agreement with Venezuela provides for an expedited verification of registry and permission to board, but only through cumbersome US State Department channels. The Netherlands Antilles agreement provides for pursuit and entry only while under tactical control (TACON) of Commander Forces Netherlands Antilles (COMFONL) in Curaçao. Each of the nonstandard agreements has its own twists to the procedure. In spite of the differences in the agreements, however, as they are exercised more frequently and as the signatory nations become more comfortable with the practicalities of the concepts of maritime interdiction cooperation, they become the basis for modest multilateral interdiction operations.

## Multilateral interdiction

### Operation Bahamas and Turks and Caicos

Operation Bahamas and Turks and Caicos Islands (OPBAT) was the first multilateral operation targeted at drug smugglers in the Caribbean. In the early 1980s the United States, the United Kingdom, and the Bahamas recognized the very serious threat that drug smugglers posed by transiting the Bahamas. Small aircraft were flying from South America and Jamaica almost daily and were dropping their illicit cargo to waiting boats, or were landing on remote airstrips. The drugs were not just 'in transit' and benign to the Bahamas, but were also having a significant corrupting influence within the Bahamas. The United States, the Bahamas, and the United Kingdom developed and implemented OPBAT, which involves provision by the US of assets, personnel, and hardware capable of tracking and intercepting the smugglers' aircraft. The Bahamas and the Turks and Caicos Islands provide law enforcement officers to ride aboard US helicopters to authorize those assets to be in their territory and to make arrests and seizures.

In June 1982, when OPBAT was formally established, only two DEA helicopters participated; they provided intercept coverage out of Nassau for only six hours per day. By 1991, OPBAT was not only multilateral but multiagency as well. Helicopters from the US Army, the US Coast Guard and the DEA were stationed at three sites throughout the Bahamas, and the OPBAT operations center was staffed by US Coast Guard personnel working for the DEA attaché assigned to the American Embassy. The US Customs Service and the Department of Defense through the Joint Inter Agency Task Force East (JIATFE), provided additional support.

OPBAT's mission is to stop the flow of cocaine and marijuana which originates in South American countries, transits through the Bahamas, and is destined for the United States. Historically, OPBAT has focused its efforts on air smugglers. As Table 12.1 illustrates, during OPBATs first full year of operations, it seized 100,000 kilograms of contraband. OPBAT seizures peaked in 1987, with over 150,000 kilograms of contraband confiscated; after that the flow of contraband dropped significantly. Since 1988, the annual flow has averaged less than 6000 kilograms annually. OPBAT has truly been a success story of how a concerted, cooperative multilateral approach can affect smuggling trends. In this case, OPBAT forced a significant reduction in air smuggling through the Bahamas.

Table 12.1  OPBAT Seizures, 1983–99

| Year of operation | Contraband seized (kg) |
| --- | --- |
| 1983 | 100,000 |
| 1984 | 39,000 |
| 1985 | 25,000 |
| 1986 | 35,000 |
| 1987 | 150,000 |
| 1988[*] | 23,222 |
| 1989 | 7,360 |
| 1990 | 3,623 |
| 1991 | 6,878 |
| 1992 | 6,834 |
| 1993 | 2,328 |
| 1994 | 1,855 |
| 1995 | 5,469 |
| 1996 | 3,156 |
| 1997 | 12,230 |
| 1998 | 8,790 |
| 1999 | 19,522[**] |

*Notes:* [*] OPBAT operations center and current asset level established; [**] seizures up to November 1999.
*Source:* US Coast Guard, 1999.

This interdiction success is, however, only part of the story. While such results are laudable, law enforcement agencies and other countries should recognize the lessons to be learned from this experience as well as the costs associated with its success. First, while air smuggling decreased, the overall flow of drugs into the US was not significantly altered by OPBAT. One avenue was closed, but other routes opened up. Smugglers will develop routes of least resistance; success in one country spells failure in another country unless there is a regional cooperative effort. Secondly, tremendous resources were committed to stopping this particular threat. Annual operating costs for Coast Guard participants alone exceeds US$14 million. When one adds to that figure about US$6 million expended annually in US Army and DEA operating costs, before long one gets a sense of the huge financial resources involved.

Thirdly, even though the air threat has been brought under control, other threats within the Bahamas have emerged, specifically go-fast vessels transiting the Bahamas from intermediate points in the Caribbean, such as Jamaica and Hispaniola, and cargo vessels with multi-ton loads of cocaine to be off-loaded in the Straits of Florida. An example of the latter is the seizure of the *M/V Ann*, carrying 1360 kilos of cocaine, in Freeport Harbor in late July 1997. OPBAT planners must continually reassess the mix of assets and strategies to meet the changing threat, and must never become over-confident that they have denied the smugglers a particular route. Fourth, and perhaps most instructive, is the degree of cooperation necessary to develop and implement OPBAT. The Bahamas had the political will to cooperate and allowed US assets on its soil, in its territorial seas, and in its airspace in order to combat the illicit flow of drugs. One of the costs associated with success in the maritime interdiction of narcotics is the managed and conscious yielding of traditional notions of sovereignty in order to maintain some semblance of sovereignty against narco-traffickers.

### Caribe Venture

Caribe Venture was first conceived and run as Caribe Storm in June 1995. This modest eight-day operation was actually a bilateral operation conducted jointly between several agencies of the United States and the Netherlands. The operation focused on the Eastern Caribbean and utilized existing maritime agreements to make the operation more widespread and effective. For the subsequent operations, the name was changed to Caribe Venture and participation was expanded to include the countries of the Regional Security Systems and the United Kingdom. These subsequent operations have occurred almost quarterly.

Caribe Venture operations are planned under the auspices of the Eastern Caribbean Working Group, which is an informal group of regional participants chaired by the US ambassador in Bridgetown, Barbados. Participants include the American Embassy in Barbados, the US Coast Guard District Seven in Miami, the US Coast Guard Atlantic Area, the JIATFE in Key West, Florida, the US Atlantic Command and the DEA. Typically, the British and the Dutch each provide their West Indies Guard Ship with an embarked LEDET, the US Coast Guard provides one or two of its cutters, JIATFE assists with planning and coordination and provides detection and monitoring capabilities as well as intelligence cuing, and the RSS countries provide patrol boats. The Commander of the US Coast Guard of the Greater Antilles Section (GANTSEC) in San Juan, Puerto Rico provides command and control of the operations.

During its first eight operations since June 1995, the combined Caribe Venture forces have made three seizures, totaling 1300 kilograms of cocaine and 4000 kilograms of marijuana. In addition to the seizures, they disrupted nine other trafficking events. However, the success of Caribe Venture operations has not been fully reflected merely in kilos of contraband seized or in numbers of people arrested, but rather in the practice of cooperation. These operations bring together planners and law enforcement officials from the various countries and promote the development of trust and confidence among them. Seemingly simple things, such as the exchange of home phone numbers and the invitation to 'call me at home', can facilitate a successful interdiction several months later when a narcotics airdrop is made in the middle of the night. Communications connectivity, command and control issues, information sharing, an understanding of capabilities, and an understanding of asset availability are all developed during the operations. Obviously these benefits carry over into the day-to-day business of maritime narcotics interdiction.

An illustrative example of this cooperation occurred one night in the middle of April 1997 when multilateral forces, through practiced cooperation, thwarted an airdrop in St Kitts-Nevis territorial seas and seized over one hundred kilos of cocaine and a vessel. The episode started about 9.00 p.m. on the evening of 13 April, when JIATFE detected an uncorrelated ROTHR air track heading north towards the northern Lesser Antilles from South America. JIATFE launched the E-2 surveillance aircraft that was on standby in Puerto Rico and, at the same time, notified the GANTSEC.

GANTSEC alerted the various islands considered possible destinations, from Martinique to Antigua to the British Virgin Islands. GANTSEC and

JIATFE also coordinated with the USCS to have a USCS airborne interceptor aircraft covertly intercept and follow the target. Later, GANTSEC launched its alert HH60 helicopter to relieve the USCS interceptor aircraft as it ran low on fuel. When it became apparent that the unknown aircraft was heading for St. Kitts-Nevis airspace, the GANTSEC watch officer called Inspector Pat Wallace of the St Kitts-Nevis Coast Guard, who in turn launched his 40-foot patrol boat. The US Coast Guard HH60 helicopter, tailing the suspected aircraft, was able to continue its pursuit into St Kitts-Nevis airspace by invoking the existing and often exercised maritime cooperative agreement. The HH60 helicopter observed the airdrop and vectored in the St. Kitts patrol boat to intercept the pickup go-fast. The go-fast abandoned the cocaine, but was nonetheless stopped and seized by the St. Kitts-Nevis Coast Guard.

The important part of this anecdote is that it clearly demonstrates how multinational cooperation can lead to success. Caribe Venture enabled the various participants to practice procedures and to exercise cooperative agreements. Handoffs of the unknown aircraft's track, the enactment of the maritime cooperative agreement with St Kitts-Nevis, and the coordination of a late night 'end game' were all executed flawlessly. As an excited Cdr Neil Buschman, operations officer for GANTSEC, exclaimed: 'Everybody could talk to everybody else'.

This type of multilateral success does not come cheaply. The US assets necessary to prosecute this one case, the E-2 aircraft, the USCS interceptor, the USCG HH60 helicopter, did not just 'happen' to be in the area; they were all part of a standing force that is available 24 hours a day. The small, but vitally important, regional coast guards require considerable investment to keep their boats running and their people trained, often at the expense of more visible programs ashore. Security Assistance funding, including International Military Education and Training (IMET) and Foreign Military Financing (FMF) in the Eastern Caribbean alone averaged about US$1.5 million per year from FY1993 to FY1997. Participant time and effort used in planning and in exercises are time and effort that could be devoted to other law enforcement duties. Finally, there would be no success without a new perspective on sovereignty – a perspective that allows for cooperation within territorial seas and airspace in order to defend against sovereignty violation by narco-traffickers.

**Summer Storm**

This 'summer of 1997' Caribbean-wide cooperative effort, conceptualized and executed under the auspices of the ACCP, was remarkably successful. The following 25 countries and dependent territories participated: Anguilla, Antigua and Barbuda, British Virgin Islands, Dominica, Montserrat, St Kitts-Nevis, St Maarten, the Bahamas, Belize, Cayman Islands, the Dominican Republic, Haiti, Jamaica, Turks and Caicos Islands, Curaçao, Barbados, Grenada, Guyana, St Lucia, St Vincent and the Grenadines, Trinidad, Suriname, the United States, the United Kingdom, and the Netherlands. In all, 828 arrests were made, and there was the seizure of 57 kilograms of cocaine, one kilogram of crack, 340 kilograms of cured marijuana, 442,000 marijuana plants, 122 weapons, eight vessels, and three vehicles. In addition, 1026 homes and 4582 vehicles were searched. While the operation did not net any single dramatic seizure or disrupt any major organizations, the coordination and cooperation were impressive, and the positive impact on local communities was substantial.

Summer Storm was developed within the ACCP. As Commissioner Ornell Brooks of Belize explained in June 1997 at Orient 97 in Key West, Florida, the regional Commissioners of Police, tired of counternarcotics law enforcement being a political issue, decided to take the lead in the regional counternarcotics effort. The concept was introduced at International Drug Enforcement Conference XV (IDECXV), held in the Bahamas during April 1997. More detailed planning followed at the annual ACCP conference in Jamaica in May 1997. The operation was executed 18–26 June 1997.

Summer Storm's regional coordination center (RCC) was located at the Barbados Police Regional Training Center and was directed by Commissioner Brooks. The region was divided into three zones, roughly described as central and western Caribbean, northeastern Caribbean, and south and southeastern Caribbean. Each zone had its own zone coordination center (ZCC) directed by a Superintendent or Assistant Superintendent of Police. Each participating country established a tactical operations center (TOC) headed by a senior police officer. The operation was run primarily with indigenous police assets, although support was provided by the US, the UK, the Netherlands, and, on an informal basis, France.

Operation Blue Skies, which was a joint US Coast Guard–DEA operation using deployed helicopters and local police officers, was planned to dovetail with Summer Storm and to provide maritime patrol assets to it. The US Coast Guard also participated by providing Belize with a cutter for their portion of Summer Storm. The UK provided a ship to operate with Jamaica, the Dutch contributed assets to the effort, and SOUTHCOM provided helicopter support. JIATFE and the

US Coast Guard provided intelligence support and, together with the DEA, provided some personnel and operations center equipment support.

As with Caribe Venture, the real benefit of Summer Storm was not in the amount of drugs seized or in the number of arrests made, but in the cooperation and contacts that were established. Some of the participants of Summer Storm had also been major players in Caribe Venture. A significant synergy occurred with Summer Storm in the linking or interlacing of different 'protocols'. For example, Blue Skies took the OPBAT concept and successfully attempted to 'regionalize' it in the Eastern Caribbean. Blue Skies and the US Coast Guard participation in Belize's Summer Storm took the Cooperative Maritime Agreements and used them in conjunction with a larger police operation. This interlacing of protocols and the associated complex network of jurisdictional authority can be confusing, not only to the operators, but especially to political leadership. The Commissioners of Police assumed the responsibility for involving and co-opting their respective political leaders, and did quite well on this front, for the most part.

While the monetary costs for Summer Storm were relatively modest, the political cost, in at least one country, became quite high, as the following case shows. The British Navy ship *HMS Liverpool*, with an embarked US Coast Guard LEDET, sailed from Jamaica after a port call during her participation in Jamaica's Summer Storm. While en route to another assignment, the *Liverpool* sighted a Jamaican fishing vessel and, from her small boat, asked routine questions of the vessel. After questioning the vessel, *HMS Liverpool* departed the area with no further interest in the fishing vessel. The fishing vessel returned to port and complained to the press of being stopped in Jamaican waters, following which the government of Jamaica made a considerable issue of the incident in the press. While there were in fact issues worthy of discussion surrounding the incident, there is ample indication that the various ministers in the Jamaican government were unaware of *HMS Liverpool's* participation in Summer Storm, or even of the existence of Summer Storm. The political costs of the resultant imbroglio are still uncertain, but it is clear that US–Jamaica relations have deteriorated as a result of the handling of the incident. Furthermore, the PNP has come under considerable attack from the opposition party for how it has handled the situation. Unfortunately, because of the strained political relations between the two governments, between then and the end of 1997 Jamaica and the US were unable to work out *ad hoc* cooperative arrangements for interdicting known narco-trafficking events in the vicinity of Jamaica.

Where does the multilateral approach go from here? Recent EU and UNDCP studies developed a number of regional approaches. One of the EU proposals relating to maritime interdiction is the concept of a multinational ship. While this rather far-fetched concept is certainly not as radical an idea as it might have been ten years ago, it embraces concepts that still may be too difficult for sovereign nations to accept. Yet, only through such nontraditional multilateral approaches can the nations in the Caribbean Region successfully stem the flow of drugs through their countries. What are the benefits and practicalities of this multinational ship concept?

## A multinational ship

One small recommendation among many listed in the EU-sponsored study 'Maritime Counterdrug Cooperation in the Caribbean' of 15 May 1997 is '...the acquisition of a logistical and maintenance platform capable of touring the region on a preplanned schedule. This should allow for flexibility as damage to the assets is frequent. The platform would also provide excellent opportunities for hands-on training. Mechanisms should be implemented to facilitate the loan and exchange of capable personnel within the regional coast guards to enhance their technical capabilities'. This concept was first developed in April 1997 as part of a brainstorming session on innovative ideas to increase cooperation and effectiveness among the United States, the RSS countries, and European countries with interest in the Caribbean. This writer and several other individuals explored the concept of a multinational ship. Cdr Ed Daniels of the US Coast Guard's Atlantic Area Staff later developed some of those ideas into a point paper entitled 'Caribbean International Support Tender'. He subsequently had the opportunity to introduce this idea to the EU study team, which adopted only the small portion quoted above.

The concept of a Caribbean International Support Tender is to provide a platform that can support regional coast guards and navies in training and in maintenance. It would also support multilateral counternarcotics operations and would be able to assist in disaster relief and other missions, such as oil spills. Support and assistance aspect of the proposition notwithstanding, the more intriguing concept would be to make the International Support Tender a truly multinational ship, conducting real-time operations in addition to support functions.

The ship itself could be a fairly low cost, low technology US Coast Guard cutter such as an older US Coast Guard Oceangoing Buoy Tender (WLB). The WLB tender has berthing for 58 people, a 120,000 pound cargo carrying capacity, and sufficient space for maintenance shops and training classrooms. The ship only cruises at about 12 knots, its top speed, but could carry high speed Rigid Hull Inflatable Boats (RHIB) for operational missions requiring short-range high-speed intercepts. Another option for the tender would be a converted Ocean Surveillance ship (T-AGOS) vessel. This low-speed vessel could be adequately out-fitted to meet mission needs and would probably require less crew to operate it. The crew would be multinational with officers and enlisted members provided by the US Coast Guard, the US Navy, the Dutch, the British, the French, as well as by RSS countries. Included as part of the crew would be experienced trainers and maintenance experts, disaster relief specialists, search and rescue experts, marine environmental experts, and intelligence specialists.

Personnel training for the coast guards and navies of the Eastern Caribbean region is currently provided through a few essentially unco-ordinated programs. There are resident courses available for a few stu-dents at US Coast Guard and US Navy training centers. The US Atlantic Command (USACOM) has in the past sponsored Operation Tradewinds, a multifaceted training exercise in the region, which includes US Coast Guard cutters visiting the various nations for several days of classroom and underway training. Presumably, Operation Tradewinds will con-tinue under the auspices of SOUTHCOM, which assumed responsibility for the Caribbean from USACOM on 1 June 1997.

The US Coast Guard conducts Operation Visits In Support of Training Assistance (OPVISTA) three or four times a year. The OPVISTA concept is for a US Coast Guard cutter to visit a country for several days: the first two or three days includes classroom and inport training, the last two or three days includes underway drills and combined operations. Finally, the US Coast Guard conducts occasional 'professional exchanges' with the coast guard and navies of the region. The International Support Tender would combine many of these uncoordinated training efforts and offer continuity from year to year so that one year's training could be built on previous years' training.

Maintenance of vessels has been a long-standing problem among the small nations of the Eastern Caribbean. Ships and patrol boats have often been acquired with little or no thought toward long-term main-tenance needs. Hence, several of the nations in the region are unable to provide a credible, continuous response capability because their vessels are in need of repair. One maintenance assistance program in the Eastern Caribbean – the Technical Assistance Field Team (TAFT) – provides maintenance assistance for the standard 40-foot Monarch patrol boats that were purchased for the various coast guards and navies in the region. This maintenance team consists solely of three US Coast Guard mechanics stationed in Puerto Rico who travel throughout the region. The International Support Tender would take over and expand the TAFT. Specialists assigned to the tender would be able to assist countries with setting up preventative maintenance systems (PMS) and would be able to perform intermediate level maintenance on the vessels. These specialists would also provide on-the-job training for the engineers of the various navies and the coast guards. In addition, the tender would be able to maintain a centralized supply system for spare parts and would have the expertise to tap easily into supply systems in the US for additional parts.

Several innovative multinational operations in the region have not reached their full potential because of the absence of a Forward Operating Base (FOB) to support patrol boats engaged in these operations. The tender would provide a ready made support platform that could provide maintenance and personnel assistance to patrol boats from various nations during an operation in a particular area. Patrol boat operations could be extended by billeting relief crews aboard the tender. Repairs and PMS could be done on the tender right in the theater of operations. The tender could also provide command and control of small multinational operations. A robust communications suite with suitable tactical display capability would enhance its efficiency. A small intelligence detachment could fuse, sort, filter, and distribute important tactical information that would otherwise be unavailable to many of the countries in the region.

The tender would be a natural facility to support disaster relief operation as well. With its large cargo capacity, relief supplies could reach a hurricane-stricken island well before destroyed runways may be reopened. It could also provide medical assistance and could make damage assessments. Moreover, it could provide limited emergency water, and could obviously provide critical communication support.

The potential for marine environmental disasters, or oil spills, is of particular significance to small economies heavily dependant on tourism. Contingency plans and exercises sponsored by the International Maritime Organization, like the one held in Grenada in early 1997, would benefit from the year-round presence of a platform that could provide command and control, could deploy booms, and could assist in the recovery of the spilled oil.

Perhaps the most intriguing aspect of the International Support Tender is its potential to become a multinational ship conducting counternarcotics operations in the territorial seas of all the countries in the region. With the introduction of the shiprider concept in the cooperative maritime agreements, the practice of cooperation developed during multinational operations such as Caribe Venture, and the political will and resolve demonstrated during regional operations such as Summer Storm, it is not too large a step to combine these elements into a standing force in the context of a single multinational ship. Imagine a ship with officers and crew from the United States, France, the Netherlands, the United Kingdom, and all of the nations of the RSS. With each of these people having law enforcement authority and exercising jurisdiction within their respective territorial seas, the ship could sail unimpeded through the Eastern Caribbean, flying the flag of the country whose territorial seas it entered. Certainly a single ship could not begin to stop the flow of narcotics through the region, but the symbolic value of cooperative commitment along with the very real cooperation that would grow from such a venture could indeed begin to turn the tide, at least in this particular region.[4]

## Conclusion

Multilateralism in the context of maritime counternarcotics efforts in the Caribbean has been successful. But it clearly has not reached its potential. Contemporary multilateralism builds on the early unilateral efforts of the United States and on the early bilateral efforts of the US and the Bahamas, and of the US and the UK. It follows too the bilateral cooperative efforts that grew out of the 1988 UN convention.

Multilateralism is possible because of practiced cooperation between the US and various countries in the region over the past several years. Exercises such as Caribe Venture, Tradewinds, and OPVISTA have all built confidence among the nations. Not only have these exercises built confidence, but they have built relationships – especially at various operational levels. These relationships, probably as much as any agreement, account for nascent bilateral and multilateral successes. These multilateral successes come at a cost. The millions of dollars required to operate OPBAT, to keep ships, aircraft, and sensors in the Caribbean, Security Assistance funding for the purchase and maintenance of assets for the regional navies and coast guards – all contribute to the formidable monetary costs of maritime interdiction. There are political costs as well, including issues of sovereignty and the associated political fallout.

Multilateralism is really the only effective approach to combating narco-trafficking in the region. Thus, the US and Caribbean nations must build on current multinational success and explore and develop new multilateral approaches – not just in maritime interdiction, but also across the counternarcotics spectrum. Certainly NATO has been an expensive multilateral arrangement, but could the deterrence of aggression and the defense of two continents have been achieved without this multilateral approach and its associated costs? In much the same way, the US and Caribbean nations will never look back on their successes at countering narco-trafficking in the region without having forged strong multilateral approaches and paid the costs of doing so, whether those costs be monetary, political, or perceived opportunity costs.

## Notes

1  Internal memo, dated 30 January 1996, Office of Law Enforcement, US Coast Guard District Seven.
2  In addition to the Bahamas and the United Kingdom, the following countries also have nonstandard agreements with the US: Barbados, Colombia, Haiti, Jamaica, the Netherlands Antilles, Panama, the Turks and Caicos, and Venezuela.
3  In July 1997, the US and Venezuela signed an agreement whereby Venezuela would allow boardings of Venezuelan vessels by US Coast Guard LEDETs embarked on Dutch, UK and French ships.
4  Since this chapter was first drafted the concept has become a reality. In September 1999 the US Coast Guard Cutter *Gentian* was commissioned as the Caribbean Support Tender, with crew from the US, Trinidad and Tobago, the Dominican Republic, the Bahamas and Guyana. The tender is used only for training and maintenance at this point.

# 13

# Regional and Global Action to Combat Drugs in the Caribbean

*Tim Wren*

The Caribbean is a multilingual, multiethnic and multi-cultural region reflecting the historical and current influences of several major powers – Britain, France, the Netherlands, Spain and the United States. The economies of many countries in the region are dominated by a single industry – sugar, bananas, bauxite, and more recently, tourism and financial services – or a combination of these industries. As a result of their small size and their dependence on foreign trade these economies are particularly vulnerable to external influences. Preferential trade agreements are under threat from global trade liberalization, and in recent times foreign development aid has been diverted or reduced and economic restructuring is causing increased unemployment. Against this background of uncertainty the drug trade has become a significant phenomenon.

As earlier chapters show, Caribbean countries long have been used as corridors for trafficking cocaine between South America producers and the drug markets of North America and Europe. Moreover, the availability of cocaine and increased local production of marijuana have led to the exploitation of the Caribbean as a consumer market in its own right. One dramatic effect of this drug abuse has been increased crime, and a significant increase in HIV infection is attributed to a growth in prostitution as a means of funding addiction. The effects of corruption spawned by the drug trade are less visible, but in recent years they have reached the most senior elected officials and their families. Corruption and crime erode public confidence in government, hinder free market reform, and undermine the legitimacy of the democratic process itself. Understandably, the drug trade is seen as the greatest threat now faced by the democracies of the region. These problems are too great to be tackled by any single nation, which makes international and regional initiatives necessary. The task of this chapter is, thus, to offer an appreciation of the nature and operation of some of these initiatives.

## The United Nations International Drug Control Programme

The United Nations International Drug Control Programme (UNDCP) is the principal international agency charged with drug control responsibilities. In particular, it is mandated to do the following: be the worldwide centre for expertise and information on drug abuse; anticipate the evolution of the drug phenomenon and recommend countermeasures; provide technical cooperation in the different fields of drug control with a view to elaborating methodologies and approaches; and help governments set up adequate drug control structures and define comprehensive national and regional master plans.[1] Programmes carried out at regional, sub-regional and national levels aim to reduce illicit drug production and abuse, and to improve the effectiveness of control over the illicit supply of drugs. UNDCP activities support the wide-ranging Political Declaration and Global Programme of Action, adopted by the UN General Assembly at a special session in 1990. Caribbean countries, in lending their support to the Programme, agree with the rest of the international community about the importance of pursuing comprehensive anti-drug strategies.

The work of the UN in helping Caribbean countries to fight the drug problem was initially co-ordinated by the United Nations Fund for Drug Abuse Control (UNFDAC), which opened its Caribbean regional office in Barbados in 1988. After the establishment of the UNDCP in 1991 (by the amalgamation of UNFDAC, the Division of Narcotic Drugs and the International Narcotics Control Board), those responsibilities passed to the UNDCP Caribbean regional office, with Barbados remaining the host country. The Caribbean regional office covers 29 countries and territories, of which 16 are independent sovereign states, six are British dependencies, and two are Associated States of the Kingdom of the Netherlands. The office also maintains links with the three French overseas departments – French Guiana, Guadeloupe and Martinique – and the two United States-administered territories in the region – Puerto Rico and the US Virgin Islands.

The UNDCP provides technical assistance and sponsors projects to strengthen countries' institutional capacity to fight the drugs. For example, it provides technology to help combat trafficking, and to developed a cadre of highly trained persons to tackle all aspects of the phenomenon. It also aids with the harmonisation of drug laws enacted by Caribbean countries. The UNDCP advocates the adoption of Master Plans or National Anti-drug Strategies by governments. The Master Plan puts the national drug situation in perspective by presenting a comprehensive assessment of drug control concerns and priorities and outlining strategies to achieve the priorities during a specified period. Ideally, each Master Plan should create realistic goals by analysing specific drug problems, evaluating the impact of existing programmes, and assessing national resources for desired initiatives. Although a Master Plan is a government document, the active participation of both the public and private sectors is recommended in order to build a national consensus on drugs and to rationalise anti-drug activities.

Caribbean countries are interdependent and should benefit from a unified approach to combating drugs. The UNDCP has been actively promoting cooperation and coordination among Caribbean countries in developing strategies to control drugs. A major legal training project, which began in 1993 and concluded in 1995 and to which a follow-up is being planned, provided the 18 Commonwealth Caribbean countries with an effective and improved system for the prosecution and adjudication of drug cases. The US$1 million project, executed in conjunction with the UWI, emphasized training to enhance the forensic skills of police prosecutors, crown counsel, and magistrates. In addition, manuals on prosecution and adjudication were produced for prosecutors and magistrates. Another objective of the project was the harmonization of drug-related laws in the 18 countries. In this respect, three model bills – Drugs (Control and Prevention of Misuse), Confiscation of Proceeds of Crime and Mutual Assistance in Criminal Matters – were drafted and sent to relevant governments.

UNDCP national projects have focused on demand reduction, prevention and control, treatment of addicts, and alternative activities in drug-prone communities. Promoting increased public awareness and education is also a major component of these projects, and this is targeted primarily at the youth. To promote the adoption of an integrated approach to fighting drugs, projects are implemented at two levels: government and the community. The government performs the role of facilitator, providing resources and information, and coordinating plans. But drug abuse is essentially a community problem and can only be effectively tackled through involving the community and giving communities a direct say in the development and implementation of action plans that promote community empowerment.

Almost every country and territory covered by the UNDCP regional office has had a national project between 1991 and 1996, and success in reducing demand for illicit drugs has been achieved in several instances. In 1995, the UNDCP launched the region's first Certificate Programme in Addiction Studies, at the three UWI campuses in Barbados, Jamaica, and Trinidad and Tobago. Aimed at educators, health professionals, medical staff and law enforcement officers, the programme is intended to enhance drug prevention and treatment skills. The programme offers a curriculum covering areas such as the pharmacology of drug abuse, youth and drugs, and fundamental concepts of addiction. In addition to UWI, the Addiction Research Foundation of Canada and the Inter-American Drug Abuse Control Commission (CICAD) are working with the UNDCP on this project. Other regional projects involving the UNDCP between 1992 and 1996 include assisting countries in upgrading forensic laboratory facilities and expertise for the better identification and analysis of illicit drugs, improvements to customs services' capability in drug interdiction, and the coordination of police activities. Moreover, two important regional initiatives are in the pipeline: the development of a drugs database for the region, and the creation of a strategic programme to combat money laundering.

## The Inter-American Drug Abuse Control Commission

The Inter-American Programme of Action of Rio de Janeiro was developed at a ministerial meeting of the OAS and approved by the OAS General Assembly in 1986. Among other things, the Inter-American Programme of Action mandated the formation of the Inter-American Drug Abuse Control Commission (CICAD). This organization is tasked by the OAS to develop, coordinate, evaluate and monitor the measures set out in the Programme of Action of Rio de Janeiro. CICAD is the most important drugs policy forum in the hemisphere. It has considerable political influence on action taken by national governments and on public awareness and opinion. The commitment of governments to act in concert through CICAD demonstrates that they have a unified front to address the problem. CICAD facilitates cooperation between and among the countries of the Americas, with support from governments outside the region and from international organizations. A major part of CICAD strategy is the development of national drug control councils, which develop national drug control plans, execute programmes and create mechanisms for professionals to coordinate anti-drug efforts.

The work of CICAD was reviewed at the OAS Ministerial Meeting held in Ixtapa, Mexico, in April 1990. The Declaration and Programme of Action of Ixtapa, which resulted from the review, mandated the formation of an Experts Group to develop Model Regulations Concerning Laundering Offences Connected to Illicit Drug Trafficking and Related Offences. These CICAD Model Regulations, published in 1990, provide generally for criminalization of the laundering of the proceeds of illicit drug trafficking offences, improved regulation of financial institutions, the availability of their records in law enforcement proceedings, and financial institutions' reporting of suspicious transactions. In October 1997 the Experts Group reconvened in Santiago, Chile, to discuss training, typologies and implementation of the resolutions arising from the Summit of the Americas. In addition, CICAD has developed model regulations to prevent the illicit diversion of precursor chemicals. Guidelines on demand reduction, information exchange and compilation of drug-related statistics have also been developed and applied. Not surprisingly, CICAD is dominated by its Latin American membership, and active participation by Caribbean governments in the work of CICAD has been limited. Meetings are regularly attended by only three or four of the larger islands, although new members, such as Barbados have been admitted recently.

The first Summit of the Americas was a meeting of Heads of State and Government of the Americas convened in Miami, Florida, 9–11 December 1994. The summit issued a Declaration of Principles and a Plan of Action to foster a 'Partnership for Development and Prosperity, Democracy, Free Trade and Sustainable Development in the Americas'. This Declaration of Principles reaffirmed governments' commitment, *inter alia*, to preserve and strengthen democracies. In the Plan of Action the governments reaffirmed their commitment to: ratify the 1988 UN Convention; enact asset forfeiture legislation; consider international sharing of forfeited assets; implement the CFATF recommendations and the CICAD Model Regulations; encourage reporting of suspicious transactions; work to identify regional narcotics trafficking and money laundering networks, prosecute their leaders, and seize their assets derived from criminal activities; and hold a working-level conference, followed by a ministerial conference, to consider a coordinated hemispheric response to money laundering.

The Ministerial Conference on the laundering of the proceeds and instrumentalities of crime was held at Buenos Aires, Argentina, 2 December 1995. Ministers agreed to recommend to their governments a plan of action which included a recommendation to the OAS to establish a Working Group to pursue a coordinated hemispheric response and implementation of legal, regulatory and enforcement actions to fulfill the requirements of the 1988 UN Convention, the CFATF recommendations, and the CICAD Model Regulations. Finally, the ministers concurred that their governments intended to institute ongoing assessments of the implementation of the Plan of Action to ensure its full and effective implementation.

## Other bilateral and multilateral initiatives

Several countries, for example, the USA, Canada, the UK, France, the Netherlands and Germany, have appointed drug liaison officers (DLOs) to countries in the Caribbean region. These DLOs are usually operational police or customs officers operating within diplomatic missions and they work closely with national law enforcement agencies. While their primary role is the interdiction of drugs destined for their own countries, they often have the opportunity to enhance the skills of their local counterparts and play vital roles in assisting local operational activities. Cooperation within the Caribbean is much less developed. None of the region's police forces has similar liaison arrangements. This shortcoming is particularly noteworthy for transit countries that are very close to cocaine and heroin source countries. The lack of language skills is a further constraint on cooperation. However, there are several important intra-regional projects and programmes that deserve recognition.

The Martinique-based CIFAD, for instance, was created in 1993 by France to take part in international cooperation in the Caribbean and Latin America. CIFAD provides an extensive range of training programmes for French law enforcement officials and other personnel from the region who specialize in fighting drug trafficking and drug addiction. The training courses are run by CIFAD permanent staff and outside specialists. The REDTRAC, located at the Jamaica Police Academy, opened for its first training course in September 1996. Under the direction of a former Deputy Commissioner of the Jamaica Constabulary Force, REDTRAC offers residential accommodation for up to forty students and has two well equipped classrooms. The centre is funded by UNDCP, and an advisory committee chaired by K.D. Knight, Minister of Security and Justice, oversees its activities. The REDTRAC staff includes a former senior DEA agent, and the centre is developing a training curriculum on drug interdiction and money laundering investigation for police and customs officers from the region.

The Dublin Group comprises all the EU countries plus Australia, Canada, and the United States – major donor countries[2] engaged in the global fight against drugs. It coordinates financing for drug abuse control in all its aspects: law enforcement, demand reduction, treatment and rehabilitation, with police officers and other professionals dealing with these areas trained in Europe and North America. Small vessels and radio networks have been donated to coast guards and logistical assistance is provided for crop eradication exercises. The range of this assistance is extensive and is coordinated in the Caribbean through local, 'mini' Dublin Groups which comprise diplomatic representatives of the donor countries and include international organizations such as the UNDCP, the European Commission and the OAS. These groups have been established in Barbados (also responsible for most of the Eastern Caribbean), the Dominican Republic, Guyana, Jamaica, Suriname and Trinidad and Tobago. Donor coordination meetings are also held in Belize, Haiti and Cuba.

The EU itself is also pursuing anti-drugs initiatives in the Caribbean. In 1996 the European Commission established a Caribbean Drugs Liaison office based in Barbados to coordinate all EU assistance to the region. The role of the office includes technical and financial support as well as coordinating the efforts of EU delegations located in the Caribbean. The EU is also funding a demand reduction project in Trinidad and Tobago costed at US$1.4 million, which is being implemented by the National Alcohol and Drug Abuse Prevention Programme (NADAPP). At its meeting in Madrid in December 1995 the European Council called on the Council of Ministers and the Commission to produce a report on the drugs situation in both Latin America and the Caribbean, as well as proposals for action. A team of experts was established and given broad terms of reference to study law enforcement, judicial/legal support, money laundering, supply reduction, demand reduction, and coordination issues. The team visited the Caribbean region in early 1996 and their report was presented at the Regional Meeting on Drug Control Cooperation in the Caribbean.

That meeting was held in Barbados, 15–17 May 1996, and it was organized by the UNDCP. Representatives of 29 Caribbean countries and territories, donor countries from the Dublin Group and various regional and international organizations participated. The meeting adopted the comprehensive Barbados Plan of Action,[3] which calls for the strengthening of national drug control councils, the harmonisation and strengthening of drug control laws, greater law enforcement co-ordination and cooperation, particularly enhanced training, improvement of forensic science facilities, enhancement of money laundering investigation and witness protection, and improved strategies to reduce the demand for drugs and the strengthening of maritime cooperation. The Barbados Plan of Action also calls for a high-level annual meeting to ensure follow-up and implementation. It was followed up in 1997 with a high-level meeting which produced a declaration of principles, and a plan of action which focuses on trade, development, finance and the environment, and justice and security. The European Union was committed to spending ECU 20 million (US$25 million) over the years 1996–2000 on anti-drug projects. This represents three times the normal level of such spending in the region, and the US government has indicated its preparedness to commit to a similar level of funding. A two-year training project to address money laundering commenced in 1998, with commitments of ECU 5 million from the EU and $500,000 from the US.

The Caribbean Customs Law Enforcement Council (CCLEC) comprises 34 countries and territories in the Caribbean, Latin America, North America and Europe North America. It was established in 1977 and its mission includes raising awareness levels within the Caribbean of the values and importance of customs services, and improving the level of cooperation and exchange of information among members. The CCLEC has proposed a regional Airports Anti-smugglimg Initiative intended to improve the region's customs drug interdiction efforts. The CCLECs Joint Intelligence Office (JIO) in Puerto Rico was established in 1989 in partnership with the World Customs Organization (WCO). The JIO gathers and disseminates customs intelligence and acts as the support centre for the CCLEC network of enforcement liaison officers. It also coordinates requests for assistance from members. The CCLEC secretariat is in St Lucia.

The International Criminal Investigative Training Assistance Programme (ICITAP) was created in 1986 under authorization by the US Congress to meet the need for professional police training in developing nations and new emerging democracies. ICITAP is a component of the Criminal Division of the Department of Justice, and it works with the US Agency for International Development (USAID) and the UN in carrying out its objectives, which include developing sound civilian police organizations that operate under internationally recognized human rights standards within sustainable criminal justice systems. To accomplish this mission ICITAP provides training in basic police procedures, 'train-the-trainer' instruction, forensic medicine and forensic testing of evidence by specialists, and specialist techniques to investigate organized crime, financial crimes, and alien smuggling. ICITAP also offers technical assistance in establishing forensic testing capabilities, developing training programmes, developing policies and operational procedures, and improving administrative and management capabilities of law enforcement agencies. One of ICITAP's key objectives is to increase awareness among police and prosecutors of the significance of higher standards of evidence gathering and of reliance on evidence presentation in courts. Well-trained scene-of-crime specialists supported by competent forensic scientists offer a legitimate alternative to confessions and other practices open to abuse.

Since 1986, ICITAP has conducted projects in 26 countries, mostly in Central and South America and the Caribbean. During the mid-1990s projects were conducted in Colombia, Costa Rica, the Dominican Republic, El Salvador, Guatemala, Haiti, Honduras, Mexico, and Panama. ICITAP was instrumental in the creation of the ACCP and the Central American Chiefs of Police Association (CACPA) to facilitate the co-ordination of agencies combating regional criminal activities in the two regions. ICITAP also supports the development of the Regional Organised Crime Information Sharing System (ROCIS), that will link Caribbean island police forces for the purpose of enhancing their effectiveness against international crime.

The US is the most active of all bilateral donor countries in the region and actively encourages countries to enter into bilateral anti-drug agreements. These include drug interdiction and overflight agreements, asset forfeiture and asset sharing agreements, and extradition treaties. The drug interdiction agreements, otherwise known as 'shiprider' agreements, allow for the pursuit and interception of suspect craft by US forces in the territorial waters of Caribbean countries. These agreements, aspects of which were discussed in Chapters 6, 9 and 12, are in force in most of the Caribbean.

The US Department of State's INCSR provides the basis for the certification, by the US President, of 'major drug- producing' or 'drug-transit' countries.[4] Denial of certification results in most bilateral assistance being cut off and a mandatory negative US vote against a decertified country in six multilateral development banks. The Foreign Assistance Act of 1961 requires, *inter alia*, a report on the extent to which countries that have received US Government assistance in the previous two years have 'met the goals and objectives of the [1961] United Nations [Drugs] Convention . . .'.

Similarly, certification depends in part on whether that country, during the previous year, has cooperated with the United States, or has taken its own steps to achieve full compliance with the 1988 UN Convention, which identifies various obligations for the countries that are party to it. In general, it requires the parties to take legal measures to criminalise and punish all forms of illicit drug production, trafficking, and drug money laundering, to control chemicals that can be used to process illicit drugs, and to co-operate in international efforts towards these ends. In 1996 and 1997, Colombia was one of several countries decertified.

The *INCSR*, therefore, covers a range of countries, from major drug producing and drug transit countries where drug control is a major element of national policy, to mini-states, where the capacity to deal with drug issues is limited. Understandably, the report varies in the extent of its coverage on the various countries. With regard to the Caribbean region, the 1996 report identified the following as major drug producing or drug transit countries: The Bahamas, Belize, Colombia, the Dominican Republic, Guatemala, Haiti, Jamaica, Mexico, Panama and Venezuela. It also designated the following as major money laundering countries: Aruba, the Cayman Islands, Colombia, Costa Rica, Mexico, the Netherlands Antilles, Panama and Venezuela.

## Money laundering

Money laundering entails the surreptitious introduction into legitimate banking and other commercial channels of assets derived from, or produced by, illegal activity. The purpose of the money launderer is to make illegally produced assets appear to be legitimate and to avoid the scrutiny of law enforcement authorities and possible prosecution. Money laundering generally occurs in three stages: placement; layering; and integration. Money motivates all forms of organized criminal activity and criminals turn to anything which makes a profit: drug trafficking; illegal arms trading; extortion; financial fraud or other crimes. Organized criminal groups, including the drug cartels and other trafficking groups, have huge amounts of capital at their disposal. Although there are no exact figures available, estimates of the funds generated by illegal activity exceed hundreds of billions of US$ per year. For example, it is estimated that over US$500 billion per year is generated world-wide by the drug trade. Of this amount, approximately 80 per cent could be available to the cartels and other trafficking organizations as profits.

There are no reliable estimates of profits generated by trafficking in the Caribbean, or of the amount of money that is laundered in the region. It is true to say, however, that by using these resources, which certainly exceed the gross national product of many countries, drug cartels and other criminal organizations wield vast economic power, and consequently, also potentially considerable political and social power. They engage the best lawyers, accountants, business managers, and bankers to launder their assets and to defend them in criminal and civil proceedings. When threatened, they use their power to corrupt, intimidate or kill their opponents. Hence, the integrity of financial institutions and economies in the region is threatened. This, in turn, threatens the political, social and economic foundation and stability of societies.

But the amounts of money involved also provide a means to attack the criminals. Organized crime has its own economics, and given the scale of activity, its use of the financial system represents a point of vulnerability The ability to trace the flow of illegal funds into financial systems, and seize and confiscate this money, allows law enforcement agencies and the criminal justice system to strike back at organized criminals and attack their economic power. Successful anti-money laundering operations have repeatedly demonstrated that they do cause serious disruption to organized crime, as they lead to the arrest of leaders of organizations and not just foot soldiers. For example: the DEA's Operation Dinero utilized an undercover bank in Anguilla and successfully forfeited multi-millions of dollars of Colombian drug assets, identified connections between Colombian cartels and organized crime in Europe, and led to the identification and arrest of fugitive drug traffickers. In addition, these operations often provide valuable evidence regarding the crimes which gave rise to generated assets in the first place. As will be seen below, fighting is done through several regional and international initiatives.

The Financial Action Task Force (FATF) was established by the leaders of the G-7 Group of industrialized countries and the President of the European Commission at the economic summit held in Paris in July 1989. FATF membership now includes 26 States and territories of the OECD, the EU and the Gulf Cooperation Council. In February 1990 the FATF published the original 40 recommendations,[5] which *inter alia* encourage FATF states to: become party to the 1988 UN Convention; enact legislation which ensures that financial institutions maintain adequate records and that those records are available to law enforcement agencies; and increase international cooperation in the investigation and prosecution of illicit drug trafficking and related money laundering offences and asset forfeiture proceedings. The FATF has always been conscious that these recommendations should be adopted more widely than its own membership, and hence it actively encourages other countries world-wide to adopt the recommendations.

The CFATF is an association of 21 Caribbean Basin states which have agreed to implement common counter-measures to address money laundering. It was established in 1992 as the Caribbean's first regional anti-money laundering effort, modeled on the Paris-based FATF, and was created following the first regional meeting on money laundering in the Caribbean, which was hosted by the government of Aruba in June 1990. This conference, attended by representatives of fifteen states plus the five countries of the FATF with direct interest in the region,[6] developed 19 recommendations – the CFATF recommendations – intended to be complementary to the forty FATF recommendations. The meeting also recognized a lack of understanding of the extent of vulnerability to money laundering within the region. At a regional ministerial meeting in November 1992 hosted by the government of Jamaica, the CFATF produced an accord embodied in the Kingston Declaration on Money Laundering. The Kingston Declaration endorsed the 1988 UN Convention, the OAS Model Regulations and the FATF and CFATF recommendations. Most importantly, it called for the establishment of a secretariat and charged that body with coordinating the implementation of these agreements, regulations and recommendations by member governments.

The CFATF secretariat itself was created in 1994 and is hosted by the government of Trinidad and Tobago. A technical meeting of the CFATF in March 1996 agreed to consolidate the constitution of the CFATF including defining terms of membership and funding arrangements. This new constitution, titled Memorandum of Understanding among Member Governments of the CFATF, was adopted by the Ministerial Council of the CFATF in San José, Costa Rica in October 1996 and was signed by 21 governments.[7] The most important work of the CFATF is done by its member governments. The work programme includes an annual review of the status of implementation (self assessment), a more detailed country by country review of adoption measures (mutual evaluation), and the coordination of technical assistance and training.

Self-assessments provide member governments with a snapshot of the level of progress each country or territory has made in implementing the recommendations. Equally important, they provide the secretariat with information which will enable it to analyse technical assistance needs of members. As a result of the initiatives being studied by the UNDCP and the EU the importance of the self assessment process is increased. Training efforts undertaken by donors and other states can only be correctly focused and produce the maximum benefit for the region if they are premised on an accurate analysis of members' needs. Each member is best situated to determine what its needs are; the most readily available mechanism for analysing needs is a self assessment programme, which sets objective standards to assess implementation. CFATF members have agreed to pursue the self-assessment programme on an ongoing basis. Similar surveys are also used by the Offshore Banking Group, CICAD, the Summit of the Americas money laundering workshops, and the Commonwealth Secretariat. Recognizing that each request inevitably places a burden on the officials who have to respond, coordination has been improved and, with the agreement of participating countries, more data are now exchanged.

The objective of the mutual evaluation programme is to create a constructive consultative approach to assist governments with the implementation of recommendations. Examiners, drawn from member countries, are senior officials with responsibility for supervising of financial institutions, law enforcement agencies, or legal development. The country under examination provides an analysis of the money laundering problem together with details of the measures in force or planned to address the problem. During an on-site visit the examiners meet with officials responsibile for legal policy, financial market supervision, prosecution and investigation of money laundering, together with representatives of financial institutions, to discuss their approach to money laundering. A detailed report is prepared by the examiners describing their findings and identifying possible improvements to the country's anti-money laundering system. This confidential report is submitted to the CFATF plenary for adoption. Summaries of these reports are included in the CFATF annual report. The Cayman Islands, Trinidad and Tobago and Costa Rica were examined in 1995, and Panama was examined in 1996. In March 1995 the CFATF secretariat participated in the examination of the Netherlands Antilles and Aruba which were visited by the FATF as an extension of its evaluation of the Kingdom of the Netherlands. The Bahamas, St Vincent, Barbados and St Lucia volunteered for evaluation in 1997.

The CFATF secretariat does not have resources to provide its own training projects, but is tasked 'to identify and act as a clearing house for facilitating training and technical assistance needs of members, including dealing with requests for training and technical assistance from members and advising on sources of assistance'. While conducting research for a UNDCP project in 1995,[8] the secretariat contacted donor governments and various training organizations to gather information on donor countries' programmes for money laundering training. It concluded that there was no organized strategy to deal with training assistance and, almost without exception, bilateral training efforts were conceived as short-term projects with inevitable short-term effects.

Furthermore, when individual national agencies had instituted their own assistance programs, efforts over-lapped and were duplicated. Indeed, courses dealing with the same content were simultaneously provided by several donor governments. The same study noted concerns expressed by senior police officers and other officials that so many courses, seminars and workshops were convened that staff were less available to do their work. It was also observed that, while interesting, too many of these courses revolved around the laws, procedures and experiences of trainers from North America or Europe, rather than being tailored to the specific needs of the students, focusing on their countries laws, resources and general environment.

The selection of participants for these courses also needs more thought. Most operational training for police officers has been provided for constables or sergeants. The selection of these students, who carry out investigations, is logical up to a point. However, it fails to take into account that these officers follow the policies of their senior officers. Moreover, there has been little meaningful training in money laundering or asset confiscation for the supervisors or managers of drug investigation teams, or for the heads of Criminal Investigation Departments. Consequently, these managers and their Police Commissioners have not established or introduced policies which require inquiry into the financial aspects of drug cases on a routine basis. This failure in the development of force policy and direction for operational investigators is probably the most significant factor in the failure to trace and confiscate drug assets to date. The senior officers who set objectives for departments and oversee investigations must have a working understanding of the issues involved if they are to direct the tracing of drug assets and the detection of money laundering activity.

Finally, training must survive beyond the initial infusion of capital, effort, and other resources. It should be institutionalized and housed in economically self-sufficient or regionally funded institutions created with, but not wholly dependent on, donor assistance. This will ensure that training is available on a continuing basis to meet changing circumstances and needs. Short-term training programs, organized both bilaterally and multilaterally by donor countries and international organizations, have been widely available in the region. For example, as part of an external relations programme, the FATF has convened awareness seminars for the financial sector, and CICAD has followed up their model regulations with training workshops in Central America and the Caribbean. The UNDCP has provided drugs-related training for police officers and prosecutors who deal with money laundering and financial investigation issues. Some examples of bilateral assistance include courses arranged by US federal law enforcement agencies, the secondment of investigators and prosecutors by the United Kingdom to St Vincent and Trinidad and Tobago, drugs training courses run by the Royal Canadian Mounted Police (RCMP) in Canada, and the secondment of experts by the Netherlands to assist Aruba and the Netherlands Antilles establish financial information units.

## Training and investigation

Training should revolve around four main principles: policy-makers and supervisors should receive training; trainers should be trained; training should be relevant; and training should conform with long-term strategic goals. Several initiatives have been proposed by the CFATF to the UNDCP and to donors. These include police and customs training programs, and multi-sector conferences and seminars including representatives from the judiciary, law enforcement, supervisors of financial institutions, and the financial sector itself. As described earlier, these proposals have attracted commitments from the EU and the US amounting to more than $5 million to finance the project over 2 years.

There are differences in law between the civil law and common law jurisdictions, and legal differences among countries sharing the same legal tradition. Consequently, legal training should be tailored to the laws of each country or groups of countries having similar laws. Cases exist which illustrate how few practitioners in the legal profession – the judiciary, prosecutors and defence – have experience or meaningful training in the application of the money laundering and related asset forfeiture laws of their jurisdictions. Some training has been provided by donor governments and multilateral organizations including, for example, the UWI/UNDCP Legal Training project. Further training on a continuing basis is required.

The powers to investigate and confiscate drug assets typically apply in the more serious cases of drug trafficking. While the laws of countries assign responsibility for action by banks and other financial institutions, initiatives for any effective application of these powers has to come from the police. Despite the number of drug cases being detected these measures are not being used on a regular basis. Each of these cases presents an opportunity to confiscate the convict's assets derived from drug trafficking, rather than just impose a prison sentence, but this is not being done on a routine basis. It should become force policy that drug traffickers' assets will be thoroughly investigated in all cases. The question of available resources is, however, important. Of the 21 members of the CFATF, the majority have populations of less than two million. Most members are also categorized as 'less developed nations'. Police forces are often small and under-resourced, and judicial systems lack sophist-ication. Almost all jurisdictions have experienced increases in crime and violence related to increased drug trafficking activity.

Although the implementation of money laundering counter-measures is a primary responsibility for law enforcement agencies and the judicial system, the financial services industry, comprising banks, non-bank financial institutions, offshore banks and international business cor-porations cannot be overlooked. In 1995 all CARICOM Central Banks adopted common money laundering guidelines. This followed a resolu-tion of a CARICOM Heads of Government meeting which had been proposed by the CFATF. These guidelines are applied to all commercial banks and have a preventative effect. Generally, they are not enforceable in the sense that failure to comply has a legal basis for sanctions, but they constitute an important code of conduct.

Training for the financial sector is patchy. Commercial banks affiliated with Canadian, US and UK banks have done the most in providing in-house training for employees, establishing compliance officers, and in implementing specific anti-money laundering policies and procedures developed by their corporate parents. Indigenous commercial banks do not generally provide the same standard of training for employees, nor appoint compliance officers. Anti-money laundering policies and pro-cedures which are implemented by these institutions rarely go beyond the terms of the money laundering guidelines issued by Central Banks.

Training offered to non-bank financial institutions is almost non-existent. This sector of the financial services industry has been largely ignored by regional governments and foreign trainers. Consequently, they have not been sufficiently engaged in the anti-money laundering dialogue and their degree of vulnerability is yet to be fully understood. Moreover, the issue of company registration should be addressed. Where offshore companies are available for legitimate purposes, such as IBC, there is an inherent vulnerability to their use for criminal purposes. In many instances the means for initial and subsequent controls on com-pany registration could be strengthened as a preventative measure.

Banks and other financial institutions are required to properly identify customers, retain records of transactions, monitor account activity and report suspicions to the police, among other things. The requirement to report suspicions is both voluntary and mandatory, depending on the laws of countries. Whatever the basis for reporting, reports do not occur as frequently as might be expected, and in some cases never. This is due to a variety of factors. The banks may not have confidence in the police to handle sensitive information about their clients. Staff may be concerned about personal risks provoked by making reports about a customer who knows them and perhaps their family. In any case, there should be a particularly close level of cooperation between the investigators and the banks. Most banks will identify a 'compliance officer' responsible for this sort of liaison. The relationship between the bank and police should be based on mutual confidence and trust, and there is a need for reciprocal exchange of information. The police can help banks and other financial institutions to identify patterns of criminal activity, but bankers will want to ensure that information disclosed will be treated confidentially. Wherever possible, bankers should be appraised of the progress of investigations and should be informed if suspicions are not substantiated by the investigations.

## Coordination and cooperation

Similar to the CICAD and UNDCP coordination, the CFATF secretariat communicates with each member country through a primary contact person. This person's post varies from country to country. In the majority it is the Attorney General; in some, the Director of Finance; and in yet others, it is the head of the drugs police. The primary contact person should communicate with the key individuals in individual departments or agencies at the local level. There is also need for regular coordination among government departments and the financial sectors. To this end ministers have agreed to establish National Committees on Money Laundering. Among other things, these will promote and monitor the implementation of policy recommendations; develop a national consensus on counter money laundering measures; develop national policy positions in respect of money laundering initiatives; select the country's representatives to multilateral organizations and meetings; provide a standing point of contact for external organizations; and oversee the implementation of decisions from international meetings. In addition to policy level coordination there is a need for operational coordination. Particularly when new systems and procedures are being established, or old systems revised, the police need to interact with prosecutors, the judiciary, financial supervisors, financial institutions and their associations, customs and the inland revenue entities. The coordinator of this work plays a key role in developing awareness and promoting cooperation.

The Caribbean region is a recognized corridor for the transhipment of drugs to North America and Europe. Consistently, there are significant numbers of drug seizures and related arrests involving nationals of Caribbean, Latin American, North American and European countries. These arrests generate cases which often require evidence and extradition among Caribbean and other jurisdictions. The exchange of mutual legal assistance between Commonwealth jurisdictions is available through rogatory letters authorized by law. Such procedures are routine among Commonwealth countries. Consequently, letters rogatory are widely available and mutual legal assistance is not generally a problem between these states.

Separately, extradition between Commonwealth states may be effected where it is permitted by domestic legislation. This exists widely in the form of the Fugitive Offenders Act which was passed in 1881 by the United Kingdom and has been adopted by the Commonwealth. This legislation does not apply, however, between Commonwealth and non-Commonwealth jurisdictions. Here, specific legislation is needed, authorising rogatory letters or mutual legal assistance pursuant to treaties. In addition, the development of model legislation and treaties for mutual legal assistance, as well as modern extradition treaties between Commonwealth and non-Commonwealth jurisdictions would be of great utility in the region, as more governments identify the need for bilateral confiscation agreements and mutual legal assistance treaties to allow for the reciprocal freezing and confiscation of drug assets. Some governments have established procedures to share confiscated assets, which are often used to benefit a police force directly, but are also used to fund education, prevention and rehabilitation programmes.

## Conclusion

As this and other chapters in this volume show, the political will and tangible resources of Caribbean countries, other nations in the Hemisphere and international organizations are now being increasingly channeled towards disrupting the trade and the organized criminal activity related to it. Recent years have witnessed enhancements in the nature, scope, and value of assistance provided to the region and of the regional and international initiatives to combat drugs. The resources of non-governmental organizations, government agencies, and private sector organizations can and should be applied to create an effective and co-ordinated response to what is now justifiably characterised as the most serious threat to stability and economic development in the Caribbean.

# Notes

1   See *Report of the UNDCP Caribbean Regional Office*, Barbados, April 1996.
2   All EU countries, plus Australia, Canada and the United States.
3   *Report of the Regional Meeting on Drug Control Co-operation in the Caribbean, held at Bridgetown, Barbados, 15–17 May 1996.*
4   This report is produced annually by the Bureau for International Narcotics and Law Enforcement Affairs.
5   The 40 FATF recommendations were revised and updated in June 1996.
6   The five are: Canada, France, The Netherlands, the UK and the US.
7   CFATF member governments are: Anguilla, Antigua and Barbuda, Aruba, The Bahamas, Barbados, Belize, Bermuda, the British Virgin Islands, the Cayman Islands, Costa Rica, the Dominican Republic, Grenada, Montserrat, Nicaragua, the NA, Panama, St Lucia, St Vincent and the Grenadines, Trinidad and Tobago, and the Turks and Caicos Islands. (Dominica, Guyana, Jamaica, St Kitts and Nevis, Suriname, and Venezuela have requested renewed membership.) (Colombia has requested observer status.)
8   The Investigation and Prosecution of Money Laundering and Asset Forfeiture Cases in the Caribbean Region', unpublished paper by A. Carlos Correa, June 1996.

# Index

Printed in the United States
108615LV00002B/6/A